Praise for

Christianity and Wokeness

"Owen Strachan has done a great service to the Church not only by taking aim at one of her most dangerous foes (wokeness), but also by pointing her again and again to her all-sufficient Savior and head. Few men possess the mix of intellect, winsomeness, academic rigor, pastoral sensitivity, and raw courage that drips from every page of this book."

> **—Voddie Baucham Jr.,** dean of the School of Divinity at African Christian University and author of *Fault Lines: The Social Justice Movement and Evangelicalism's Looming Catastrophe.*

"This is an alarming and remarkably insightful book. It shows how 'wokeness' is a deeply anti-Christian movement that even today is increasing racial divisiveness, anger, resentment, and hostility because it wrongly evaluates people based on the color of their skin rather than who they are as unique, individual members of the worldwide human race."

> **—Wayne Grudem,** Distinguished Research Professor of Theology and Biblical Studies at Phoenix Seminary

"Whenever the Church faces a major threat to the purity of sound doctrine and a biblical worldview, God raises up a strong voice to confront that destructive error. That is what we have in this book. Refuting one of the most damaging ideologies of the day, Owen Strachan dissects and dismantles the present-day 'woke' movement with theological precision and a polemical rebuttal. Paul charged that a spiritual leader in the Church must 'be able both to exhort in sound doctrine and to refute those who contradict' (Titus 1:9). In other words, if truth is to be cherished, error must be exposed—and denounced. Strachan does both in this book. Lest you fall prey to the secular agenda of the day, you will want to carefully read and internally digest this book. Truth is its own best defense."

> **—Steven J. Lawson,** president of OnePassion Ministries in Dallas, Texas

"With regard to what is commonly referred to as 'wokeness' (e.g. Critical Race Theory, liberation theology, social gospel, etc.), there are those who would suggest that it is safe for Christians to 'eat the meat and spit out the bones.' But in *Christianity and Wokeness: How the Social Justice Movement Is Hijacking the Gospel—and the Way to Stop It*, Dr. Owen Strachan reminds believers in Christ of precisely why both the 'meat' and 'bones' of wokeness must be rejected. The evangelical Church will benefit greatly from the scriptural and scholastic heavy-lifting Dr. Strachan has undertaken in this extremely helpful and timely work."

> **—Darrell Harrison,** dean ⬛⬛⬛⬛⬛⬛⬛⬛⬛⬛ ost of *Just Thinking* podcast

"Woke teaching, Critical Race Theory, and intersectionality should not be in the toolchest of a Christian. They are dangerous ideologies opposed to the Gospel, biblical unity, and biblical truth. This book is an excellent introduction to these destructive heresies and a powerful presentation of the only truth that brings lasting reconciliation: the Gospel of Jesus Christ."

—**Ken Ham,** founder and CEO of Answers in Genesis

"This work should be read by those on both sides of the divide. Owen Strachan's treatment of the subject as it pertains to the disciplines of sociology, economics, and politics is acute. However, my greatest delight is that his goal is not to win an academic or political victory, but to bring his reader to Christ. He sets before us the Scriptures as the ultimate standard and the Gospel as the ultimate answer for the human predicament."

—**Paul Washer,** founder and director of HeartCry Missionary Society

"Moved by concern for the Church, Owen Strachan has provided a valuable and insightful resource on Critical Race Theory, intersectionality, and woke culture. *Christianity and Wokeness* offers a perceptive analysis that explains why these ideologies are inconsistent with the Gospel and how they will wreak irreparable harm if left unchecked. Gracious yet firm, Strachan exposes the woke movement by showing how it is fundamentally incompatible with biblical Christianity. Conversations about race, ethnicity, social justice, and unity are important. But the Gospel, not wokeness, is the answer to these and other challenges. Thankfully, Strachan is a faithful guide for navigating these crucial questions."

—**Tony Perkins,** president of the Family Research Council

"The issues behind CRT are complex. The law of God diagnoses the disease, and the Gospel provides the cure. Owen Strachan has provided a non-emotional, winsome, and detailed analysis of CRT and the 'wokeness movement.' He has exposed its faulty assumptions, has shown where the movement violates the biblical worldview, and has given us a fair warning about how, once again, the Gospel is at stake. I highly recommend the reading of this book. Let its truth sink in, then go and proclaim the Gospel with conviction and passion."

—**Miguel Núñez,** senior pastor of International Baptist Church of Santo Domingo and founding president of Wisdom & Integrity Ministries

"Woke evangelicalism is in many ways an echo of the Emerging Church Movement that flourished at the start of the new millennium. Like that movement, the woke doctrine actively subverts the clarity and simplicity of the Gospel. In *Christianity and Wokeness*, Owen Strachan meticulously analyzes the trend, showing that wokeness is actually a false religion, incompatible with biblical Christianity. This is a refreshingly bold and compelling critique—a must-read resource for evangelicals who want to understand and properly navigate the prevailing cultural current."

—**Phil Johnson,** executive director of Grace to You

"As a pastor in Africa who has been coming to preach in the U.S. for a quarter of a century, I keep noting with interest the new trends that come up in the Church there. In the recent past, the biggest trend has been the subject of social justice. If you are keen to know why there is so much controversy concerning this matter, I highly recommend this book by Owen Strachan to you. It gives a lucid understanding of the concept of social justice and also argues convincingly as to why the Church should guard its doors against it."

—Dr. Conrad Mbewe, pastor of Kabwata Baptist Church and founding chancellor of the African Christian University in Lusaka, Zambia

"Like Rip Van Winkle, many Christians today are sleeping through a revolution. The divisive, deceptive, and destructive forces of wokeness, identity politics, and Critical Race Theory are hard at work deconstructing American society, popularizing Marxism, upending justice, attacking Judeo-Christian ethics, promoting reverse racism, and belittling the reconciling Gospel of Jesus Christ. The book you hold in your hand is a wake-up call to the dangers of wokeness and a summons to stand in opposition, armed with Gospel truths that alone set people free. Let's start our own revolution by retelling the truth about God, creation, sin, and redemption in Jesus Christ. Owen Strachan has provided us with a book for our time. You *must* make time to read it! The future of the Church and the nation cannot be taken for granted."

—Philip De Courcy, pastor of Kindred Community Church in Anaheim Hills, California, and teacher on the daily radio program *Know the Truth*

"For Christians who long to see divided peoples come together, to see injustice and oppression vanquished, and to see sins from our past dealt with thoroughly, the ideas of Critical Theory, intersectionality, and 'woke' theology can initially appear very attractive. Unfortunately, all that glitters is not gold. In this book, Owen Strachan has served the Church by helping us distinguish the fool's gold of 'woke' theology from the real gold of Gospel truth. Strachan not only understands the cultural trends that are currently seducing the Church, but he also understands and explains how these trends look and feel in local congregations. As a pastor, I found that Strachan's analysis not only confirmed and deepened my own cultural observations, but also rang true to the way these lies look and feel when they touch the people I serve. Strachan does not stop with cultural analysis; he proceeds to a delighted exposition of the Gospel that alone is able to reconcile people to God and each other! Pastor, buy this excellent book and give it to your people—by doing so you will help them see the lies that surround us more clearly. You will also help them believe that the Gospel is sufficient to produce reconciliation, unity, and justice in the world in a way that 'woke' theology never could."

—J. Ryan Fullerton, lead pastor of Immanuel Baptist Church in Louisville, Kentucky; co-founder of the Immanuel Network; and co-author of *Experiencing God through Expository Preaching*

"*Christianity and Wokeness* is an excellent book, written by a uniquely gifted man. Owen Strachan is a rare combination of a professor, prophet, and pastor. As a professor, Owen has carefully done his research. As a prophet, Owen has courageously declared the truth. As a pastor, Owen has skillfully shepherded the flock of God. In other words, *Christianity and Wokeness* is a rare mix of academic excellence, unwavering conviction, and pastoral sensitivity. My prayer is that this book will serve myriads of believers looking for biblical clarity amid great cultural confusion."

—**Jason Wredberg,** lead pastor of Redeemer Bible Church in Minnetonka, Minnesota

"The social justice agenda is multifaceted and has become a living room conversation through nightly news reports, politics, and small group Bible studies from your local church. It would be a gross error to underestimate this woke movement as a toothless tiger or a nonvenomous snake. The woke movement is a multi-headed dragon that is devouring our society on matters of politics, economics, education—and sadly, religion. The woke movement has introduced a new religion of victimhood that has replaced the true Gospel of Jesus with the grievance gospel, and Jesus's Church with a woke church. We need faithful men who will respond with crystal-clear biblical teaching that reveals the devious woke agenda and presents the pure Gospel of King Jesus to a dying world. I'm grateful that Owen Strachan has taken on this subject, providing a biblical response to CRT and the wicked woke agenda. We need more men who will stand firm in our era."

—**Josh Buice,** pastor of Pray's Mill Baptist Church in Georgia and founder and president of G3 Ministries

"The Christian Church has become divided over the topic of racism and oppression, particularly in how one identifies and addresses such sins. These differences have stemmed from ideologies that are alien to Scripture but appear in biblical dress. Owen Strachan takes on these challenges with pastoral sensitivity, carefully explaining the genesis and development of such ideologies and how they have impacted modern cultural thinking. He is remarkably thorough without overwhelming the reader with minutia. Strachan also provides insightfully clear biblical analysis, highlighting many key points that can ably serve as fruitful topics of discussion within the Church. I heartily commend this work to all who wish to engage thoughtfully and biblically on these vitally important issues today."

—**Ekkie Tepsupornchai,** senior pastor of Western Avenue Baptist Church in Brawley, California

"As the clouds of wokeness and Critical Race Theory (CRT) darken the evangelical horizon, Dr. Owen Strachan's book shines a light of clarity so that every believer can define terms and understand this seismic cultural shift. Strachan's book is a one-stop source, making a complex topic simple and easy to understand. Strachan provides powerful insights and analysis through the bright lens of Scripture. While most evangelicals have found it challenging to get up to speed on this movement, Strachan's book provides a pivotal starting point for everyone on these critical issues."

—**Virgil Walker,** executive director of operations at G3 and cohost of the *Just Thinking* podcast

"One of the reasons why wokeness has become so acceptable in the Church today is because many Christians—especially white Christians—are afraid to denounce it. One of the most effective things about wokeness is that it shames white people into silence or compliance. Too many seem to believe speaking for wokeness or not speaking at all are their only options. But there's a third option—a fearless and faithful option: the only viable option for men like Owen Strachan. At a time when so many people are unwilling to speak about this with truth in love, I'm grateful for *Christianity and Wokeness*. In a succinct, simple, and sanctifying manner, Strachan masterfully affirms that light cannot fellowship with darkness and that Christianity cannot fellowship with wokeness."

—**Samuel Sey,** blogger at SlowToWrite.com

"I must confess my bias: I devour anything Owen writes. His theological clarity speaks for itself. Now add to that his courage in tackling such a hot topic. Here in South Africa, we live daily with the reality of racism (past and present) and its bitter legacy. Yet this makes Christian unity shine all the brighter against such an ugly backdrop. American prosperity heresy and church-growth methods have already ravaged the Church in this land. The last thing we need now are imported wokeness myths dividing the body of Christ. May God use Owen's book to equip African watchmen on the wall and to unify the Church around biblical truth."

—**Tim Cantrell,** senior pastor of Antioch Bible Church and president of Shepherds' Seminary Africa in Johannesburg, South Africa

"The best thing I have ever read on wokeness. We have a Marxist disease that is plaguing our country. Men and women must speak up, and Owen Strachan has done so clearly and concisely. His book will be required reading for my church. I heartily recommend it."

—**Tommy Nelson,** senior pastor of Denton Bible Church in Texas

"Dr. Owen Strachan has once again provided a great service to the Church—this time with *Christianity and Wokeness*. He boldly and pastorally tackles some of the most pressing issues of our day with precise cultural analysis and clear theological reasoning. This book will prepare the reader 'to contend for the faith that was once for all delivered to the saints' (Jude 3). I found myself filled with hope as I was pointed to the sufficiency of Scripture and the need for rigorous biblical thinking in order to stand firm on the Gospel in difficult days. But ultimately, I was thrilled with Christ and the power of the cross."

—**Gavin Peacock,** associate pastor of Calvary Grace Church and author of *A Greater Glory: From Pitch to Pulpit*

"This is not just another endorsement for just another book. Rather, I want to commend to you a well-written, well-reasoned book which evaluates perhaps the most destructive theological and cultural movement of our generation. Owen Strachan's *Christianity and Wokeness* deals methodically and fairly with the arguments, providing both insightful commentary and biblical solutions. In my estimation, opponents of a non-woke position must respond to Strachan's book if they are to continue any further. It is my earnest hope that Christians will abandon this toxic ideology and deal with sin issues using biblical tools, seeing Christ as our only hope for salvation and reconciliation. I pray this book is used greatly by the Lord to help the Church break free from its slavery to a false and anti-Christian system."

—**Nate Pickowicz,** author and pastor of Harvest Bible Church in Gilmanton Iron Works, New Hampshire

"Every generation must make a renewed defense and articulation of the true Gospel, because the Gospel is under assault in each successive generation. Wokeness is that assault in our generation. In fact, there has probably been no greater threat to the true Gospel in the twenty-first century than the religion of wokeness. I use the word, 'religion,' because wokeness is an altogether different religion from historic Christianity, with its own alternative definitions of sin, atonement, and virtue, etc. As a pastor I cannot commend this book highly enough. The Church of Jesus Christ needs to know and understand Satan's schemes and how to combat them with God's Word. This book by Dr. Owen Strachan is just that—a biblical, tour-de-force defense of the Gospel that equips the Christian to stand in the day of battle. I know of no other work which so clearly identifies the dangers of this new religion and also courageously proclaims the beauty and excellency of true Christian unity, which can only be established in the Gospel of our triune God. I thank God for this book. May it bolster our generation to love and defend the true Gospel."

—**Grant Castleberry,** senior pastor of Capital Community Church in Raleigh, North Carolina

"As a Christian believer called and gifted to be a Christian teacher, Owen Strachan has written this insightful and important book. He engaged the entire family of ideas that constitutes the chant of the 'woke.' He does it respectfully but with a penetrating honesty about its narrow, contentious, and destructive ideological framework and purpose. His knowledge is detailed and thorough in its scholarship while his writing is plain, clear, and accessible to any who show interest—and who shouldn't—in understanding this philosophical stance that threatens to redefine humanity. He isolates the destructive aspects of the 'woke' culture while writing as a confident Christian who has experienced the power of the Gospel and knows that Jesus as risen Lord has indeed placed all things under His feet. Strachan's analysis of difficult terms and ideas along with their accompanying bibliography shows an acute comprehension of the issues but also reclines into very practical counsel concerning how to think and act in light of the onslaught of challenges provoked by 'wokeness.'"

—**Tom J. Nettles,** senior professor of historical theology at the Southern Baptist Theological Seminary

"This book could not be more timely. In it, Dr. Strachan accurately highlights the destruction of CRT thinking not just in the culture, but more importantly, the Church. *Christianity and Wokeness* shows convincingly why CRT must be refuted and rejected by all who want to remain faithful to the biblical Gospel."

—**Albert Kilgore,** pastor-teacher of Mission Bible Church East Valley in Arizona

"As the ideology of wokeness spreads like gangrene throughout many churches, we need men who will stand and speak the truth in a way that is able to win minds and hearts. Owen Strachan delivers on this great need in his latest book.

"With the mind of a scholar, Owen defines wokeness with great care and addresses the serious nature of its worldly ideology. Rather than paint with a broad brush, he uses precise strokes to provide an accurate picture of both the problems with wokeness and the solution that is solely rooted in the Gospel.

"With the heart of a pastor, Owen addresses the real social evils of America in both the past and present. He demonstrates that the solution can never be found in the worldly ideology of wokeness but only in the hope of the Gospel of Jesus Christ. In a true sense, this book is not waging war against wokeness but fighting to preserve the purity of the Gospel that alone can address the problems that plague our world.

"Although the gates of hell will never prevail against the Church, threats to the Gospel continually arise that must be battled. Dr. Strachan does not wring his hands and fret over wokeness but strengthens his hands and fights for the Gospel. He invites you to join in the fight and stand for truth. This is the book you need to prepare for the battle."

—**Tom Buck,** senior pastor of First Baptist Church of Lindale, Texas

"Wokeness, Critical Race Theory, and intersectionality are amongst the most volatile—and troubling—issues confronting the Church today. Unfortunately, too many engage these matters—and the problems of race and injustice often lurking behind them—with reckless generalities and incendiary rhetoric. However, in *Christianity and Wokeness*, Strachan surgically defines terms, unpacks history, traces arguments, and wields Scripture to reveal the dangers within these ideologies and why Christians should be on guard. In so doing, Strachan frames our cultural and ministry moment and points Christians to a more biblically faithful path forward. Thus, *Christianity and Wokeness* is an important book, and it's arriving at a strategic moment. Whether you agree or disagree with Strachan's appraisal, this book is necessary reading for every Christian who seeks to better grasp Critical Race Theory, intersectionality, and wokeness and to understand why many of us see these ideologies as serious challenges before the Church."

—**Jason K. Allen, Ph.D.,** president of Midwestern Baptist Theological Seminary and Spurgeon College

"I was thoroughly blessed and informed by this book. Dr. Strachan is aware that the Church is in a battle for its Gospel integrity, but he does not leave out woke proponents or the unsuspecting who are deprived of biblical insight. I encourage friends and foes to read objectively, with a willing mind ready to confront the lies you may have heard from the woke camp."

—**Seymour Helligar,** pastor of Grace Community Church of Long Beach

"The Church has always had to stand firm and resist being tossed to and fro by every doctrinal fad of the day. Hard postmodernism is one of the most significant fads of our day. Biblically driven believers will appreciate Dr. Strachan's 'Machenesque' clarity and courage as he brings us up to speed on this graceless and particularly acidic ideology and helps us recognize the cultural, theological, and spiritual dangers of wokeness."

—Blake White, lead pastor of South Side Baptist Church in Abilene, Texas

"As Judas's kiss betrayed our Lord, so wokeness, feigned in love, betrays His Gospel. Promising to be as soothing as oil, wokeness is a drawn sword pointed at the heart of our Savior's Bride. Dr. Strachan has discerned the serpentine twang behind its smooth words, and he has carefully cast the bright light of Scripture for us to safely wade our way through the miry bog of this novel ideology. As Issachar's men of old (1 Chronicles 12:32), he's shown himself to know the Word and the times in which we live by writing this volume. I'm thankful he's articulated the problems of wokeness while not losing sight of the problems wokeness seeks to address, all the while pointing us to the one true solution to all our problems—the glory of God in a Savior crucified for our sins. May God use this book to bring Christ His honor so that His Bride finds her solace, not in the cunning words of strange men, but rather under the tender care of Her Bridegroom's arm, near to His heart, and within the sound of His comforting voice."

—Jacob B. Reaume, pastor of Trinity Bible Chapel in Waterloo, Ontario

"Given the importance of this topic and the confusion that surrounds it, I am grateful that Owen Strachan wrote this book. But I am also glad for the way he wrote this book. It's clear without being superficial. It is informed without being esoteric. It is principled without being indifferent. It is uncompromising without being uncompassionate. Above all, Owen seeks to be biblical. His burden is not to divide people by ideology but to unite people in the only enduring way possible—through the Gospel of Jesus Christ."

—C. J. Mahaney, senior pastor of Sovereign Grace Church of Louisville

"This book should be required reading for every pastor and aspiring pastor in America. Woke theology, like the Judaizing heresy, is an irredeemable poison that's being injected into the Body of Christ by leaders who should know better. Like Paul in Galatians, it must be clearly, carefully, relentlessly, and above all courageously opposed with the Bible, and that is exactly what *Christianity and Wokeness* does. While it seems the fear of man has silenced most of the evangelical watchmen we look to for guidance, at a time when the stakes could not be higher, Dr. Strachan has produced an easy-to-read book that makes it absolutely obvious on which side the faithful should stand. I thank God for this work and its brave author and publisher, and I pray it has the widest possible exposure."

—Jon Benzinger, lead pastor of Redeemer Bible Church in Gilbert, Arizona

"Suddenly, so it seems, almost everyone has gone woke. Wokeness, a progressive and liberal ideology, is threatening to take over every sphere of life—politics, commerce, sports, social media, and, sadly, even the Church. Because wokeness has become the new morality, the Church can no longer stay neutral. Christians can no longer remain on the sidelines. And since the very Gospel is at stake, it's high time for all who name the name of Christ to defend the name of Christ from this great threat to the followers of Christ. This is why the Church needs this book. With great precision and persuasiveness, Owen Strachan uses his theological proficiency to outfit Christians for this battle that is being waged against us. After explaining how wokeness has thoroughly integrated into the very fabric of our culture and has gained a major foothold in the Church, Strachan masterfully exposes this new morality as the old lie of the Serpent. He then proceeds to dismantle it with fourteen tightly argued biblical objections. Rather than leaving his readers to gaze over a bloody and disarrayed battlefield, Strachan pastorally and with great precision picks up the scattered debris by carefully applying God's antidote—the Gospel of Jesus Christ—to the wounds of the Church. This is the battle of our generation, and this is one of the most crucial books of our day that every Christian warrior needs to have in their arsenal. It's a must-read!"

> **—Jeffrey D. Johnson,** pastor of Grace Bible Church in Conway, Arkansas, academic dean of Grace Bible Theological Seminary, and owner of Free Grace Press

"In one of the most challenging times in the history of the world, strong winds of error are shaking the professing Church in new ways. Many of these errors are linked together by a worldview (CRT) that has graduated from the academy and taken root in popular culture. With great skill and a love for God's Church, Owen Strachan diagnoses that worldview and identifies answers. He does this with a gracious but urgent biblical clarity. This book is a timely gift to the Church and a resource that every pastor should have on hand to help shepherd God's people in these confusing days."

> **—Richard Caldwell Jr.,** pastor-teacher of Founders Baptist Church in Spring, Texas

"Since his opening encounter with our first parents in Eden, the Enemy of our souls has employed a consistent strategy; he uses biblical terms with his own dictionary. Wokeness is yet another warhead from the same arsenal hurling 'arguments and opinions raised against the knowledge of God' (2 Corinthians 10:5). In these pages, Strachan unmasks how Critical Race Theory hijacks the glorious truths of forgiveness, justice, reconciliation, and even salvation itself and replaces them with cultural meanings amounting to social saccharine. These pages provide vital perspective for thinking biblically in a world adrift in cultural confusion."

> **—Rick Holland,** senior pastor of Mission Road Bible Church in Kansas City, Kansas

Christianity and Wokeness

CHRISTIANITY

AND

WOKENESS

How the Social Justice Movement
Is Hijacking the Gospel—
and the Way to Stop It

Owen Strachan

Foreword by JOHN MacARTHUR, bestselling author of
Only Jesus and chancellor of The Master's University

REGNERY
FAITH

Regnery Faith books may be purchased in bulk at special discounts for sales
promotion, corporate gifts, fund-raising, or educational purposes. Special editions
can also be created to specifications. For details, contact the Special Sales
Department, Regnery Faith, 307 West 36th Street, 11th Floor, New York, NY
10018 or info@skyhorsepublishing.com.

Unless otherwise marked, all Scriptures are taken from THE HOLY BIBLE,
ENGLISH STANDARD VERSION.® Copyright © 2001 by Crossway, a
publishing ministry of Good News Publishers. Used by permission.

Scriptures marked KJV are taken from the KING JAMES VERSION, public
domain.

Regnery Faith™ is an imprint of Skyhorse Publishing, Inc.®, a Delaware
corporation.

Visit our website at www.regnery.com.
Please follow our publisher Tony Lyons on Instagram
    @tonylyonsisuncertain.

10 9 8 7 6 5 4 3 2 1

Library of Congress Cataloging-in-Publication Data is available on file.

Cover design by John Caruso
Cover photo by Daniel Day

Hardcover ISBN: 978-1-68451-243-0
First paperback ISBN: 978-1-68451-705-3
Ebook ISBN: 978-1-68451-253-9

Printed in the United States of America

To John MacArthur and Voddie Baucham Jr.

Swifter than eagles and stronger than lions (2 Samuel 1:23)

CONTENTS

Foreword

by John MacArthur

Critical Race Theory (CRT) has been an aggressive force in academic circles since the late 1980s, radically affecting the way many college professors, politicians, Millennials, and students from Generation Z view the world (Western culture, in particular). CRT is basically neo-Marxism on postmodernist steroids—a deeply uncongenial point of view cynically weaponized for the deconstruction and dismantling of social structures. Wherever it is introduced, CRT deliberately provokes and feeds on disunity. It intensifies ethnic hostility, promotes crass identity politics, foments resentment, and imputes guilt or victimhood to people according to their skin color.

In recent years, even among people who have never consciously heard of CRT, the values and vocabulary of this worldview have become familiar elements in everyday discourse. Buzzwords like *systemic racism, implicit bias, whiteness, white privilege, cultural appropriation, colonization, microaggression,* and *social justice* constitute the essential vernacular of Critical Race Theory. Those terms are now fairly commonplace around the water cooler, on the nightly news, across the spectrum of social media, and recently, even in church. The prevalence of so much

CRT jargon (and the widespread embrace of the ideas those expressions represent) shows how thoroughly this way of thinking has become ensconced in our culture and in so many minds.

It is especially disappointing—and disconcerting—to see doctrines borrowed directly from CRT infect the Church and spread so quickly. In recent years, many leading evangelical voices have begun to parrot Critical Race Theorists, suggesting (for example) that Christians in this generation will never truly be able to fulfill the command to love our neighbors until we glean from the lessons and language taught by the purveyors of CRT. They claim CRT hands Christians "a set of analytical tools that explain how race has and continues to function in society." Many have insisted that these are *indispensable* tools that "can aid in evaluating a variety of human experiences" in a way that, presumably, Scripture cannot.

Even though the predictable and inescapable result of CRT is division, it has lately been aggressively promoted even by ministries that were originally founded on the principle that Christian unity is an essential expression of Gospel faith. Church leaders who would self-identify as "Gospel-centered" seem to have shifted the *actual* focus of their message to "social justice" and other themes borrowed from CRT's tapestry of pet issues.

Meanwhile, Gospel doctrines like original sin, atonement, justification, and the glory of Christ are being eclipsed by lectures about social inequities and ethnic injustices that can never fully be atoned for—but for which reparations should nevertheless be paid. In many pulpits across the evangelical movement, Gospel language is being supplanted by socialist rhetoric.

It is especially frustrating that this is happening among formerly conservative evangelicals—even while observant critics in the secular realm have begun to see and point out the destructive tendencies of CRT. Some of the keenest minds in the academic world have begun to marshal their energies (using both scholarship and satire) to expose the dangerous fallacies of the system. Critical Race Theorists have argued that math education is inherently racist, that the very notion of objective truth is rooted in white supremacy, and that Western values—moral standards, in particular—are tools of oppression. According to CRT, every major aspect of our culture is riddled with racism.

The divisive effects of such a worldview are now obvious. CRT has not helped, much less healed, social strife and ethnic divisions. It has made those problems exponentially worse. And perceptive people have noticed. In the realms of politics and education, CRT is finally being held up to critical scrutiny by a few articulate and influential academicians and thought leaders.

Unfortunately, evangelicals—always late to every party—are enthusiastically jumping on another cultural bandwagon just as its wheels are about to come off. As an "analytical tool," CRT has no more use than a wrecking ball. It can demolish core social structures and leave society itself in ruins, but it cannot clean up the mess, much less build anything worthwhile.

I am heartily thankful for the courage and clarity that Owen Strachan has shown in dealing with these issues. I'm especially grateful that he has compiled his excellent critiques of Critical Race Theory in this succinct, straightforward digest. He demonstrates persuasively why CRT is not merely a harmless theory, or even a valid analytical tool. It is in fact a dangerous worldview that is incompatible with Christianity at the most fundamental level.

This volume will be helpful to anyone striving to understand these things. It is the perfect resource to hand to anyone who wonders what all the fuss is about.

Tolle lege.

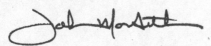

Introduction

Shakespeare once wrote, "There is a tide in the affairs of men," an observation that surely rings true in historical assessment.[1] The character in *Julius Caesar* who spoke these cunning words went on to commend following that tide for personal gain as much as is possible. That is not my mindset in citing the Bard. Rather, I believe that there are indeed certain moments in cultural and societal life when one is conscious of greater movements afoot. In our time, the system I call "wokeness" pulls us all in some way, driving us onward, with most people in our civilization and the Church of Jesus Christ having very little sense either of where they are going or what rocks the turbulent waters conceal.

This book is an exercise in tide-identifying and rock-spotting. Because—like any theory-driven discipline—wokeness has its own vocabulary, definitive literature, and intramural discussions, many people in general and many Christians in particular do not grasp it and are not studying it. Yet every day, we hear the imperatives: "White" people should "be less white," according to material presented in a

---

[1] William Shakespeare, *Julius Caesar*, Act 4, Scene 3.

training session for Coca-Cola employees, as just one head-spinning example.[2] Headlines and social media posts announce to us yet more "antiracism" initiatives, more compulsory "social justice" teaching sessions, more "racial equity" funding measures, more instances of people being "racist" who we never imagined as such. The imperatives and accusations pile up: "Be less white." "Your silence [on racial matters] is violence." "No justice, no peace." Some of this advocacy is soft, and some of it is hard, but in aggregate form, it threatens to overwhelm us. It adds to a common line addressed to people of all colors and backgrounds: *be woke—or else.*

Consequently, many Christian men and women are profoundly confused. Actually, that description is too weak: Many men and women are dazed and destabilized, disoriented and disheartened. They sense that a tide is carrying them and that a movement may well be marshaling strength against them, but they have little idea how to respond, what to do, or where the paddles in the boat are stowed. *Christianity and Wokeness* aims to help you resist the tide. It functions as an introductory overview and condensed theological analysis of "wokeness." I use this term to describe the collective ideas and activism of Critical Race Theory, intersectionality, and people who identify as "woke" more generally.

I have written this text, in short, to bring Christians (and any interested friends and conversation partners) up to speed on wokeness and then to give an answer to this system. Though I critique the movement strongly, readers should note that the very act of framing and engaging its thought is itself an act of respect per the conventions of scholarship. Wokeness, Critical Race Theory (which I'll refer to with the abbreviation "CRT"), and intersectionality are complex ideologies that require careful handling and studied contemplation.

This last comment matters. Ours is an age when people frequently comment harshly online without so much as viewing a video, listening

---

[2]   Jade Bremner, "Coca-Cola Faces Backlash over Seminar Asking Staff to 'Be Less White,'" *Independent*, February 24, 2021, https://www.independent.co.uk/lifestyle/coca-cola-racism-robin-diangelo-coke-b1806122.html.

to a podcast, or reading an article. This is truly a "speak quickly and judge angrily" era (contradicting the admonition we find in James 1:19–20). In the pages that follow, I make no bones about rejecting CRT, but only after honoring its major proponents (authors primarily, many of them gifted writers) by reading, digesting, and praying about their arguments and narratives. Furthermore, my text is not the last word on the matter; if you want to continue your study of wokeness, Critical Race Theory, and intersectionality, I encourage you to consult the "Recommended Reading" section at the book's end.[3]

It may be tempting to read this book as a work of dismissal and scorn. It is surely not that. It is an exercise in traditional intellectual exchange, grounded in genuine respect for the serious and consequential case made by the other side (both inside and outside the Church of Christ). Wokeness, CRT, and intersectionality have found audiences for some understandable reasons; "race," ethnicity, justice, sexuality, and related concepts are no small issues and have to be sorted out by people in varying situations. My hope is that this book can help you toward that end.

The book has an intentional flow: Chapter 1 gives an overview of wokeness and its related movements in contemporary culture; Chapter 2 presents a summary of how wokeness is entering the Church; Chapters 3 and 4 get into the ring and offer a thorough evaluation of wokeness according to Scripture; Chapters 5 and 6 trace the biblical vision of

---

[3]   As a word of overview: Though wokeness, Critical Race Theory, and intersectionality are, in technical terms, distinctive, they are so closely connected that we will use the terms somewhat interchangeably in this book. When I use the term "wokeness," I use it to signify the shared ideas found in these movements and ideologies. Where specificity is called for, we will be specific, but as will be clear, the common cause of these three ideologies is so close as to render them effectively allies in a common war against unequal power, with special opposition going against white, heteronormative, religious people and the "supremacist" order they have created to the disadvantage of numerous underprivileged minority groups. Said differently, the person who is woke surely agrees with CRT ideology, and the person who agrees with CRT very likely agrees with intersectional ideology.

identity and ethnicity[4] and offer the God-given solution to ethnic division; and Chapter 7 builds on the theological foundation to consider the vexing details of the history of racism in America.

There is more ground we could cover and more books I could reference. Without apology or qualification, this project is, as noted, an introductory work. It is not an exhaustive tome. It is instead intended to function as a launchpad into this conversation and should be read as such. Each chapter in this project could be twice as long, cite many more sources, and make a fuller case against wokeness. Yet this shorter volume will, I pray, help readers who want an accessible entry point into the debate hosted by our society and by the Church.

My goal here is not to produce a generic introduction to wokeness. I have intentionally written a *Christian* introduction. It is thus unequivocally and unapologetically biblical. All that follows is staked upon the Word of God—the inspired, inerrant, authoritative, sufficient, and totally *good* Word of God. I am not bashful about writing as a Christian (knowing that not everyone who reads the book will be one, and gladly so). Rather, I intend for this book to show that Christianity not only has an oar to dip into the troubled waters around us, but that it is the one true safe harbor in our world. It is not one path among many to God; it is the system of systems, the body of doctrine that both refutes every worldly ideology and gives us nothing less than divine truth about us, our fractured world, and God.[5] Christians not only *can* speak to this ideology; Christians *must* speak to it, for ours is the faith

---

[4]   I use "ethnicity" because, as we shall see, "race" is not actually a positive biblical reality, but a construct. On this point, ironically, I agree with CRT advocates, much as many of them state that race is a social construct, but then practically operate in many senses as if it is real. There is in truth a confusing interplay of reality/nonreality with the typically "woke" conception of race. See Chapters 3 and 5 for more.

[5]   To read more on the connection between the personal God of the Christian faith and the Word that God has authored through human authors, see Carl F. H. Henry, *God, Revelation, and Authority*, vols. 1–6 (Wheaton, Illinois: Crossway Books, 1999).

once for all delivered to the saints by God (Jude 3).[6] We are not sup-posed to tuck this faith away in a closet, but we are summoned by the Apostle Paul to "contend for the faith" God has given us, battling not flesh and blood, but principalities and powers that war against the Church and her Warrior-Savior (Ephesians 6:12).

But enough table-setting. To the ramparts; to the law and testimonies. As we begin, I encourage you to read and meditate on these verses, which are the driving concern of everything that follows (emphasis mine):

> See to it that no one *takes you captive* by philosophy and empty deceit, according to human tradition, according to the elemental spirits of the world, and not according to Christ. (Colossians 2:8)

We destroy arguments and every lofty opinion raised against the knowledge of God and *take every thought captive* to obey Christ (2 Corinthians 10:5).

---

[6]   Unless otherwise specified, the normative translation used in this project is the English Standard Version (ESV).

CHAPTER 1

How Wokeness Is Entering the Culture

*The Bible is authoritative on everything of which it
speaks. Moreover, it speaks of everything.*

—*Cornelius Van Til*

In a famous training session captured on video in 2016, a speaker named Ashleigh Shackelford opposed "racism" in memorable fashion.[1] Standing before a room of women, many of them white, Shackelford bluntly told them that "all white people are racists." Not only that, but she pronounced that they had no real hope of changing: "No, you're always going to be racist, actually," she said. "Even when you're on a path to be a better human being."

This video went viral. It shocked many and seemed like an outlier a few years ago. In truth, it laid out the core program of the system I call "wokeness." In this system, there is no grace and no love. There is only grievance, resentment, and condemnation. Shackelford revealed as much in her next comments: "I believe all white people are born into not being human." She saved her toughest words for last: white people, she said, grow up "to be demons."

---

[1] David Nussman, "'All White People Are Racist Demons,'" Church Militant, September 10, 2020, https://www.churchmilitant.com/news/article/all-white-people-are-racist.

This is strong water even in leftist circles. Yet while Shackelford said some things that her peers might not say (at least, not out loud), her core argument is not at all unusual in woke circles.[2] According to standard woke ideology, in general terms "white" people are racist, the historic oppressors of others, and thus as a collective unit, "white" people are guilty.[3] As Shackelford made clear, there is no real solution for this guilt; there is only acknowledgement of it, ongoing awareness of it, and the undertaking of certain works to oppose one's nature as a "white" person.[4]

What exactly was transpiring in this strange video? Wokeness was advancing. The movement loosely called "wokeness" is now making many inroads into secular society. It is also infiltrating the Church, with many social media users being pulled to affirm wokeness through hashtags, social media statements, and other means. Such action may at first blush seem to fit with a compassionate response to cultural trends, including clashes with police and unrest in different places. Many evangelical leaders argue just this: They claim that wokeness is the way forward for the Church. As we shall see, however, wokeness is a major threat to the Christian faith.

In watching the video mentioned above, and in observing many trends within Christian circles, I could not help but think of a nearly one-hundred-year-old book. In 1923, liberal Christianity was gaining

---

[2] Wokeness should never be assumed to be the dominant prism of any person or ethnic group. Here, for example, is a comment on the video of Shackelford's presentation: "I'm a black woman. This is disgusting. This is racist. This is not funny and it's not cute. People need to stand up against this." Recognizing thought diversity is a major way to avoid being taken captive by false ideologies.

[3] "Racism is deeply embedded in the fabric of our society. It is not limited to a single act or person. Nor does it move back and forth, one day benefiting whites and another day (or even era) benefiting people of color. The direction of power between white people and people of color is historic, traditional, and normalized in ideology.... Whites hold the social and institutional positions in society to infuse their racial prejudice into the laws, policies, practices, and norms of society in a way that people of color do not." Robin DiAngelo, *White Fragility: Why It's So Hard for White People to Talk about Racism* (Boston, Massachusetts: Beacon, 2018), 22.

[4] I'm putting "white" in quotation marks because it is a concept that is treated as real but—in my judgment—has no basis in biblical teaching nor reasonable fact. More on this in Chapters 3 and 5.

major popularity. Liberalism retained the vocabulary of traditional Christianity but changed the meaning of the terms. Salvation was not primarily about personal salvation, but social change. Man's core prob-lem was not his own sin, but societal brokenness, political corruption, and economic oppression. Christianity was modified by Harry Emerson Fosdick and the liberal Protestants to remake the public order, not rescue the damned sinner. A hundred years ago, this ideology was entering churches, seminaries, and sound Christian organizations with impunity. Amidst a great uproar, theologian J. Gresham Machen wrote:

> [W]hat the liberal theologian has retained after abandoning to the enemy one Christian doctrine after another is not Christianity at all, but a religion which is so entirely different from Christianity as to belong in a distinct category.[5]

Machen famously defined liberalism not as a different form of Chris-tianity, but as a different thing altogether. Though it used similar terms and sounded like traditional faith, liberal Christianity was "not Chris-tianity at all," Machen argued. The long tail of twentieth century theol-ogy has shown clearly that he was right.

Today, the Church faces a new challenge. Like liberal Protestantism, which denied the historic truthfulness of the faith, supernatural miracles, and a sin-cleansing atonement for individual sinners, wokeness is not merely a different form of Christianity, a remixed version that fits fluidly with conservative evangelical faith. Built on Critical Race Theory (CRT), wokeness uses theological language and even the very system of Christian theology, albeit without any need for grace and God. Wokeness per Machen is thus in a "distinct category" from sound biblical doctrine. Wokeness, in the clearest terms, is not Christianity at all.

In what follows, we will show this by defining what wokeness is not, addressing what it is, and examining what a related discipline called

---

5 J. Gresham Machen, *Christianity and Liberalism* (Grand Rapids, Michigan: Eerdmans, 1923), 6–7.

"intersectionality" argues. Our study is not an exhaustive overview of wokeness, CRT, or intersectionality.[6] Rather, it is a critique of a late twentieth- and early twenty-first century intellectual and social movement. Though I will touch on tension points and offer critique in places, in this chapter (and Chapter 2), I will generally describe it, rather than deconstruct it.

What Wokeness Is Not

Before we delve further into what wokeness is, though, let's put a pause on our study. As much as we need to know what wokeness is, we first need to know what wokeness is not. Here are a few stances and convictions that are not woke, despite what you may have heard. The following principles and actions are righteous, stemming from Christian wisdom, not from any worldly system:

- Wanting societal harmony across backgrounds and skin colors does not make you woke.
- Wanting peace in fiery settings with a history of ethnic tension does not make you woke.
- Seeing massive failings in American and Western history, namely long and sustained patterns of racist thought and practice, does not make you woke.
- Being troubled by Christians' complicity with racism in the past does not make you woke (on this and the previous point, see Chapter 7).
- Adopting children from a different region or with a different skin color does not make you woke. Nor does an "interracial" marriage.

---

[6] Readers wanting more depth in these areas can consult the "Recommended Resources" at the book's end.

- Grieving the needless deaths of human beings who are made in the image of God and bear God-given dignity and purpose does not make you woke.
- Doing everything you can and know to do to build bonds with people different from you in various ways does not make you woke.
- Enjoying global culture and those who differ from your own background does not make you woke.
- Knowing that Jesus Christ was a Middle Eastern Jew and not a white American with flowing golden locks does not make you woke.
- Praying for greater diversity in your church through the saving of fellow sinners does not make you woke.
- Wanting greater justice in a world that is filled with hostility, pain, and injustice does not make you woke.
- Working to be more thoughtful with one's language regarding personal differences does not make you woke.
- Recognizing that you have in yourself the sinful potential to spew the hate of partiality and to act on this in short-term or long-term ways does not make you woke.
- Identifying troubling trends of partiality in one's national, regional, communal, or familial heritage does not make you woke, nor does wanting to leave such evil behind.
- Rejoicing in Gospel-driven fellowship across all common boundary markers in this world does not make you woke.

These statements matter because many people today are confused about what wokeness is. Many wonder if they are instinctually woke because they hate "racism"[7] and ethnocentrism, love humanity as made

---

[7] I'm using this term, but as noted, I do not do so believing in discrete "races." The reason I use it is because some wrongly do believe in "races" and, furthermore, in the superiority of one "race" over another.

in God's image, want to work as much as possible against sin of all kinds, humbly acknowledge their own failings (and troubled societal history), and generally seek unity in the Gospel. But this is not wokeness in action. This is basic biblical Christianity.[8]

This starting point is very important because Christians must see today that wokeness is not our only option. It is a relatively new and vigorously promoted option, yes. Many folks around us—inside the Church and outside it—are buying into it wholeheartedly. But wokeness does not have the market cornered, and Christians therefore must not confuse a godly approach to one's ethnicity and background with the adoption of woke thinking and acting.

It's not hard, though, to see why folks would make this mistake. Here are some reasons why: Critical Race Theory is complicated and has its own language and discourse, and most people do not read many books on complex intellectual movements. Additionally, most people do not track nuanced developments in legal studies. Positively, most people do want civic unity and do grieve the wickedness of past racism. Finally, most people support the police even as they want relations between law enforcement and citizens to improve in different hotspots around the nation.

In such a climate, with wokeness speaking so strongly and with such widespread cultural acceptance today, many Christians may well think that wokeness is the way forward. Many of these people, we note carefully, have noble hearts and good intentions. Nonetheless, the truth is they are in danger. This is not unlike how previous generations faced the devil's choice of embracing socialism as their operative ethics or being rejected by their non-Christian peers. Embracing this system seemed to

---

[8]   See Chapters 5 and 6 for a more sustained presentation, where we substantiate this claim through a survey of the Bible. As a side note, it is also true that the mindset just described also characterizes many non-evangelical people. Though they do not know Christ savingly and are sinners under real threat of divine judgment, thanks to God's common grace they nonetheless want to be fair, want people around them to thrive, oppose racism where they see it, and hope for better days in their land. In reading many people this way, I diverge quite radically from the way woke theorists and activists view common folk, as will become clear.

make sense, for our world is filled with economic unrest stemming from numerous factors. Yet to embrace an ungodly ideology is to lose Christianity, however long the switchover takes.

Today, we face a similar hard bargain. Many Christians are susceptible to being co-opted by wokeness—their Christianity remaining intact externally, but with a new internal host. Great discernment is needed. After all, do wokeness and Christianity share vocabulary and even a common burden for justice? Yes, this is true. There are surely what I call "connection points" between the two systems of thought and similar usage of terms like justice, love, and unity. But here we must ask: What is justice? What is unity? More broadly, what does it mean to be human? To answer these good questions, we cannot ask the people around us. We cannot learn such higher truth in an afternoon seminar. We have to go to God. We need the teaching of Scripture.

Our dependence on Scripture is intentional and unmissable. Though many today operate as if academic theory and social activism should supplement Christian thought and practice, in truth the Bible is sufficient for these things. (The Bible is sufficient for *all* things that pertain to life and godliness—see 2 Peter 1:3.) Simply put, the Bible gives us exactly what we need to find unity, hope, and justice in this world. The Bible, furthermore, fuels a life of "scriptural reasoning"—of thinking well about all things according to the conviction that God is God, and everything else is not. We'll say more there, but our intellectual engagement as Christians must involve: (1) total trust in all that God's Word teaches and (2) the wise and reasoned application of a biblical worldview to the hard questions around us. That is just what this book will do: we deconstruct our culture's systems through biblical reasoning (cultural deconstruction) in order to reconstruct a true worldview founded in the Gospel of Christ (Gospel reconstruction).[9]

---

9   Methodologically, I follow Cornelius Van Til, who advocated a presuppositional approach to apologetics in which the believer practices what can be called both "cultural deconstruction" and "gospel reconstruction." For more on Van Til, see Greg L. Bahnsen, *Van Til's Apologetic: Readings and Analysis* (Phillipsburg, New Jersey: Presbyterian & Reformed, 1998), 30.

All this may sound rather high-flown. So let's cut straight to the point: The answer to the problems that ail us—and they do really ail us—is not wokeness. It is biblical truth. It is the image of God. It is, above all things, the person and work of Jesus Christ. All this we shall explore in the pages to come.

What Wokeness Is

We have now thought about a few markers that do *not* signal that you are woke. If the convictions mentioned previously don't make you woke, though, what does? Wokeness is first and foremost a mindset and a posture. The term itself means that one is "awake" to the true nature of the world when so many are asleep.[10] In the most specific terms, this means one sees the comprehensive inequity of our social order and strives to highlight power structures in society that stem from racial privilege.

In intellectual terms, wokeness occurs when one embraces the system of thought mentioned above called Critical Race Theory.[11] CRT teaches that all of societal life is structured along racial power dynamics. Race is a "social construct," according to CRT; it's not biologically based and exists only in our imagination.[12] (Again, I actually agree on this point

---

[10] For more on the background of the term "woke," see C. Eric Lincoln and Lawrence H. Mamiya, *The Black Church in the African-American Experience* (Durham, North Carolina: Duke University Press, 1990), 372. I am not using the term in this project according to its past usage, but its present usage. The Cambridge English Dictionary, for example, defines the word as follows: "a state of being aware, especially of social problems such as racism and inequality." Accessible online at https://dictionary.cambridge.org/us/dictionary/english/wokeness.

[11] Critical Race Theory first arose in the field of legal studies. It was formally launched at a 1989 workshop near Madison, Wisconsin, by a group of lawyers and legal scholars. Richard Delgado and Jean Stefancic, *Critical Race Theory: An Introduction*, 2nd edition (New York and London: New York University Press, 2012), 4. For many of CRT's early formative writings, see Kimberlé Crenshaw, ed., *Critical Race Theory: The Key Writings That Formed the Movement* (New York: New Press, 1996).

[12] Delgado and Stefancic, *Critical Race Theory*, 8–9. CRT is now influential in numerous disciplines, including sociology (e.g., Robin DiAngelo) and psychology (e.g., Beverly Daniel Tatum).

with CRT proponents due to biblical teaching, not their ideas.) Yet race is America's original lie that has led to America's original sin: racism.

Racism occurs when one racial group oppresses, dehumanizes, and demeans another. According to woke voices, this is what "white people" do. Woke theorists and activists argue that America was and is shot through with racism.[13] The specific terms capturing this truth are "structural racism" and "systemic racism."[14] It is not only that individuals can say or do racist things; it is that the entire civilizational order is infected with racism. This problem cannot be the application of virtue in any individual sense. Systemic racism can only be addressed through political and economic means.

The intractability of this evil owes to its origins. According to woke history, America originally was rigged to be a power game that only "white" people would win.[15] Slavery and Jim Crow perpetuated such inequity. Then and now, white people think of themselves as superior to "black" people; this is the disease of "whiteness." While "whiteness" is a mentality, it is predominantly believed and practiced by "white people."[16] Such people benefit from a system grounded in "white suprem-

---

[13] Racism is "ordinary, not aberrational." Delgado and Stefancic, *Critical Race Theory*, 7.

[14] See, for example, Ibram X. Kendi, *How to Be an Antiracist* (New York: One World, 2019), 18.

[15] Some CRT theorists do not actually believe that race is a tangible, discrete truth. But they treat it as if it is to advance the interests of underprivileged peoples. This is called "strategic essentialism." See Helen Pluckrose and James Lindsay, *Cynical Theories: How Activist Scholarship Made Everything about Race, Gender, and Identity—and Why This Harms Everybody* (Durham, North Carolina: Pitchstone, 2020), 72–73, 195.

[16] Note the discussion by DiAngelo, *White Fragility*, 33. Though some theorists bob and weave when it comes to connecting "white" people with the problems with whiteness, DiAngelo (a "white" person) shows no such hesitation: "White supremacy describes the culture we live in, a culture that positions white people and all that is associated with them (whiteness) as ideal." The connection is unbreakable: white people inherently practice "whiteness," and so necessarily participate in and benefit from white supremacy, the result of "whites" in collective form. Other racial groups—notably Asian-Americans—partake in and benefit from this system as well. See, for example, how in Washington state an "equity report" grouped white and

acy" and promote it all the time.[17] They do so intentionally, both individually and systemically, through campaigns of violence by police, disproportionate incarceration of minorities, unfair housing decisions, unequal distribution of public resources for schooling and other causes, limited access to health and nutrition, and much more.[18] Again, to be clear, CRT theorists and activists argue that a racist America creates these conditions, often purposefully and with intent to do real harm to people of color.

But that is not all it argues—not by a long shot. "White supremacy" functions at the unintentional and even seemingly invisible level as well. "White" people, for example, commit "microaggressions," voicing subtle and unintended stereotypes (e.g., "I don't see color") that negatively imply power over ethnic minorities. They believe and pass down expressions of "white privilege" along these lines. Most any difference in cultural and social practice is read by CRT theorists and activists in monocausal terms—it stems from racism. The solution to one's personal racism is to become an "antiracist."[19] There is no middle ground

---

Asian American students together, treating the latter group as "white," effectively. See Helen Raleigh, "Asian Americans Emerging as a Strong Voice against Critical Race Theory," *Newsweek*, March 9, 2021, https://www.newsweek.com/asian-americans-emerging-strong-voice-against-critical-race-theory-opinion-1574503.

[17] Consider the discussion by Jemar Tisby, *The Color of Compromise: The Truth about the American Church's Complicity in Racism* (Grand Rapids, Michigan: Zondervan, 2019), 16–17.

[18] For sourcing, see as one example Michelle Alexander, *The New Jim Crow: Mass Incarceration in the Age of Colorblindness*, 10th anniversary edition (New York and London: New Press, 2020 [2010]), x–xiv. Alexander's focus is on imprisonment but references many other ills as well.

[19] Kendi, *How to Be an Antiracist*, 23. Note that being an "antiracist" is not a nature but a posture: "We can knowingly strive to be an antiracist. Like fighting an addiction, being an antiracist requires persistent self-awareness, constant self-criticism, and regular self-examination." Note carefully: One is never cured of racism in this framework. One does not gain a "new nature," to use a biblical phrase descriptive of the born-again believer. The language here is religious ("self-examination") but also deeply psychological: Racism is akin to an addiction. Racists can manage their condition, but never overcome it.

between encouraging racism and fighting racism; there is only racism and antiracism.

We Have Seen the Enemy, and It Is Color-Blindness

The enemy of "antiracism" is as much "color-blindness" as it is intentional racial oppression. This may be one of the most surprising finds that readers will make in seeking to be part of the cure, not the problem. The high-minded civil rights ideals of Martin Luther King Jr., to cite just one figure, are strongly—even severely—critiqued by CRT theorists and activists. "Color-blindness" is not the goal; a society where children are judged by the content of their character, not by their skin color, is not the goal. Rather, the defeat of "whiteness" is the goal.

Ibram X. Kendi, perhaps the leading woke theorist today, puts a fine point on the matter: "The most threatening racist movement is not the alt right's unlikely drive for a White ethnostate but the regular American's drive for a 'race-neutral' one."[20] This is basically what DiAngelo says as well: "In some ways, racism's adaptations over time are more sinister than concrete rules such as Jim Crow."[21] DiAngelo is more restrained with her language, but her point is actually sharper than Kendi's. We are not merely in a different racist order today; according to her, we are in an order that is worse, far worse, than in the days when Jim Crow laws dominated society. This is a stunning argument, truly shocking to behold.

Here again we see something vital about wokeness. Though it announces itself to us in positive terms, telling us we should be for "racial equity" and "justice" and "unity," it conceals thunder. It is not a movement of unity at all, nor does it preach tolerance. In actuality, it saves its strongest firepower not for extraordinary offenders, but for ordinary men and women who live quiet, normal American lives. These people, it turns out, are the true villains. If this language sounds strong,

---

[20] Ibid., 20.
[21] DiAngelo, *White Fragility*, 50.

consider what Kendi—a much-praised professor at Boston University—has said: Such people, mostly "white," constitute the "most threatening racist movement" today, worse than actual white supremacists who create real terror and division. The "regular American" is worse than the cross-burning Klan member; as DiAngelo suggested, America today is worse than in the days of Jim Crow, and "white fragility" and all it disguises are to blame.

Let us think for a moment about how explosive these claims are. In common non-woke thinking, the average "white" person in America is much like the average person in any country that looks and lives like many others. Countries, after all, often have one ethnicity represent a major part of their population. There will be real problems and sins in such circumstances, yes, but there may well also be what we call a "majority culture" that is practiced by many that is not inherently wicked. Ethnic differences are not necessarily evil; nor are the cultural habits, customs, inclinations, and practices that crop up around them. Having a majority culture practiced by a citizenry that to some extent looks alike and has a shared heritage is not necessarily a sign of sin.

But wokeness reads "white American majority culture" as very evil itself. Wokeness argues that the existence of racism in America means that "white" people fall prey to a special form of evil beyond normal Adamic fallenness. This is because of America's "white supremacist" order; the country and public order themselves are corrupt, not just the "white" populace. As we shall explore in Chapter 7, America's past does indeed contain real and systemic sin. Countries can and do enshrine unrighteous thinking in law; Christians know this and stay vigilant against it. But woke scholars and activists argue that the America of today is much like the America that formalized slavery, Jim Crow, and segregation. In addition, the average "white" person today is much like an intentional racist of the American past, whether or not they actually say or do anything traditionally identified as racist. Such people deserve this description because they are part of the majority culture.

In woke thinking, the average "white" person participates in American majority culture, a culture that is irrevocably stained with racism.[22] The well-meaning "white" housewife in my current state of Missouri who goes about her daily business, tries to be a good neighbor, and lives a quiet existence is not fundamentally considered a decent citizen by virtue of God's common grace.[23] There is no common grace in wokeness; there's just the righteous (the woke) and the guilty (ordinary white people). This housewife is not just a *part* of the broader unjust framework, though; according to Kendi and others, she is the very burning core of the problem. Even as she posts photos of her kids on Instagram, bakes pumpkin muffins in the fall, and volunteers at her local homeless shelter, she is actually a "white supremacist." She not only participates in the collective problem; in a real sense, she *is* the problem.

"Antiracism" as the Way Forward

The only way, as noted previously, that our Midwestern housewife can address her sins is by becoming an "antiracist." According to the woke, beneficiaries of "whiteness" must identify themselves as "racist" and thus embrace, in a kind of secular conversion experience that is often marked by a public declaration, being an "antiracist" through confession.

---

[22] Please note at this point that there is no such thing as an "average white person," nor is there such a thing as a "white mentality" or a "black mentality," much as we hear otherwise. There may be patterns that exist among certain people groups, but these archetypes—so often cited in public discussion today—are not grounded in definitive research or thinking. Recognizing this truth is Step 1 out of woke entrapment, whether one is a Christian or not, though Christianity always accords with reality and is the only logical endpoint of any true search for reality.

[23] When we speak of God's "common grace," we do not mean that this is a second grace, wholly distinct from God's "special grace" (which is His saving grace). We do mean that God is a perfectly gracious God who shows grace in different forms to sinners of all kinds. This two-fold unity shows up in other areas of our theology of God as well: there is a "will of decree" and a "will of desire" that we find in our scriptural study, yet the will of God is not broken up into two wills but is one will with two effects.

To become an "antiracist" means that one commits to a complete personal and social revolution. The system of white supremacy that one has either benefited from or simply left unchallenged must fall. The way it falls is by aggressive and sweeping action at every level to reimagine America (and the West) as an "antiracist" society.

Common proposals include reparations for descendants of slaves; restructuring hiring practices to ensure diverse personnel; protesting and opposing—even violently if necessary—stubbornly "racist" entities and individuals; reeducating youth to show the systemic wickedness of America as a country; practicing "lament" and the personal confession of one's inherent racism (especially if "white"); performing public acts of secular repentance to right wrongs; and, most generally, the destruction at every turn of "white supremacy" anywhere it can be found.[24]

CRT's teaching is plain: "white supremacy" truly is everywhere. Following Critical Theory, which contends that the seemingly peaceful cultural order of the West hides major power imbalances, CRT involves looking at ordinary life and society through the lens of racial power dynamics.[25] In America, the argument goes, common people are not leading lives of quiet dignity; they are either oppressing others or being oppressed. Inequality rules the social order just as it rules the economic order. In CRT, life is a zero-sum game. Some win; most lose. Guilty people—"white" people—can only embrace personal negation and perform ritual works.

This is all very philosophical, though. Rest assured that woke ideology is not made for classrooms. It is made for revolutions. We have witnessed one in recent months under the banner of "Black Lives Matter." While not all CRT theorists or activists would commend such open

---

[24] See Tisby, The Color of Compromise, 192–212.

[25] To understand Critical Theory, one can do no better than Roger Scruton's book Fools, Frauds, and Firebrands: Thinkers of the New Left (London: Bloomsbury Continuum, 2017 [1985]), 115–58. Scruton notes that Critical Theory sought to bag big game from the beginning: It questioned the very nature of reason itself (138–39). Destabilizing reason allowed for the destabilizing of entire worldviews. We note for our purposes that Critical Race Theory makes exactly the same move with similarly outsized ambitions (see Chapter 3).

hostility, the movement assembled around "BLM" includes voices that do promote both social destruction and physical violence. The official BLM platform, which was sanitized in late 2020 after coming under strong criticism, formerly opposed the "nuclear family," for example, and endorsed LGBT identity.[26] In the summer of 2020, marches under the BLM banner—which included many Antifa members—endangered many American cities. Under the banner of "protesting" police brutality, a complex subject deserving of careful analysis, activists torched property, attacked counter-protestors, and even murdered individuals. A stunned America watched as its cities burned day after day with only a tepid governmental response in many places—and even some endorsement in others.

The response to such behavior was mixed among BLM supporters; but for many, such violence and mayhem was not lamentable, but a sign of righteous agitation and even real progress. This is because of America's evil societal nature. As a society built on "white supremacy," America deserves to be targeted, demolished, and built afresh on "antiracist" principles, they say. Again, in some cases the need for such cleansing is stated metaphorically. But it is impossible to miss that in many instances, when the theory escapes the classroom, it does not land softly. As numerous examples show, teaching that "white supremacy" deserves nothing other than destruction has led to real-life consequences.[27] For its unbiblical teaching and its ungodly violence, Black

---

[26] The interested reader can find quotations from BLM's former platform in Matthew Wright, "Black Lives Matter Removes Page Encouraging the 'Disruption' of the 'Western Nuclear Family' during a Massive Cleanup of Their National Website," *Daily Mail*, September 22, 2020, https://www.dailymail.co.uk/news/article-8759959/BLM-removes-page-mentions-disrupting-Western-nuclear-family-website.html. At some point in September 2020, the platform was reduced substantially (this appears to have been in response to criticism from Marcellus Wiley and others).

[27] I think, as just one example, of the murderous shooting of former police chief David Dorn in the St. Louis area. Dorn was a "black" man, but that did not spare him the wrath of the mob.

Lives Matter and woke activism must be rejected—by Christians, certainly, and by any citizen besides.

Intersectionality and Opposition to All Inequality

To have your eyes opened to your own racism is the great awakening that CRT seeks. But coming alive to the true power dynamics that course through our world in racial terms means one begins to see many more unjust imbalances in the social order. Indeed, when one becomes "woke," one not only becomes an "antiracist," but also an opposer of numerous other evils and a liberator of many other groups. One recognizes the "intersectional" nature of injustice, meaning that one discovers that the causes of many underprivileged minority groups overlap.[28] This "intersection" means that a thorough vision of "social justice" involves opposing unjust power dynamics across the board. "White privilege" is the first culprit, but numerous other social arrangements incubate oppression, including the following:

- Men who have leadership positions naturally oppress women, and "toxic masculinity" predominates

---

[28] Kimberlé Crenshaw first proposed this concept in "Demarginalizing the Intersection of Race and Sex: A Black Feminist Critique of Antidiscrimination Doctrine, Feminist Theory and Antiracist Politics," *University of Chicago Legal Forum*, vol. 1989, issue 1, article 8, available at https://chicagounbound.uchicago.edu/cgi/viewcontent.cgi?article=1052&context=uclf. Here is an excerpt that explains her thinking: "The point is that Black women can experience discrimination in any number of ways and that the contradiction arises from our assumptions that their claims of exclusion must be unidirectional. Consider an analogy to traffic in an intersection, coming and going in all four directions. Discrimination, like traffic through an intersection, may flow in one direction, and it may flow in another.... Black women sometimes experience discrimination in ways similar to white women's experiences; sometimes they share very similar experiences with Black men. Yet often they experience double-discrimination—the combined effects of practices which discriminate on the basis of race, and on the basis of sex. And sometimes, they experience discrimination as Black women—not the sum of race and sex discrimination, but as Black women" (ibid., 149).

- Imperial intellectuals use the construct of reason to oppress minority groups in the academy
- The rich oppress the poor (fiscal inequality is inherently wrong)
- Physically able people oppress physically disabled people (this is "ableism")
- "Cisgender" and "heteronormative" straight people oppress "sexual minorities"
- Adults oppress children (especially religious ones, including those who "homeschool")
- Christians oppress "religious minorities"[29]

This list could go on. Though the concern for "intersectional justice" began as a feminist project, it has quickly expanded its mission and now stands for a huge body of burdens. The scarlet thread running through intersectional interests is that common forms of inequality represent injustice. Society must be rethought, rebuilt, and reconstructed.[30] Though intersectionality rejects "binary" thinking in terms of the sexes, it is ironically binary to its core. You are either an oppressor in

[29] For a discussion of many of these categories, see Patricia Hill Collins and Sirma Bilge, *Intersectionality: Key Concepts* (Cambridge, United Kingdom; Medford, Massachusetts: Polity Press, 2016). See also Beverly Daniel Tatum, *Why Are All the Black Kids Sitting Together in the Cafeteria? And Other Conversations about Race*, rev. ed. (New York: Basic Books, 2017), 101–8. Tatum considers the Christian religion a "system of privilege" over minority religious expressions, and thus, while serving as president of Spelman College (whose official seal contains the phrase "Our Whole School for Christ"), she organized a multifaith baccalaureate service which included readings from the Muslim (Islamic) and Bahá'í faiths. Tatum took these measures even while self-identifying as a Christian. Ibid., 108, 296–97.

[30] Ironically, however, intersectionality also has produced disagreement among Critical Theory advocates. To give one example, CRT scholars have been criticized by Marxist scholars who deem the category of class (or economic standing) to be a more impactful and comprehensive social factor than that of race. Michael J. Dumas, "Doing Class in Critical Race Analysis in Education," in *Handbook of Critical Race Theory in Education*, eds. Marvin Lynn and Adrienne D. Dixson (New York: Routledge, 2013), 115–18.

different areas of life, or you are oppressed. There is no middle ground. Your skin color and access to privilege determine which category you're in, not your character.

The broader project of "social justice" thus advances the "rights" of minorities of many kinds to remove inequality—or even difference itself—from our world. Men must be removed from positions of authority, and boys must be trained to see strong manhood as akin to "toxic masculinity." Income must be taken and redistributed. Capitalism should be strenuously resisted, for it was built on the back of racism. Reason must be opposed by "personal narratives" driven by a belief in "standpoint epistemology," the view that one's minority status gives one a unique ability to see truth that privileged peoples necessarily cannot comprehend.[31] Public spaces must be redone to accommodate the fluid "gender identities" of individuals. And more broadly, all forms of personal identity (and "orientation") must be affirmed without question and accepted as a positive reality. (As I have noted, a thorough critique of these views comes in Chapters 3 and 4; we're seeking, in all fairness, to describe the system in a compact way here.)

As if these undertakings were not ambitious enough, public policy must at every turn advance "antiracist" and "intersectional" interests. The law and courtroom justice have to shift from a retributive focus (holding evildoers to account) to a distributive and reparative emphasis (creating a more equal society through "humane" laws and verdicts). There is a lively debate among CRT theorists over whether the movement should train its guns on traditional targets (the law), everyday interactions (sociology), or the public square (policy and politics).[32] Regardless, in all sectors, the movement advances, and it does so not only along the

---

[31] A working definition of standpoint epistemology: "Feminist standpoint theorists make three principal claims: (1) Knowledge is socially situated. (2) Marginalized groups are socially situated in ways that make it more possible for them to be aware of things and ask questions than it is for the non-marginalized. (3) Research, particularly that focused on power relations, should begin with the lives of the marginalized." T. Bowell, "Feminist Standpoint Theory," *Internet Encyclopedia of Philosophy*, https://iep.utm.edu/fem-stan.

[32] See Delgado and Stefancic, *Critical Race Theory*, 19–38.

lines of those opposing racism, as per CRT, but in numerous areas where "inequality" equals injustice, according to intersectional advocates.

Where Did All This Ideology Come From?

In two words: Karl Marx. And two more: Friedrich Engels. This duo sent shockwaves through the West following the publication of *The Communist Manifesto* in 1848. Alongside the economic argument, they made this foundational claim: "Hitherto, every form of society has been based, as we have already seen, on the antagonism of oppressing and oppressed classes." Therefore, "the history of all hitherto existing society is the history of class struggles. Freeman and slave…lord and serf, guild-master and journeyman, in a word, oppressor and oppressed."[33] This perspective on human identity and societal ordering fit fluidly with Darwinian cosmology, the spread of which Marx cheered in his era.

There is a great deal to evaluate in Marxist ideology. We will not dive into it in this book, but we do need to note just how influential this framing of society was. In truth, humanity is divided into two groups: saved and unsaved. But Marx reframed our fundamental categories along economic lines—"class struggles," to be precise. He saw history playing out as a great conflict between oppressors (those who control the means of production) and the oppressed (those who are not economically privileged).

Marx located this critique more specifically in societal institutions. Jeffrey Johnson concisely captures the anti-authority dimensions of the bibliographic wet bomb that Marx (and Engels) sent into society through *The Communist Manifesto*:

> Marx believed that the great moral problem of society could be reduced to the institutions of authority within society. He held that because authority by its very nature is oppressive, all authoritative structures and institutions must be destroyed.

---

[33] Karl Marx and Friedrich Engels, *The Communist Manifesto*, 9.

And when all decentralized divisions of authority have been dismantled, a globalized classless society must take its place in a new world order. In this new world order, people will no longer have to relate to each other as superiors and inferiors, rich and poor, leader and follower. Not until there are no class divisions, diversity, or hierarchical stature of authority will society be free of oppression. Only then will the world be rid of evil and experience utopia.[34]

This worldview was rooted in atheism: godlessness. But Marx did not only shake his fist at the divine. He hated the world God had made. He despised what theologians call "creation order." He wanted to wipe out every trace of divine making from the earth. We quote Johnson again on this count:

But most importantly, because our present institutions derive their delegated authority from God, these institutions (individualism, family, church, and state) must first be deconstructed and stripped of their authority in order to fully eliminate God from society. In fact, for Marx, deliverance from the evils of capitalism cannot occur until all traces of God are removed from this world.[35]

Critical Theory would adapt Marx's categories and critiques in the mid-twentieth century. It applied the Marxist grid not solely to considerations of class, but also to anthropology more broadly. As Marx maintained, everyone is either an oppressor or an oppressed person. The Frankfurt Critical Theorists like Theodor Adorno and Max Horkheimer argued that bourgeois institutions mediated the oppression in question. People outside of the cultural mainstream came off as essentially

---

[34] Jeffrey Johnson, *What Every Christian Needs to Know about Social Justice* (Conway, Arkansas: Free Grace Press, 2021), 28–29.

[35] Ibid, 29.

righteous in their struggle against cultural norms. In essential terms, minority groups gained favored status during this time. The challenge to institutions first posed by Enlightenment thinkers gained serious stream as the Critical Theorists challenged the integrity of the "bourgeois" social order.

In fact, *reason itself* was lost in modern society, driven as it was by capitalist ideology. Commenting on the thought of Frankfurt School theorist Max Horkheimer, Roger Scruton noted that:

> Reason, he argues, is corrupted by the capitalist order and loses its natural focus in human life…. For bourgeois reason, therefore, humanity is strictly *imperceptible*. The true critical philosophy is the one that, by turning the gaze of philosophy on philosophy itself, sees the poisoned sources of its own polluted reasoning.

Scruton summarizes Horkheimer's burden: we must "pass beyond philosophy into 'critical theory' and discover the true possibility of emancipation, which begins with the emancipation of thought itself."[36] In simpler terms, to understand humanity, the Critical Theorists argued that one must recognize the corrupted nature of society, but not only of society—of ordinary reason itself. It is for this reason that Voddie Baucham Jr. has argued that such thinking—including Critical Race Theory, derived from this system—is gnosticism.[37] He means that according to this ideology, there is a higher knowledge that only some possess; ordinary perception alone will not do. The structures of reality, whether economic or cultural or "racial" (in our time), may look sound, but they are not. They must be exposed, for they actually contain surging injustice within them. Only some can see this—the woke.

---

36 Scruton, *Fools, Frauds, and Firebrands*, 138.
37 Voddie Baucham Jr., "Ethnic Gnosticism," in *By What Standard?: God's World… God's Rules* (Cape Coral, Florida: Founders Press), 105–16.

As readers will now grasp, this system is precisely what Critical Race Theory uses to make its case. The world is fundamentally flawed; only a few enlightened folks can see it. The world is not divided along the lines the Bible says it is (saved and unsaved), but between the oppressor and the oppressed; liberation is not found in any theological solution, but through identification of the oppression—often hidden—that society transmits. This is Marx's own tool, updated and revised.

There is intellectual lineage here. CRT owes its major categories to Critical Theory, which owes its major categories to Marx. Yet this combative mentality of unfair victimization was whispered long before Marx. The ultimate source of this ideology does not sound like the voice of God, but like the slithery hiss of a serpent.

The Traps Are Set: The Ironies of Our Current Culture

The previous material shows us that we are walking in a cultural fog today. We hear sharp directives coming through the mist but have little sense of what to do and where to go. We do know one thing for sure: many traps are set. It has become very hard to be a person of virtue on "racial" matters today, but it has become very easy to be a racist. Wokeness in general has electrified American and Western culture and made them zones of resentment, perpetual guilt, and grave danger.

In this climate, there are in fact so many traps set by wokeness that you are caught no matter which way you turn. John McWhorter has captured this reality in critiquing what he calls "Third Wave Antiracism." McWhorter observes the following ironies of woke ideology that, in his words, mean that this system's ideas ultimately "translate into nothing whatsoever." This is a lengthy quotation, but a helpful one:

1. When black people say you have insulted them, apologize with profound sincerity and guilt. **But** don't put black people in a position where you expect them to forgive you. They have dealt with too much to be expected to.

2. Black people are a conglomeration of disparate individuals. "Black culture" is code for "pathological, primitive ghetto people." **But** don't expect black people to assimilate to "white" social norms because black people have a culture of their own.

3. Silence about racism is violence. **But** elevate the voices of the oppressed over your own.

4. You must strive eternally to understand the experiences of black people. **But** you can never understand what it is to be black, and if you think you do you're a racist.

5. Show interest in multiculturalism. **But** do not culturally appropriate. What is not your culture is not for you, and you may not try it or do it. But—if you aren't nevertheless *interested* in it, you are a racist.

6. Support black people in creating their own spaces and stay out of them. **But** seek to have black friends. If you don't have any, you're a racist. And if you claim any, they'd better be *good* friends. Just know that you still aren't allowed in their private spaces.

7. When whites move away from black neighborhoods, it's white flight. **But** when whites move into black neighborhoods, it's gentrification, even when they pay black residents generously for their houses.

8. If you're white and only date white people, you're a racist. **But** if you're white and date a black person you are, if only deep down, exotifying an "other."

9. Black people cannot be held accountable for everything every black person does. **But** all whites must acknowledge their personal complicity in the perfidy throughout history of "whiteness."

10. Black students must be admitted to schools via adjusted grade and test score standards to ensure a representative number of them and foster a diversity of views in

classrooms. **But** it is racist to assume a black student was admitted to a school via racial preferences, and racist to expect them to represent the "diverse" view in classroom discussions.[38]

Wokeness is a strange thing, as McWhorter's incisive analysis makes clear. It offers liberation, but it entraps. It speaks the tones of justice, but it causes injustice. It tells "white" people they need to honor the "black" experience, but it gives only one side of the "black" experience. It reads an entire group of people as intractably guilty and reads the opposite group of people as irreversibly innocent. It does all this by building on an American past that does have real problems and sins in it and by pointing to events of the current day as proof that the injustices of the past are not in any meaningful way overcome, but fester in our time. The case made by woke ideology is in no way unifying. Instead, the synthesis of the past with the "oppression" of the present ends up not defeating those past evils, but resuscitating resentment, victimhood, and societal leveling. Such a program will yield division, not healing.

Conclusion

What is wokeness? Wokeness is, as we have noted, a mindset, a mood, and a set of principles and beliefs. It takes different forms; CRT is woke, intersectionality is woke, and belief systems that make use of the concepts and framework of these ideologies are woke, whether wittingly or unwittingly. While wokeness is the overarching category, then, and is found in different ideologies, it has certain key ideas. Based on the preceding analysis (with more to come), here are seven key commitments of wokeness.

---

[38] John McWhorter, "John McWhorter: The Neoracists," *Persuasion*, February 8, 2021, https://www.persuasion.community/p/john-mcwhorter-the-neoracists.

1. The world is fundamentally divided into oppressors and oppressed people.
2. A major form of oppression today comes from "whiteness."
3. "Whiteness" is not a neutral system, but creates a culture of "white supremacy" that most benefits "white" people (and also others who fail to challenge it).
4. The evils of this culture show up in disparities between groups, which reveal inequities, which reveal injustices (disparities lead to inequities, which lead to injustices).
5. "White supremacy" must be vigorously opposed through "social justice," "antiracism," and the targeting of "white privilege."
6. More broadly, any form of "privilege" and "oppression" stemming from heteronormative "white" capitalist patriarchalist structures must be opposed.
7. We can create a just, fair, diverse, and inclusive society grounded in equality of outcome by targeting inequities through political, legal, cultural, and fiscal means so that inequitable authority is deprivileged and minority groups are empowered.

As I am at pains to say, the movement promoting these unsound ideas (and many others) is both formal and informal. Some proponents have terminal degrees in related fields and are full-time scholars working on these matters. Others are teenagers logging into social media accounts on chrome laptops and retweeting hashtags. Others are marching in the street and carrying bullhorns as they oppose the police. Some are fully aware of the broader commitments of this ideology (as contained in different but complementary structures), while others have basically no knowledge of the broader body of thought and activism they're supporting. Like any movement of this vastness—like socialism, or postmodernity, or atheism, or naturalism—we find many different varieties of wokeness, but they all traffic in on the ideas cited above. The activist throwing a brick into the window to defeat "white supremacy" is woke. The mom reading a book on "raising an antiracist baby" to teach her two-year-old about "implicit bias" is woke. The teenager tearfully confessing her failure to challenge "white supremacy" is woke.[39]

Wokeness is like the major movements of years past: It appears in many forms, and though ubiquitous can be hard to identify. It is similar to postmodernism, Marxism, and in religious terms, Protestant liberalism. You can spot figures who argue for it in intellectual terms, creating scholarship that advances the movement academically. But the street-level activism is no less important. Wokeness is creating a major groundswell at the popular level that is not nearly so formal. The movement is here, in many forms, and it is executing a takeover of the public order.

Wokeness, as we have seen, is many things, but it is not sound thinking. Yet as our next chapter shows, it is not only influencing our society; it is making real inroads into the Church of the Lord Jesus Christ. As an ideology alien to the Bible, it represents a massive threat. In fact, no less a figure than John MacArthur—a leading evangelical statesman of our time—has called it the greatest danger to the Church that he has seen in six decades of Gospel ministry. Clearly, this is no small challenge. This is a once-in-a-lifetime crisis; it calls for a once-in-a-lifetime stand on God's truth.

DISCUSSION QUESTIONS

1. What are some examples of biblical practices that are often confused with being "woke"?
2. How is power a central concept in the thinking of Critical Race Theory (CRT)?

---

[39] Note that in all my examples, I am citing volitional involvement in wokeness. You may live in a woke culture, and you may be confused by it for many reasons without being woke. There are different levels of woke engagement to be sure, but the point stands: you are woke at some level when you embrace, use, support, and commend woke ideas and actions. I'll give more definition on this count in Chapter 2.

3. Which category is more important in CRT's framework—
   individuals or groups? Why?
4. According to wokeness advocates, what are some things
   a person must do to prove his or her antiracism?
5. Why does wokeness often lead to a push for "equality" in
   areas *beyond* race?

CHAPTER 2

How Wokeness Is Entering the Church

You don't end racism. You repent of it.

—Darrell Harrison

The Urbana missions conference has had an outsized influence on the American Church. In years past, Urbana introduced many young Christians to the need for Gospel proclamation in all the world. In 2015, however, the conference made headlines for different reasons. A young speaker named Michelle Higgins took the platform and gave what was for many listeners an introduction to "woke Christianity." In her talk, Higgins said the following to a reported audience of sixteen thousand:

Do you see that racism is the age-old idol in our closet that we can't manage to tear down? Do you see it in our houses of worship, my brothers and sisters, right beside the little sexism idol and the classism idol and the cool-car idol and the good-job idol and the college-degree idol? Do you see it? Tear it down and admit, with torn shirt, ash in our hair, on our hands and knees, "Oh, God, we have committed adultery with white supremacy!" The evangelical church has taken the dominance and power of Eurocentrism and made it its side-piece, or part-time lover.

She continued the theme:

> Maybe we haven't been convinced that white supremacy is
> our idol, is our little god, but we do know that we have all of
> the techniques, all of the people that we need to eliminate
> both racial and class-based injustice on this continent. We
> have all we need except the will to do it, and that may be
> because we're so comfortable that we don't want to change.
> That may be that I'm so comfortable with my wonderful,
> high-class dentist, I don't want to pay for somebody to get
> some good teeth![1]

Higgins's talk shocked many evangelicals. Instead of the unifying
message of the Gospel and the need for it to go to the ends of the earth
out of love for sinful humanity, Urbana featured a fiery denunciation of
a Church committing "adultery" with "white supremacy." For perhaps
the first time, many evangelicals realized then that there was a new tune
in Christian circles. Not only a new tune, but new material for confession
of sin: "white" students at Urbana were encouraged to confess the sin
Higgins identified, that of ordinary "white supremacy"—an experience
they likely had not expected at a missions conference.

Leaving the World We Had Made

Nearly six years later, I distinctly recall the force of Higgins's charge
and the shocked response of many brothers and sisters in Christ. In the
wake of Michael Brown's death in Ferguson and the social unrest it
caused, many of us prayed for the Church to find real unity in Christ. A
good number of us from a variety of backgrounds assumed that if we
pursued such oneness, listened to one another well, acknowledged the

---

[1]   InterVarsity Christian Fellowship USA, "Michelle Higgins—Urbana 15," You-
Tube, January 26, 2016, https://www.youtube.com/watch?v=XVGDSkxxXco.

real failings of the American past and the American Church, and priori-
tized fellowship, we would be able to endure and overcome the societal
division that was surfacing in a serious way some six years ago. This was
a common refrain: if we held our Christian family together even as some
members expressed strong opinions and strong emotions, we would find
our way out of the tension.

We assumed this because in the frankest terms, many of us did not
know what was advancing. We did not realize that a godless ideology
was creeping into the Church. Alongside real sorrow over social upheaval
and the deaths of image-bearers, this ideology was a separate thing
entirely from biblical justice, biblical grief, and biblical cultural engagement. In fact, we did not realize that this ideology would express itself
in the very terms of Scripture and link itself to good and right ambitions
of God's people. Many of us, after all, had grown up in supposedly "post-
racial" America. We heard MLK's "I Have a Dream" speech in public
school and resonated with its vision. At a common grace level, we had
friends of different skin colors and different backgrounds, and we loved
different cultural products from other communities.

It is not that we were cleansed of the possibility of "racism" or ethnocentrism. We weren't (just as our country wasn't). We all must watch
our hearts regarding partiality of any kind (treating some better than
others for various reasons per James 2), and we must all remain vigilant
against sins of every kind until we die or Christ returns (Proverbs 4:23).
But we grew up in a society that had made real societal progress along
"racial" and ethnic lines. We were encouraged in a generically humane
way to treat people fairly, value people for who they are, and work across
traditional dividing lines to build friendships. None of this meant that
the Kingdom of God had arrived. Yet all of it was indeed positive, showing that America was progressing, if in no way perfect.

In addition, I can't fail to say that it was thrilling to encounter new
culture in this period. Born in the early 1980s, I was a teenager in the
1990s. What a time to be alive! Hip hop was exploding as a cultural
phenomenon, Michael Jordan was dominating the basketball court, the

Fab Five of Michigan made baggy shorts popular (would that those days would return), and there was an excitement and a freshness to much of the culture of this era that gripped many of us. Yes, I was a short "white" kid from rural Maine who wore glasses[2] and won my school's spelling bee. It didn't matter—I was drawn like cold filings to a magnet to such "urban" culture. I loved it. I still do. It shaped me, just as it shaped many others of all backgrounds and skin colors.

The explosion of urban culture had many effects. For my part, it made me look up to people I had nothing in common with, at least on paper. The toughness, the strong manhood, the intellect packed in verse after verse of multi-syllable rap lines, the edgy coolness of so many athletes, the leadership showed in sporting events, the perseverance of artists and athletes to transcend fatherlessness and broken homes and achieve amazing things—it all affected me, even in a small town in Maine.

My local college, the University of Maine at Machias, was a National Association of Intercollegiate Athletics (NAIA) Division Two program. Its basketball team was not in a powerhouse collegiate system, but it did not matter. The players for the UMM "Clippers" were from all over the world, and I loved that global flavor, as did many in our local community. Zeke was from Bosnia and had family members who suffered in conflicts back home; Gary was silky-smooth and like many of the players from Canada; Barry was from Israel and later played at a high level in his home country; Albert, hailing from Toronto, was so fast you could only guess which direction he was going and commit to it; Chad had a scholarship to a Big Twelve school and lost it, yet could singlehandedly will his team to victory; and Earl was from a tropical island and once threw down a tomahawk dunk in traffic that I can still see in my mind twenty years later.

I adored many of these players, looked up to them, and was inspired by them. My experience was my own, but many others forged such

---

[2]   When playing sports, I actually wore Rec-Specs. There are no public pictures of this, and there never will be.

connections in this era as America opened up in different ways. At home, my little sister was originally from a South American country, and she had a real effect on me. Her skin color was not exactly like mine or like several people at our small church, but that did not matter a bit. My father and mother loved her, I loved her (and always will), and she loved us. God gave our family a blessing in the form of my sister—a Christian, and a woman who loves and serves her family well—and I am so thankful for my parents' commitment to adoption.

None of this means that every issue America faced in its past magically vanished in the 1990s. But it does reflect, at a certain level, how America operated. In a good number of places, this society made progress. We see it in the legacy of public leaders like U.S. Supreme Court Justice Clarence Thomas, the intellectual dynamism of a figure like Thomas Sowell, and the genuine change that has come to a country that once tolerated terrible evil at the level of policy and law.

Yet as all this transpired, little did we know that there was a movement that was spreading in academic circles in this time, beginning as we saw in the last chapter in the legal world, then moving into sociology and related disciplines, and finally going mainstream in the last few years. This movement would upend much of the consensus of the previous several decades. It would convince many people who did not harbor "racial" prejudice that they did; it would teach many people who had made real cross-cultural connections that they could not transcend differences of skin color. Most devastatingly, it would introduce in many churches the idea that Christianity incubates "white privilege" and, still more strongly, "white supremacy."

This is where we are today: The old world has gone. The new world has come. As we saw from Ibram Kendi in the previous chapter, in our new public order, America's greatest danger is not *actual* white supremacy of the sort promoted by the Klan, for example. It's normcore, middle-America white supremacy. It's the "white supremacy" that supposedly festers unchecked wherever groups of ordinary "white" people gather. One of the gravest threats to "racial equity" and "inclusion" is the

Church composed of a significant percentage of "white" people. This is what we hear from numerous voices today as CRT, wokeness, and intersectionality advance in a major way in the Church. Here are several ideas that we are hearing from various voices:

- Evangelicals are hearing that they are "white supremacists" by nature.
- Christians are being called to "repent" for their "whiteness" and reject their inherent "white fragility."
- Christians are told that they are complicit in the racist sins of their forebears.
- Christians are urged to read complex realities and events in monocausal terms, with racism as the cause (for example, poverty, crime rates, shootings, and educational disparities).
- Christians are encouraged to align with Black Lives Matter, an organization with a polar-opposite worldview on matters of the natural family, the sexes, and human sexuality.
- Christians are told to see "capitalism" as oppressive, unfair, and unjust, with socialism of various kinds as the preferable system.
- Christians are told that "white interpretation" has held the Church captive to a white agenda for too long, necessitating scholarship and research rooted in standpoint epistemology
- Christians are urged to support "reparations" and distributive justice (over retributive justice).
- Christians hear that they should support cultural relativism and that making judgments (along moral and other lines) about cultural practices is wrong.
- Christians are directed to add their voice to "defund the police."

The point is clear: the American Church is receiving all kinds of woke messages and exhortations today. Wokeness, Critical Race Theory, and intersectionality are making real inroads into the Church. Few know enough about these ideologies to respond to them biblically; fewer still are speaking up to distinguish the truth from the counterfeit. As a result, some Christians are going woke—or are pondering if they should. They are doing so because of the arguments and activism of influential books, including several we will now consider briefly.

Five Influential Woke Christian Books

In the following analysis, I will examine five of the most influential "woke" books that have entered evangelical circles in recent decades. The present section will feature both descriptions and limited critique of their ideological positions. (A fuller critique of wokeness is just around the corner in Chapters 3 and 4.) It is important to hear what these authors are espousing in their own words. Though there is a spectrum of conviction among the authors I engage, and though I cannot and do not know their heart as God surely does, it is nonetheless true that they are indeed promoting woke ideas, and this advocacy bodes ill for Christ's Church.

Michael O. Emerson and Christian Smith,
Divided by Faith (2000)

Michael O. Emerson and Christian Smith are professors of sociology who conducted a joint study on the issues of evangelicalism and race in the late 1990s.[3] It is arguable that no book has been more influential in the "evangelical" wokeness movement than *Divided by Faith*.[4] Emerson and Smith's study landed at the top of the Gospel Coalition's (TGC) 2016

---

[3] Michael O. Emerson and Christian Smith, *Divided by Faith: Evangelical Religion and the Problem of Race in America* (Oxford, United Kingdom: Oxford University Press, 2000).

[4] Emerson is now the provost of North Park University (Chicago, Illinois), an institution affiliated with the Evangelical Covenant Church (ECC). Smith is a professor of sociology at the University of Notre Dame.

recommended reading list on the topic of racial division.⁵ Through a combination of over-the-phone surveys and in-person interviews, the authors sought to ascertain the core beliefs of white evangelicalism on issues of race. Emerson and Smith describe their research as evidence of the reality of white privilege in America, which they call a "racialized society."⁶ As much as evangelicals might voice a desire for racial reconciliation, their institutions, organizations, and unspoken values actually perpetuate racial division.⁷

As in standard woke thinking, the authors contend that although slavery, Jim Crow, and legislated segregation are no longer realities in America, racism has not lessened. It is more covert now, but no less pervasive. It has simply changed form.⁸ Vast inequalities exist, the authors argue, between whites and blacks in the areas of income, employment, and health care, among others, all of which can be attributed to systemic racial injustice as the driving factor.⁹ All white evangelicals are complicit in the racial inequalities that exist, mainly because "they support the American system and enjoy its fruits."¹⁰

Divided by Faith may seem like a dispassionate study. But as has already emerged, it is a book of thorough advocacy, and it is steeped in woke thinking. For example, the authors argue that whites and blacks should work together to "recognize" and "resist" racialized "structures of inequality" in society.¹¹ In combating racial inequality, whites, as "the main creators and benefactors of the racialized society, must repent of their personal, historical, and social sins." This is because "if historical and

---

⁵ This list is comprised of recommendations provided by numerous TGC contributors. Ivan Mesa, "7 Books on the White-Black Racial Divide You Should Read," the Gospel Coalition, September 22, 2016, https://www.thegospelcoalition.org/article/7-books-on-the-white-black-racial-divide-you-should-read.

⁶ Emerson and Smith, *Divided by Faith*, 7.

⁷ Ibid., ix, 88, 170.

⁸ Ibid., 9.

⁹ Ibid., 12–14, 132, 171.

¹⁰ Ibid., 22.

¹¹ Ibid., 55, 171.

social sins are not confessed and overcome, they are passed on to future generations, perpetuating the racialized system, and perpetuating sin."

This is a curious argument. It communicates a generational understanding of sin that is foreign to the New Testament. Nowhere is any person asked by Christ or His apostles to repent of a sin that a family member committed. Nowhere is anyone rendered guilty for crimes of previous generations (as we'll discuss in greater depth in Chapter 4). We can surely grieve past failings, but this is altogether different from repenting of them. We have enough sins to repent of in ourselves, let alone for other people.

Ironically, Emerson and Smith are "perpetuating" the very problems they indict. It is their thinking, and the ideology of others like them, that passes on "sin" and a "racialized system." They are "whites" according to their work, and they have bought into a body of thought that divides rather than unites. Instead of realizing real unity in Christ, this kind of activism leads only to polarization. Nor is it based in Christ exclusively; the chief remedy in overcoming the racial divide is for "whites" to see that the problem is not primarily one of individual responsibility, resolved through evangelism and the changing of sinful hearts. In terms common to woke literature, the problem is addressed beyond the Gospel as churches unite to dismantle institutions and structures of oppression in Christian circles and in society that the Gospel does not overcome.

Soong-Chan Rah, Prophetic Lament (2015)

Soong-Chan Rah is a professor at North Park Theological Seminary in Chicago, Illinois. In 2015, he published a book entitled *Prophetic Lament*, which was named by *Relevant* magazine as one of its top ten nonfiction books that year.[12] Rah's work is an interwoven mixture of biblical commentary on the book of Lamentations and cultural commentary on racist injustice in America. Rah argues that systemic racism is pervasive in the United States, a reality which has become more and

---

[12] Soong-Chan Rah, *Prophetic Lament: A Call for Justice in Troubled Times* (Downers Grove, Illinois: IVP Books, 2015).

more evident through the high-profile shootings of unarmed black men by white police officers.[13] In such cases, non-black Christian outsiders should lament with their black brothers and sisters, joining in their cries to God voiced out of pain and outrage.[14] The author argues that, when faced with the reality of injustice against blacks:

> Our claims must first shift from the defensive posture of "I am not a racist" to "I am responsible and culpable in the corporate sin of racism." We must move from "let's just get over it" to "how do I personally continue to perpetuate systems of privilege?"[15]

Besides using the language of lament, what are Rah's proposed remedies for the problem of suffering? Eliminating the power of one group and redistributing the power to others. Rah advocates for concrete actions in society and in the Church that seek to "dismantle" and "deconstruct" the power and wealth of majority oppressors, even while reapportioning that power and wealth to minorities, especially blacks in America.[16] In situations of injustice and oppression, white voices should keep quiet, while voices of color and feminine voices should speak.[17] Rah bases this claim on the fact that in the book of Lamentations, the literary device of personification is used to characterize Jerusalem as a woman— "her children have gone into exile" (Lamentations 1:5).[18]

Rah is on a mission to silence some in the Church. As noted, he wants "white" people, especially "white" men, to shut their mouths. He maintains that in racially charged cases such as the Michael Brown shooting in Ferguson, Missouri, in 2014, white Christians should not

---

13 Ibid., 139, 204–12.

14 Ibid., 44.

15 Ibid., 125–26.

16 Ibid., 23, 170–72, 177.

17 Ibid., 208.

18 Ibid., 59–64, 82.

"argue the details of the law and analyze the issues on legal merits," but rather should join in the lament or else be silent.[19]

This is a classic example of woke strategy. It is not the actual facts of the case that matter, and it is not American jurisprudence that matters; it is the narrative of police brutality against minorities that matters. This is a deeply problematic framing. "White" Christians and all Christians should definitely take interest in police shootings and should do so fairly, thoughtfully, and with a thorough interest in the facts of the case as weighed by the details of the law. Without law and without order, society breaks down, and justice atrophies. No, "white" people should not lay aside factual and legal analysis. As those who love our neighbors, we must be a voice for justice. No person can be silenced because of their skin color. What Rah presents as the solution to "racism" is truly partiality.

Daniel Hill, White Awake (2017)

Daniel Hill is the founding pastor of River City Community Church, a multiethnic church in Chicago, Illinois. Hill's 2017 book, *White Awake*, was backed by a joint partnership of InterVarsity Press (IVP) and the Christian Community Development Association (CCDA).[20] In this book, Hill recounts his own personal journey from being spiritually blind about white privilege in the early days of his ministry to his eventual painful awakening. Hill speaks of the pervasive and universal nature of white privilege and "the system of white supremacy" in the U.S.[21] He holds that all white people are racist, whether consciously or subconsciously. No one is immune. In fact, racism is the chief overarching sin that the Church has to deal with in the present day. "The primary enemy of God's kingdom in this realm is white supremacy," Hill declares.[22]

---

[19] Ibid., 67.
[20] Daniel Hill, *White Awake: An Honest Look at What It Means to Be White* (Downers Grove, Illinois: IVP Books, 2017).
[21] Ibid., 37–38, 147, 158.
[22] Ibid., 152.

The author speaks about his own need to repent of his sin and the sins of his community. He writes,

> I repent all the time because I believe I'm surrounded by the sickness of racism. I see the sickness in the ideology of white supremacy and have no doubt that it has infected me.... I see the sickness of systemic racism and have no doubt that I contribute to it in ways I'm not aware of. I'm surrounded by sickness, and I am sick.[23]

Hill is sure that he is racist, subconsciously so, even when he cannot pinpoint anything specific. This is a major part of the problem with Hill's writing. We are open to hearing his case that America is shot through with "white supremacy." After all, we know what actual "white supremacy" looks like, and it is hideous—a manifestation of Satanic influence in the world God has made. It looks like segregation, and lynchings, and women being abused by slave masters, and a societal order denying the humanity of people based on their skin color. That is actual "white supremacy."

But outside of groups like the Ku Klux Klan and voices among the "alt-right," where do we find such wickedness today? Hill points to "the inequitable systems that perpetuate disparities."[24] It is surely possible that we may find inequities in our systems, and if we do, we should tackle them. But while we take disparities seriously, they do not in themselves prove injustices. Some "white" people are wealthy, and some are very poor; the difference between them can reduce to injustice, but it also can owe to numerous factors, none of them stemming from "white supremacy." We are left with a passionate "prophetic" call from Hill, but very little in the way of proof of systemic supremacy.

---

[23] Ibid., 139.
[24] Ibid., 64; see also 149–53.

Eric Mason, Woke Church *(2018)*

Eric Mason is the founding pastor of Epiphany Fellowship in Philadelphia, Pennsylvania.[25] In Mason's 2018 book, *Woke Church*, he argues that the essence of wokeness means holding white people "accountable for the racial injustice we are entrenched in."[26] White people have created a privileged system of institutions and structures that keeps blacks in a state of oppression. Thus, blacks and those of other minority races must help whites "grow in their racial IQ" to realize that their conscious or unconscious racism creates the problem—but white Christians should not fear, because along with Christian activists, there will also be "saved racists" in Heaven.[27] The author states that justification, the heart of the biblical Gospel, "isn't merely a position, but a practice," maintaining that it is "an attribute and an action."[28] In the author's words, activism on issues of racial justice in society seems to be part and parcel with the attribute of being justified. Mason laments the fact that the Christian Church did not participate in and stand at the forefront of the Black Lives Matter movement, which arose in 2013.[29]

---

[25] Eric Mason, *Woke Church: An Urgent Call for Christians in America to Confront Racism and Injustice* (Chicago, Illinois: Moody, 2018).

[26] Ibid., 112.

[27] Ibid., 111, 175. The thoughtful reader must ask: "Are there saved thieves in Heaven, saved adulterers, or saved murderers?" The formulation of the category of "saved racists" is perplexing. It seems that the primary identity of this group throughout their time on Earth is that of persistent racists, even though they somehow wind up inheriting salvation along the way.

[28] Ibid., 45–46. Later in his book, Mason asserts that social justice should not be viewed as "the content" of the Gospel (104–5), but it is not clear how this statement jibes with his earlier statements about justification. There seems to be a basic confusion between justification and sanctification in Mason's thought. Biblical justification is solely forensic—it is God's legal declaration that a sinner is not guilty and positively righteous in his sight. John Murray rightly notes, "Justification is not any religious exercise in which we engage however noble and good that religious exercise may be." John Murray, *Redemption Accomplished and Applied* (Grand Rapids, Michigan: Eerdmans, 1955), 118; see also 117–31.

[29] Mason, *Woke Church*, 107–8.

What is Mason's solution to the pervasive nature of racism in America and even within Christian circles? "Deconstructing an unjust system," Mason contends, as Paul did in the case of Philemon the slaveowner and Onesimus the slave (Philemon 10–16).[30] Besides a dismantling of perceived racist institutions in society, Mason makes a case for the simultaneous rise of distinctively black institutions. There should be a push for organizations in which blacks have full control, sole ownership, and total empowerment. Mason remarks, "I fear that if we partner with whites that they will find a way to subjugate blacks and make us dependent on them in a way that kills our freedom of a truly black led institution."[31]

Sadly, Mason's last statement reflects fear rather than faith. As a gifted Christian preacher and thinker, Mason spoke powerfully for numerous conferences, events, publishing houses, and other organizations. He owed such opportunities not to cynical "white" patronage but to God, and in human terms to fellow Christians who recognized his soundness and gifting. As just one example, I was eager to have Mason speak for the Council on Biblical Manhood and Womanhood when I led it. Mason was a vital voice in training men to pursue Christ, and I was thrilled when he spoke for us. My "partnering" with him—as just one small example—was in no way motivated by trying to "subjugate" him, make him "dependent" on me, or "kill" his freedom.

In reality, in the case of Mason and many others of diverse backgrounds and skin colors, evangelicalism really did become more unified in the last several decades. Professors were appointed at schools that had known little diversity in past days. Pastors' conferences featured godly men who had little in common in terms of background but seemingly everything in common in terms of shared faith in Christ. Evangelical youth packed out Christian hip-hop concerts, adored artists of various skin colors, and genuinely took joy in the creative gifts of such performers. It was not skin color that united us, after all, but God's grace.

---

[30] Ibid., 63.
[31] Ibid., 100.

But as wokeness has infiltrated the Church and taken people captive to varying degrees, this unity has been lost. Distrust reigns. Resentment festers. It is truly tragic. While I do not know the state of anyone's heart—only God does—I do pray for such disunity to recede, and for godly leaders to once again savor the oneness we have in Christ.

Jemar Tisby, The Color of Compromise (2019)

Jemar Tisby was the chief executive officer of the Witness: A Black Christian Collective.[32] As of late March 2021, he had joined arms with Ibram X. Kendi and is now the assistant director of narrative and advocacy at Kendi's Center for Antiracist Research (of Boston University).[33] In 2019, Tisby published his *New York Times* bestseller, *The Color of Compromise*, a historical account of the Christian Church in America and its attitudes toward race since the founding of the colonies. Tisby walks through the various eras of American history, from the Colonial era to the Revolutionary War era to the Civil War era to the Jim Crow era to the Civil Rights era, before landing in the present day.

Tisby's sustained thesis in this book is that white Christians in America have been complicit in racism against blacks throughout history and "history demonstrates that racism never goes away; it just adapts."[34] Racism involves a differential of power between groups, and a multitude of white American Christians have been "complicit in creating and sustaining a racist society."[35] The overtly racist strategies of days past—slavery, lynch-

---

[32] Jemar Tisby, *The Color of Compromise: The Truth about the American Church's Complicity in Racism* (Grand Rapids, Michigan: Zondervan, 2019).

[33] This surprised many people familiar with Tisby's Christian profession, for Kendi has made a public point of disavowing "savior religion" of the kind central to evangelical Christianity.

[34] Ibid., 19, 154–55, 160, 171, 175, 191. For an early statement of this notion from one of the founders of CRT, see Bell, *Faces at the Bottom of the Well*, 13. It is also important to note that Tisby gets his definition of racism from Beverly Daniel Tatum, a psychologist who espouses Racial Identity Development Theory, the field of psychology's ideological equivalent to Critical Race Theory. For this definition, see Tisby, *The Color of Compromise*, 16.

[35] Ibid., 17. The chief concern that arises in reading Tisby's book is how many complex facts of American history he minimizes, glosses over, or entirely ignores.

ings, and segregation—have made way for a more subtle, yet no less pervasive form of racism that fills evangelicalism's institutions, social systems, and practices.

Tisby makes some salient points about American history. Yet there are two considerable problems with his book. First, he largely fails to tell the story of how a diverse coalition of voices, including many "white" people, campaigned against slavery and Jim Crow. His narrative is effectively one-sided, and if you didn't know the end to the story, you would have little idea that many people of varying backgrounds and skin colors paid dearly to end these evil systems. The struggle to end slavery, the slave trade, Jim Crow, and segregation required tremendous sacrifice from men and women of diverse roots and perspectives. Many identified as born-again believers, and some definitely did not. This mix notwithstanding, there are many to honor in this regard, and there is a big and important counter-narrative to the dominant "whiteness drove racism" paradigm, true as that is in numerous ways.

Secondly, Tisby makes the move already observed a few times in this text, assuming that the same evil that corrupted America societally in days past is working with similar effectiveness in the present hour. In assessing such a view, we need to be clear in our response: We will battle partiality of varying kinds until Christ returns. Yet Tisby's project offers little to substantiate the claim that we have failed in substantial form to overcome racism. At the societal level, America has changed dramatically since the days when slavery, Jim Crow, and segregation polluted its moral order. While he is right that racism has not disappeared, his book

---

Examples include the proactive participation of African traders in the transatlantic slave trade in the seventeenth century, "black" leaders who themselves supported colonization efforts in the nineteenth century, "black" slaveholders in America during the same period, Margaret Sanger and Planned Parenthood's "Negro Project" in the twentieth century, the startling rate at which "black" babies have been aborted in the U.S. since *Roe v. Wade* (1973), and the alarming number of shootings of young "black" men in recent decades perpetrated by young "black" men. Any historiographical treatment, especially one that spotlights perceived failures of justice, itself needs to do justice to the facts of history. Careful balance in weighing the evidence is imperative.

underplays the considerable progress this country has made in this area at the level of policy and law. (We will address a related matter, that of "systemic injustice," in coming chapters.)

Excursus: The Theology of James Cone

A final voice I need to mention—briefly—is that of James Cone. Cone is not alive (he died in 2018), but he is widely considered the founder of what is called Black Liberation Theology (BLT). BLT is not the same movement as CRT, but it has many shared commitments, and different Christian voices attracted to wokeness draw on both streams for their programs of change. We cannot exhaustively address BLT, but in what follows, we can introduce its major argument through the writings of its major theologian.

For Cone, BLT depends upon the Marxist system of oppressor and oppressed (hegemony). According to Cone, "the Christian faith does not possess in its nature the means for analyzing the structure of capitalism. Marxism as a tool of social analysis can disclose the gap between appearance and reality, and thereby help Christians to see how things really are." Cone believed that usage of the Marxist "tool" of the oppressor/oppressed paradigm would enable "Black Theology" to expose the true inequity and oppression of the "black" community. In his view, this is what Black Theology existed to do: "to analyze the nature of the gospel of Jesus Christ in the light of oppressed black people—so they will see the gospel as inseparable from their humiliated condition, bestowing on them the necessary power to break the chains of oppression."[36]

Christianity is thus a religion not of the "white man" and his gospel—a gospel that creates mere social equilibrium. Cone rejected such theology in favor of "a religion of liberation, a religion that says God created all people to be free. But I realized that for black people to be free, they must first love their blackness." This can be done by teaching people that

---

[36] James H. Cone, *A Theology of Black Liberation*, 40th Anniversary Edition (Maryknoll, New York: Orbis, 2010 [1970]), 5.

Christ was black. He wrote as follows of this concept: "Christ's blackness is both literal and symbolic.... The least in America are literally and symbolically present in black people."[37] This truth rendered the "black" community free of "white" theological influence, as Cone argued in his work on ethics: "The grounding of Christian ethics in the oppressed community means that the oppressor cannot decide what Christian behavior is."[38]

Cone fit in a stream of theology that gained prominence in the 1950s and 1960s in Latin America. Fusing Marxist thought with the writings of the Old Testament prophets, Liberation Theology recast the task of the Church, making it about the uplifting of oppressed peoples. Cone applied this system to the plight of the "black church." Denying substitutionary atonement—and even decrying it as a form of weakness alien to a truly liberated people—he made the move that the liberal Protestants had already executed, albeit from within his own social location. The Christian faith became a message of communal empowerment, not soul salvation. The Church found not only strength but essential content in the framework of oppressor and oppressed humanity. This Marxist concept was not only a helpful idea, but also an essential "tool of social analysis" to liberate disempowered people.

Cone's ideas demand more extended treatment. Yet even this brief survey suffices to show that Cone addressed real social conditions with a revised doctrinal program. We feel his pain and are even pierced by elements of his assessment. But we cannot accept his diagnosis nor his cure. Cone merged Marxist thought with his own conception of socially oriented Christianity. He argued for the "blackness" of Jesus at the same time that he rejected the sin-cleansing atonement of Christ. He addressed the "black church" with intellectual force and real passion, appealing to people to abandon the traditional Gospel for a more radical one. In his day and ours, Cone's ideas draw attention, but evangelicals must not embrace them. As is clear from the theologian's own writing, he did not

---

[37] James H. Cone, *God of the Oppressed* (Maryknoll, New York: Orbis, 1997), 126.
[38] Ibid., 191.

seek to pass on a traditionally evangelical Gospel, but to reject, revise, and supplant it.

Four Different Responses among Evangelicals to Wokeness

We understand why Cone and the previous voices gain audiences. They often put their finger on a real problem in our past or present, only to both diagnose and address that problem unbiblically. As we have noted, few people have yet spotted this trend. In a good number of congregations, the Church has not thought deeply together about biblical justice as opposed to social justice in its many manifestations. As a result, we are presently seeing evangelicals sort themselves out into four general categories. The boundaries between these groups, we note, are not thick; many folks are moving between categories as the Church figures out what Critical Race Theory is, what a biblical vision of justice is, and how Christians should live in a day of fresh division and hostility between different groups. Nonetheless, the lines are clarifying, and the stakes are high.[39]

The first category is the **non-woke**. That's the category to which I belong, in case that is not sufficiently clear, as do a strong number of Christians across the "racial" and ethnic spectrum. I will not seek to map this group at length, because this book broadly represents my own handling of a non-woke biblical program. The second category is populated by the **confused and undecided**. These people are watching major events play out in American society with growing distress. They do not have the inclination, time, or tools to investigate wokeness in a deep way. As a result, they don't know what to think, but are uneasy at all turns. They need a pastor to sort out these issues, but many pastors have not done so, will not do so, or are themselves trying to catch up. This is

---

[39] The words of Jude 22–23 apply to the people sketched in this section: "And have mercy on those who doubt; save others by snatching them out of the fire; to others show mercy with fear, hating even the garment stained by the flesh." We do not treat people falling into ungodliness as if they are all in precisely the same position; they are not.

understandable. But we cannot stay confused and undecided for long. The enemy is moving swiftly and has already stolen a march on us. The sheep need help, because the wolves—"fierce wolves," says Acts 20:29—seek to enter the Church and tear their faith to pieces.

The third category is made up of the **engaged yet cautious pro-woke**. This group wants to handle the vexing matter of racism well and often engages social media to do so. They may use popular hashtags and slogans, read some scattered material about racism, and speak against it. Indeed, they want to speak, and even to lead—but they haven't done a deep-dive in woke ideology. In some cases, they're skimming the surface and are guided by the crowds—by a Christianized version of what the crowds are saying, that is.

Many in this group (as in the previous two) want justice to rule our world. They have a commendable heart and passion for those who suffer. They know of the injustices of the American past and rightly despise them. In reading the books mentioned above, we understand why there is a fire coursing through woke writings. Injustice is wicked, and to a degree it is right that historical sins sit heavy upon us. As we have noted and will cover in Chapter 7, the evils of the American past and the Church's complicity in racism should not only sadden us, but anger us. This is true when we read about sin of any kind and genuine injustices done to any people. It is right, and our conscience is only correctly functioning, when we feel real passion and grit our teeth in pain over evildoing. This is how a Christian conscience, rightly working, operates.

We do not dismiss passion over the past, then. But we cannot be ruled by it, nor by anger, as Christians. We cannot fall prey to the view that our contemporary society has failed to change in meaningful ways over the centuries. We cannot hold people guilty for the sins of past generations (more on this to come). We cannot read people in a certain light because of their skin color. We cannot automatically equate our culture's pursuit of justice with biblical justice. We cannot fail to think very carefully about cultural ideologies and secular worldviews. We cannot assume that because woke leaders and activists use biblical language, and even cite biblical teachings, that the case they make is a sound one. People in this category—Category 3—fall prey to all these traps, alas.

Some in this category may say that they oppose CRT but want to honor those who are experiencing systemic injustice and societal oppression. Such a confession may seem compassionate, but it actually fits the core commitments and worldview of CRT. It thus wrongly diagnoses the situation, and it cannot avoid offering the wrong solution as a result. Where we hear such views, we should not burn fellow church members and friends down. As this book seeks to do, we should speak the truth in love to this group, for they need to be turned back from the direction in which they are going. The path they are following leads only to doctrinal compromise and personal ruin, as successive chapters show.[40] Neither the woke diagnosis, nor the woke cure, will bring about the unity, justice, hope, and healing that wokeness promises.

The fourth group is made up of the **convinced and committed pro-woke**. This group is heavily influenced by CRT. They read the literature, they encourage the activism, and they have fully bought into the critique of society and culture offered by CRT. They may be found in teaching and ministry positions, and they are actively encouraging fellow Christians to become woke. The positions outlined earlier in the chapter represent those held by different members of this group. This fourth group is the type that actively promotes CRT, wokeness, and intersectionality. Pastors in this group charge "white" people to repent for their sins. Leaders issue accusations against "white" Christians for being racist "white supremacists" due to their skin color. Theologians in this group practice "standpoint epistemology," compelling a racialized interpretive method rather than a theological one. Lay believers network in their congregations to compel fellow members to go woke and shun and condemn those who do not do so.

---

[40] As the reader can discern, the existence of these categories does not mean that we will always be able to tell neatly and decisively where someone falls on this spectrum. Wokeness is complex, and people are complex, and it will take biblical preaching, pastoral care, and biblical counseling to work through these issues. Our solution as believers is not a blowtorch of conviction; it is to stand on the truth, minister the truth, love according to the truth, and seek the good of the sheep according to the truth (John 17:17). We oppose worldly ideologies not in the end out of anger, but out of love and out of a desire to see those being taken captive be freed from the Satanic stronghold (2 Corinthians 10).

How Should We Engage the "Convinced and Committed" among Us?

This book seeks to help all Christians who are encountering wokeness. It can frankly be confusing to sort out where people stand, and thus which category suits them best. This is partly because many of us are disoriented, confused, and troubled. In such difficult circumstances, we need to be able to ask hard questions; we need to have honest conversations; we need to listen to one another in Christian humility; we need time to process, think, reason, meditate on Scripture, get our arms around worldviews, and more. What is justice? What is equity? How do we handle our fraught national heritage? How do we think through our own presuppositions and cultural background? It is not wrong to ask such questions, think hard about them, take time to mull responses we hear, and weigh different cases. It is right to do all such things. Wokeness is frankly a very difficult issue—one of the toughest the Church has faced in the last three hundred years. Christianity is not hostile to deep thinking; Christianity is grounded in it.

We must also remember that engaging wokeness is not going to war against flesh and blood. It may be presented that way, but as Christians, we war against spiritual powers (Ephesians 6:12). This means, among other duties, exposing and confronting the false teaching of men and women. But our goal here is not to condemn or cast out, but rather to help, strengthen, and call the straying back. This book is intended to steer the first and second groups toward clarity. My hope is that it will pull the third group back from the edge of a steep cliff. Yet this text has a special burden to address the fourth group, for they are in the gravest danger. This group is bringing wokeness into the Church. They represent the hard edge of "woke Christianity," and it is always the hard edge of a system that must draw the lion's share of our attention.[41]

---

[41] This is true of all apologetic and worldview engagement. If we are engaging Marxism, we must first handle the hard edge of Marxism, not more mediating voices. We must know where the system goes when pushed to its logical conclusions. Not every woke voice urges this (hence the categories I've listed out), but some do, and they are the intellectual vanguard. Switching the example, if one hundred years

Let's zoom out for a moment. As we have seen, wokeness, as with CRT and intersectionality in general, is not friendly to Christianity. Though there are shared concerns on the surface between the non-woke and woke, wokeness cannot be adapted to Christianity. As we make plain in the following chapters, wokeness is not a prism by which we discover truths we couldn't see in a Christian worldview. Wokeness is a different system entirely than Christianity. It is, in fact, "a different gospel." But it is not just that. In the final evaluation, wokeness is not just *not the Gospel*. Wokeness is *anti-Gospel*.

This reality should not shock us. As theologian Cornelius Van Til emphasized in his ministry, God and the creation are wholly distinct.[42] God is Creator; everything else is created. The Creator-creature distinction leads to a second eye-opening realization: There is an absolute ethical antithesis between God and the world, the world being fallen after Adam's sin in Genesis 3.[43] This means that the first task of Christian witness regarding other systems is not to show how God and a sinful world are the same; the first task is to make clear how God and everything else are distinct.

At the worldview and apologetics level, this means that we are not initially trying to establish how similar Christian thought is to unbelieving thought. It means instead that we must first distinguish Christianity from all other systems. While acknowledging real intellectual points of contact, we must labor to help people inside the Church and out see the distinctive beauty of God and the glory, order, and joy found in the Church created by the blood of His Son. Christianity is not just like other

ago you wanted to understand liberal Protestantism, you would not have spent much time trying to comprehend the middle group embracing this system. You would have gone to the leading lights defining this movement, pushing it, and leading out. We do this in this text—we engage most commonly the hard edge of wokeness, because the strongest voices set the parameters that ultimately determine where this modern movement will end up.

[42] Cornelius Van Til, *The Reformed Pastor and Modern Thought* (Phillipsburg, New Jersey: Presbyterian and Reformed, 1971), 5–6.

[43] Cornelius Van Til, *An Introduction to Systematic Theology*, 2nd edition (Phillipsburg, New Jersey: Presbyterian and Reformed, 2004), 64.

systems of thought, but with a Jesus twist at the end. Christianity is a different system altogether. Christianity is the true system.

Thus, a crucial part of Christian ministry is clarifying the antithesis between Christianity and every other system.[44] We recall Paul's words in 2 Corinthians 10:3–6 on this count:

> For though we walk in the flesh, we are not waging war according to the flesh. For the weapons of our warfare are not of the flesh but have divine power to destroy strongholds. We destroy arguments and every lofty opinion raised against the knowledge of God, and take every thought captive to obey Christ, being ready to punish every disobedience, when your obedience is complete.

This passage syncs elegantly with Colossians 2:8, which is cited in the introduction. There, Paul commands the Colossians, "See to it that no one takes you captive by philosophy and empty deceit, according to human tradition, according to the elemental spirits of the world, and not according to Christ." Synthesizing these passages crystallizes our theological calling as believers: We are not to be taken captive by ungodly ideologies. Instead, we are to take every thought captive in obedience to Christ.[45] This means that we must practice cultural deconstruction, analyzing and critiquing an unbiblical system, in order to do Gospel reconstruction, such that we think all our thoughts according to biblical teaching and the contours of sound doctrinal reasoning, not worldly arguments or worldviews.

---

[44] This is a Van Tillian and presuppositional concept. Here is how he frames the idea as one example: "insofar as men are aware of their basic alliances, they are wholly for or wholly against God at every point of interest to man." Cornelius Van Til, *An Introduction to Systematic Theology* (Phillipsburg, New Jersey: Presbyterian and Reformed, 1974), 29.

[45] As one example of such work, the title of Richard Pratt's introduction to presuppositional apologetics is based on this phrase in 2 Corinthians 10:5. Richard L. Pratt Jr., *Every Thought Captive: A Study Manual for the Defense of Christian Truth* (Phillipsburg, New Jersey: Presbyterian and Reformed, 1980).

Armed with such a twofold calling, we remember that it is not our job to give Jesus good PR. We are not trying to "nice-ify" the Christian faith. We are not seeking to make it palatable to the natural man. We are not downplaying the hard truths of biblical teaching in order to "get people in." We are striving as godly men and women to present the whole counsel of God in order to glorify God as witnesses and make disciples who obey all Christ commanded and taught (Matthew 28:16–20). There is no way to be faithful to God and offer the world a "reasonable" Christianity. Sadly, this is what some around us seem to think they should do. They work hard to show unbelievers that they are thoughtful, amenable, irenic, fair, and nice. They hope in doing so to make Christianity attractive and compelling, avoiding the past presentational errors of "biblicist" Christians.

Such an approach appeals to all of us in our flesh. We all want to be liked. Yet while we must bear spiritual fruit and show love to all we engage, we cannot forget the apostolic mandate (Galatians 5:22–23; Matthew 22:34–39). As with all the apostles, and as with Christ Himself, Paul's calling was not to offer people a palatable Christianity that would please the natural man. Paul's mission was, in love, to destroy strongholds, expose unbelief, rebuke false ideologies, and above all preach Christ crucified and raised for us.

Paul and his peers had no choice between "preach Christ" or "deconstruct falsehood." They had to do both. They thus trained the earliest disciples not to be taken captive by lies, but to think every thought in submission to God. This is what it means, then and now, to extend the Great Commission. The end result of our preaching, evangelism, apologetics, and missions is not a box we check to indicate a personal commitment. It is obedience to everything Christ and His apostles taught from a true convert, born of Heaven, who knows what God's Word demands and lives out their faith by the Spirit's power.

All this hard and costly work is motivated by love. In telling the truth, we love God and we love our neighbor (Matthew 22). A major temptation before us all today, though, is to manage our *social reputation*. While we must strenuously watch our *moral reputation* as followers of Christ, we cannot fear man. We must not whitewash our walls so that our doorway looks like every other Egyptian home. We see such an impulse among some who belong to the fourth group—the convinced and committed—sketched earlier. Some assume that worldly justice and biblical justice are basically the same; others know of the differences but do not want to risk the world's scorn. All who hold these ideas are in a perilous position. We can only have one master, and it will be either Christ or the Antichrist, assuming the form of the spirit of the age.

As we pray for those promoting wokeness, and as we speak the truth in love per Ephesians 4:15, we must seek the repentance and recovery of such individuals. We want unity, after all—unity in the truth of Jesus Christ and His apostles. In terms of personal friends and church members, we must follow the steps of discipline per Matthew 18:15–20 on these matters, even as we publicly confront those teaching unbiblical ideas in a broader sense. While we pray this action will not end in formal separation—we hope for repentance early on in the Matthew 18 process—church discipline is indeed the outcome faced by those who cling to divisive and ungodly ideology. Though it will pain us greatly, excommunication must be enacted for those who, after going through the Matthew 18 steps, do not repent of teaching CRT, wokeness, and intersectionality.

At the institutional level, the same principle applies. Houses divided cannot stand. Trustees, voting members, organizational leaders, educational boards, and so on must not tolerate the spread of wokeness any longer. The hour is late. The time for repentance and change is now—or else we will not have churches and seminaries and institutions and organizations left to defend.

Conclusion

The preceding survey indicates that a serious movement is underway, vying for the hearts and minds of evangelicals. We must not forget that the books summarized earlier are penned by pastors, professors, and theologians in the Church. In much of the "convinced and committed" literature cited, the formal term "Critical Race Theory" does not appear—in most volumes, not even once. However, our brief summaries have demonstrated that these works are soaked in a worldly ideology of wokeness. The enemy does not always appear in robes of darkness. He often masquerades as an angel of light (2 Corinthians 11:14). It is past time for Christians to wake up—not to the so-called "truths" of CRT, but to the deception that is creeping into our churches.

If the clarion call of this chapter sounds apocalyptic, it is not. If anything, it is too weak. As I mentioned some pages back, just one hundred years ago or so, evangelicalism was in the process of losing one church and institution after another. J. Gresham Machen witnessed it firsthand. Though fundamentalists and some conservative evangelicals earned a reputation as pugnacious, with the image of the "Fightin' Fundamentalist" enduring in our time, in actual historical fact, the fundamentalists didn't fight nearly enough. They lost, and lost, and lost some more. They lost their churches, they lost their seminaries, they lost their missions agencies, they lost their parachurch organizations, and they kept on losing until there was very nearly nothing else left to lose. They lost to one group in aggregate: liberals (modernists).[46] Though Machen made a brave, even heroic, stand, the true outcome of the fundamentalist-modernist controversy was a clear loss for the conservatives and a clear win for the liberals.

---

[46] The historical reality is that the liberals were the war party that overcame the conservatives. Tragically, there was a big faction caught in the middle, a faction that sought unity and peace at any cost. Though such a goal sounds good, it was used—and is usually used—by the liberal war party to attack theological conservatives. Among the Baptists, A. H. Strong fell into the uncomfortable middle ground; among the Presbyterians, this role fell to Clarence Macartney. Both were gifted and typically conservative men who ended their careers robed in the garments of tragedy due to a failure to stand decisively against the war party. If good men do not stand in their hour of testing, noble works will collapse. See Jeffrey Straub, *The Making of a Battle Royal: The Rise of Liberalism in Northern Baptist Life, 1870–1920* (Eugene, Oregon: Pickwick, 2018); Bradley J. Longfield, *The Presbyterian Controversy: Fundamentalists, Modernists, and Moderates* (Religion in America) (New York: Oxford University Press, 1993); and Gary North, *Crossed Fingers: How the Liberals Captured the Presbyterian Church* (Tyler, Texas: Institute for Christian Economics, 1996).

What will the outcome be in our time? Will we lose as they did? Much depends on this: whether we will contend, and contend, and contend (Jude 3). Again, the hour is late. Much is at stake. In the coming pages, we will cover much, and we will unpack this conviction and the driving thesis of the book: Christianity and wokeness are not compatible. Christianity is the truth of God found in the Word of God. Wokeness, as we are at pains to say, is a different religion altogether.

DISCUSSION QUESTIONS

1. Among professing Christians, what is the difference between the "engaged yet cautious pro-woke" group and the "convinced and committed pro-woke" group?
2. How does Paul's reminder that the Church's ultimate struggle "is not against flesh and blood" (Ephesians 6:12) apply to wokeness teaching?
3. What does it mean that there is an "antithesis" between God and the world?
4. What are some statements made by "convinced and committed pro-woke" Christian authors that surprise you?

CHAPTER 3

Why Is Wokeness an
Ungodly System?

Part One: Theological Issues

Let it not be said that I was silent when they needed me.
—William Wilberforce

Twenty-five years after I read it, I distinctly recall it: The heart beating beneath the floor. The narrator, transported in and out of sanity. The threat of discovery for the crime, looming over the reader as with the protagonist of the story. Though I encountered it in the mists of high school back in rural Maine some decades ago, Edgar Allan Poe's "The Tell-Tale Heart" still sends an electric shock down my spine when I reengage it.[1] Poe was no believer, but he understood keenly the vengeance of the human conscience. Once we acquire guilt, just and real guilt for crimes done, it is not easy to silence it.

In the short story, Poe's unnamed narrator has killed an old man. There is no true dead heart beating in the story, of course, but the narrator—going mad in his unrepentant evildoing—still thinks the dead heart makes an audible sound that others can hear:

> I paced the floor to and fro with heavy strides, as if excited
> to fury by the observations of the men—but the noise steadily

---

[1] Edgar Allan Poe, "The Tell-Tale Heart," first published in *The Pioneer*, January 1843.

increased. Oh God! what could I do? I foamed—I raved—I swore! I swung the chair upon which I had been sitting, and grated it upon the boards, but the noise arose over all and continually increased. It grew louder—louder—louder! And still the men chatted pleasantly, and smiled. Was it possible they heard not? Almighty God!—no, no! They heard!—they suspected!—they knew!—they were making a mockery of my horror!—this I thought, and this I think. But anything was better than this agony! Anything was more tolerable than this derision! I could bear those hypocritical smiles no longer! I felt that I must scream or die! and now—again!—hark! louder! louder! louder! louder![1]

Poe's book draws our attention in our study of wokeness for one primary reason: guilt. In woke ideology, past crimes have been done; though they occurred long ago, guilt for them still exists today. The evils of the past should not be buried, nor can they be buried according to wokeness. They cannot be humbly acknowledged and learned from as historic events; no, they still live. Guilt still exists. The racist heart of the American past still beats.

Or, switching the metaphor, like a meteoric rock that falls from the sky and passes through a house's roof, then its second floor, and finally its first floor, "white guilt" must pass down through the generations, even into the present. This is our fate; this is our burden. We cannot fail to pass on our guilt, for we are guilty of past crimes. In woke thought, we cannot overcome this guilt, and we cannot put it past us; we can only embrace it, live under the shadow of our failings, and seek secular means of restoration. The Gospel does not deal with this problem; in fact, clinging to the Gospel as our antidote to past evils is the worst thing we could do, for it spiritualizes an institutional problem and thus ensures it will not resolve.

---

[1]   Ibid., accessible at https://www.poemuseum.org/the-tell-tale-heart.

All this is wrong, biblically wrong. It is deeply injurious to our society, but especially to the Church. In this chapter and the next, I will give a fourteen-part critique of wokeness. In this chapter, I will issue a theological critique of wokeness (seven points); in the next chapter, I will unpack more of a cultural and societal critique of wokeness (seven points). While there is overlap between the two chapters, the focus of this chapter is on the spiritual problem before us. Here, I seek to help the Church find freedom from a truly terrible fate: unresolved guilt on false pretenses. This is truly what flows from false gospels of every kind.

First, wokeness tweaks the doctrine of humanity, losing sight of the *imago Dei* as our constituent identity.

The image of God is the ground of our positive anthropological unity as the human race. As I argue extensively in *Reenchanting Humanity*, God made the man in His image and made the woman from the man's rib (Genesis 1 and 2).[3] As a result, both the man and the woman and all their offspring bear the image of God. Every person is thus *fully human* per the image. This is our starting point for understanding every human person. We do not begin with how unalike we all are. Rather, we begin with anthropological unity—unity grounded in who God made us to be and who we are even in our post-Fall world.[4] We are image-bearers, and though sinful to the core, every human person bears this identity. This means that we are not fundamentally disunited, but united by our common theistic formation. We are one human race. Sin scrambles this unity, yes, but it endures, nonetheless.

---

[3]   Owen Strachan, *Reenchanting Humanity: A Theology of Mankind* (Fearn, Scotland: Mentor, 2019), 13–25, 136–37.

[4]   Many woke writers would contest this idea from the outset since it affirms the existence of God. To give just one example, atheism is a prominent theme throughout Ta-Nehisi Coates's memoir written to his son, *Between the World and Me*. Ta-Nehisi Coates, *Between the World and Me* (New York: One World, 2015), 28, 71, 79.

As humans, we are not fundamentally different but fundamentally alike.[5] We are one human race, not many different "races." The very concept of race, in fact, is man-made. While it is true that there are certain differences between people groups (physiologically, for example), we have no biblical grounds for splicing humanity up into many "races." Racial theory, in fact, owes to genuine racists, who made it up to exalt themselves and justify their evil partiality. Scripture makes no such move. Yes, there are distinct ethnicities and people groups recognized in the Bible (see Chapter 5). But ethnicity does not cancel out our shared anthropology. Ethnicity deepens our vision of oneness in Adam—we are unified, but distinctly and wonderfully made.

To be human does not mean that you look like someone else in a cookie-cutter way. It does not mean that you speak the same language. It does not mean that you like the same things or share the same views. To be human means that you are a man or a woman made in God's image (Genesis 1:26–27). Humanity is not a narrow biblical reality, we see. Humanity stretches across geography, across affinity, across ethnicity, and across background. The one human race is not the same such that we are robotic carbon copies of one another. No, we are one human race, our identity grounded in being made in God's image, but beautifully diverse from this essential starting point. Wokeness denies all this. It fundamentally emphasizes not human oneness, but human diversity—and diversity without any meaningful hope of unity.

Though many woke thinkers know there is no proof of "race," they use "strategic essentialism" to advance the interests of minority groups. This means that though "race" is a fiction, woke leaders act as if it is real. Their strategy is cynical and unfounded. We should reject it. Instead of denying human oneness and amplifying human diversity so that we have no meaningful unity, Christians need to amplify human oneness and celebrate God-given diversity. We are not many "races," but we are

---

[5]   Anthony Hoekema notes that all human beings, as a result of being created in the image of God, share a threefold responsibility to God, neighbor, and nature. Anthony Hoekema, *Created in God's Image* (Grand Rapids, Michigan: Eerdmans, 1994), 75.

all made by God—unique creatures invested with the wisdom and design of God, capable of both good and evil.

We cannot find ultimate unity in Adam, but we can point people to Scripture to show that the human race is not made to hate one another, but to come together in Christ. Wokeness in our time opposes such a conclusion. Despite its forceful arguments, I believe that teaching about our image-bearing nature will prove evangelistic. Instead of seeing themselves as part of warring tribes based on heritage and skin color, men and women will recognize that their identity as a human person is God-given and, by His grace, God-honoring. We are not clumps of cells, and we are not made for hatred. We are all image-bearers, whatever we look like, whatever our IQ, whatever our background may be.

Second, wokeness unhelpfully groups people according to "whiteness," a deeply problematic concept.

Wokeness does not try to tackle the ugliness of sin at its deepest level. As mentioned earlier in this book, wokeness argues that "white" people are "oppressors." They foster "white supremacy" at all times, and in fact cannot help but do so. This supremacist order has taken on systemic and structural shape. The guilty party is composed of those who promote and benefit from "whiteness."[6]

As with the novel vision of humanity discussed above, this is a novel doctrine of sin. There is no biblical word that indicates that "whiteness" is wicked. It is true that "white supremacy" is and was wicked, but if we think about history, not all "white" people embraced such a view or practiced racism. Many fought against it. Certain "white" people may be racist or ethnocentric, but "whiteness" is not indicative of "white supremacy." There are no biblical grounds for such a view; furthermore,

---

6   Richard Delgado and Jean Stefancic, *Critical Race Theory: An Introduction,* 2nd edition (New York and London: New York University Press, 2012), 82; Robin DiAngelo, *White Fragility: Why It's So Hard for White People to Talk about Racism* (Boston, Massachusetts: Beacon Press, 2018), 24; Robert Jensen, *The Heart of Whiteness: Confronting Race, Racism, and White Privilege* (San Francisco, California: City Lights, 2005), 3–11.

we should not read the existence of a majority culture or majority ethnicity as necessarily symbolic of evil. (More on this later.)

The sins of "white supremacy," ethnocentrism, and "racism" should be repented of. There are indeed people who commit these sins; all of us stumble in many ways. But to convict all "white" people of such wrongdoing is wrong and unbiblical. Doing so is nothing less than the sin of bearing false witness or false accusation against a fellow image-bearer (Exodus 20:16; Matthew 15:19). The CRT diagnosis is a radical reframing of man's chief problem. It changes our fundamental condition from one of individually willed sin to one of inherently racist "whiteness," which makes horizontal transgression against men of greater import than vertical transgression against God.[7]

The entire category outlined here is problematic. Just as "whiteness" is not uniquely wicked, neither is there any such thing as "whiteness." We do well to destabilize a monolithic conception of the same. In America, many people may have so-called "white" skin color. There may be so many of these people that we can identify elements of what is called "white majority culture." But we must be very careful here. People who have "white" skin are not the same. Let's think about a few ways this is true:

1. All skin color is not the same.
2. "Whiteness" as a category overlooks the reality of ethnicity.
3. Ethnicity is often a contributing determinant of one's experience—being Irish, or being Russian, or being West African.

---

[7] A biblical example can help here. For instance, King David committed adultery, sinning against Bathsheba, and transacted a murder plot against her husband, Uriah, to cover up the wicked deed. After realizing his wrongdoing, however, David cried out to God in Psalm 51:4: "Against you, you only, have I sinned and done what is evil in your sight...." As Hoekema rightly notes, "David did not mean that he had not sinned against people, but in the depth of his repentance he had come to the conviction that all sin is finally sin against God." David's recognition is what CRT denies. Hoekema, *Created in God's Image*, 170–71.

4. Even when identifying ethnicity, people of the same ethnic background often differ greatly in their lifestyles, experiences, and worldviews.

5. Though we often assume that ethnicity or common background yields iron unity, in actual fact, people of the same ethnicity often kill one another, hate one another, and divide from one another.

6. This is true at an even more granular level: individual family members can be altogether divergent from one another.

For all these reasons, to act as if "white" people believe, do, and want the same things is unsound. We can stretch this critique a bit more. Much as "white" people are treated in general terms by woke thinkers and leaders, there is in reality tremendous division among "white" people, including on the most foundational matters of life. In politics, for example, here is what Pew Research recently found:

> Overall, 35% of white registered voters identify as independent, while about as many (36%) identify as Republican and fewer (26%) identify as Democratic.[8]

This means that there is no one "white" political perspective, just as we would have guessed. This in turn means that "white" people support very different programs, voting for opposite candidates in society-shaping elections, for example. Supposedly monolithic people actually support polar-opposite platforms.

We find similar data regarding religion. According to Pew, 29 percent of "white" people are "Evangelical Protestant," 19 percent are "Mainline Protestant," 19 percent are "Catholic," and 24 percent are "Unaffiliated

---

[8] "The Parties on the Eve of the 2016 Election: Two Coalitions Moving Further Apart," Pew Research Center, September 13, 2016, https://www.pewresearch.org/politics/2016/09/13/2-party-affiliation-among-voters-1992-2016.

("nones").⁹ At first blush, it may seem like most "white" people are religiously homogeneous due to "shared" Christianity. That, after all, is precisely the way "white" people are often addressed and evaluated in America today. But like the political data above, even a moment's extra thought punctures such a view. Evangelicals clash sharply with mainline groups, Catholics are clearly not the same as the "nones" (though their tradition does feature nuns), and in formal terms evangelicals and Catholics have major soteriological differences.

These statistics and others we could cite tell us what common sense yields: "White" people are anything but the same. They disagree not only about religious particulars, but about the most basic convictions of life. This is not to say that we cannot observe certain sociological patterns among majority cultures. But even if such patterns exist, we should nonetheless be painstakingly careful about breaking people down according to skin color and then concluding that we know who a given person is based on that color. Is this not only true about major convictional matters, but everything in between? Do all "white" people like country music? Some love it—but don't some hate it? Don't some "white" people love NPR—while others despise it? The more questions like these that we ask, the less unanimity we find.

Our brief study shows us what we already know instinctively. There is no such thing as "whiteness," nor any such thing as "blackness" (or any variant). Race is not grounded in reality. It was an invention of sinfully partial people, and it has been both restored and treated as real in recent decades in the West.¹⁰ It is true that there are variations between people groups. But as Ken Ham has shown, the "so-called 'racial' characteristics that people think are major differences (skin color, eye shape, etc.) account for only 0.012 percent of human biological variation." On the specific subject of skin color, the presence of less melanin means

---

⁹   "Religious Landscape Study," Pew Research Center, https://www.pewforum. org/religious-landscape-study/racial-and-ethnic-composition/white.

¹⁰   For more on the history of this thinking, see Robert Wald Sussman, *The Myth of Race: The Troubling Persistence of an Unscientific Idea* (Cambridge, Massachusetts: Harvard University Press, 2016).

"lighter" skin color; more melanin means "darker" skin color. So Ham concludes: "No one really has red, or yellow, or black skin. We all have the same basic color, just different shades of it. We all share the same pigments—our bodies just have different combinations of them."[11] In scientific terms, this means, according to Ham, that the differences between people groups are "absolutely trivial."[12]

These basic truths remind us, then, that grouping humanity according to "race" as dependent on skin color is wrong. Genetically and culturally, "whiteness" as a discrete form of humanity is a fiction. There is no such thing. There are people who have common skin color, backgrounds, and even interests, yes. We can draw some parallels between people in terms of "majority culture." But even if we do so and have some justification for such sociological conclusions, we must never make the mistake of thinking in racial patterns. As we shall see in Chapter 5, there is no biblical basis for the category of "race." Humanity enjoys real distinctiveness and diversity, but that in no way paves the ground for a hard-and-fast conception of differing human identities based on skin color.

Instead of making the assumptions that wokeness does, it would be better to do what Scripture encourages us to do from numerous angles: We should get to know people as they are. We should not stereotype them. We should avoid demonizing any one people group. We should treat individuals as individuals. They may like country music, Premier League soccer, NPR, or they may swear off such interests for life. We have no idea who a given person is or what their life experience has been. Yet there is one human race and one human need. While getting to know people as God-made individuals, we should recognize that all human beings have the same problem (sin) and the same cure (Jesus Christ). This is true of "white" people; this is true of us all.

---

[11] Ken Ham, "Are There Really Different Races?," Answers in Genesis, November 29, 2007, https://answersingenesis.org/racism/are-there-really-different-races.

[12] Ibid. On these and related matters, Ham's work is some of the most helpful material on race I've encountered, for it is grounded in Scripture and fully conversant with sound science.

Third, wokeness actually foments the very sin it presumes to critique: "racism."

I was reminded of this reality when learning online of a Coca-Cola training session on whiteness in February 2021. The session encouraged its viewers to "Try to be less white." Being "white" was defined in no uncertain terms.

According to the training session, to be less white is to:

- Be less oppressive
- Be less arrogant
- Be less certain
- Be less defensive
- Be less ignorant
- Be more humble
- Listen
- Believe
- Break with apathy
- Break with white solidarity[13]

This session fit with the broader argument of wokeness. As we have noted, wokeness finds "white" people objectively guilty of racism. The normal "white" person is part of a structurally wicked order in which racism is "an integral, permanent, and indestructible component of this society."[14] The takeaway is plain: White people are racists. The only solution is to become an "antiracist," which is not primarily a positive condition, but is instead the recognition that one

[13] Karlyn Borysenko, "Shocking Images Show Coca-Cola Is Training Employees to 'Try to Be Less White,'" YouTube, February 19, 2021, https://www.youtube.com/watch?v=FRWfSoSmNqw; see also Karlyn Borysenko (@DrKarlynB), "BREAKING: Coca-Cola is forcing employees to complete online training telling them to 'try to be less white.' These images are from an internal whistleblower:," Twitter, February 19, 2021, 9:42 a.m., https://twitter.com/DrKarlynB/status/1362774562769879044?s=20.

[14] Delgado and Stefancic, *Critical Race Theory*, ix.

is an incurably racist person who must strive through concrete actions to enact antiracism.[15]

This is where we see Critical Race Theory and wokeness truly closing the door, locking it, and throwing away the key. The solution to the problem of racial prejudice *is* prejudice, just of a different kind. In CRT thinking, "The only remedy to racist discrimination is *antiracist* discrimination."[16] You must, in other words, undertake a never-ending litany of works that work against your fundamentally racist nature. You cannot overcome such a condition, but like an alcoholic, you can manage it. If you're "white," for example, you can and should try to "be less white" every day you live.

The moment you believe this ideology, you have been taken captive. And in a deeply sad irony, you have become what you so despise: You now have adopted the thought patterns and behavior of a "racist"—or, more accurately, a "partialist," to coin a term. Showing favoritism, even to a suffering group, is repeatedly denounced throughout Scripture (Exodus 23:3; Leviticus 19:15; James 2:1, 9) because it contradicts the very character of God (Romans 2:11). This is what happens with unsound thoughts and unsound character: Our thinking becomes contradictory and even nonsensical, and we champion the lie instead of the truth. Said stronger, we become what we set out to oppose. In striving to defeat racism—an honorable goal—we unwittingly end up disliking and judging people of a certain skin color. Wokeness promises justice but begets injustice.

Our discussion reveals, furthermore, that wokeness greatly minimizes the diversity and complexity of the biblical view of sin.[17] Wokeness

---

[15] Ibram X. Kendi, *How to Be an Antiracist* (New York: One World, 2019), 217–27.

[16] Ibid., 19. Emphasis added.

[17] The Apostle Paul's longest vice list, found in Romans 1, consists of no fewer than twenty-one sins (Romans 1:29–31). In his vice list in Galatians 5, Paul lists fifteen sins and concludes with the open-ended, catch-all phrase "and things like these" (Galatians 5:19–21). All human beings are created individually and uniquely by God, but after the Fall, this also means that human beings express their rebellion against God in diverse and idiosyncratic ways.

judges us without knowing the hidden motives of our heart—knowledge only God possesses (1 Corinthians 4:5). If you have heard that you are guilty of "white supremacy" simply because of your "whiteness," you have been falsely convicted and unbiblically indicted. You do have real sin, and your sin manifests in numerous ways and demands repentance on penalty of everlasting judgment. But your skin color and heritage are not inherently sinful. Such a conclusion is totally foreign to Scripture. If it were true, entire people groups could never come to Christ. Yet Scripture revels in a Gospel that saves people from every tribe, tongue, people, and nation and shows us diverse people converting to Christ throughout the book of Acts (see Chapter 6).

If you have been convicted and demeaned for your skin color or heritage (whatever each may be), you have been wronged. In Christ, you are freed from false guilt, false shame, and the trappings of a false gospel. You are also free to enjoy your heritage, background, and community. You should not do so as a Christian in a way that compromises your standing in Christ and your real unity with every Christian brother and sister. But you should not feel guilt or shame over enjoying the morally sound music, arts, language, food, and heritage of your background. Your cultural and ethnic background is not ultimate in your identity, but neither is it necessarily tainted. Instead of living in fear, judgment, imposed guilt, and insecurity (which is just practical godlessness), we should live in thankfulness to God, who has given us our heritage and written our backstory.

The foregoing is true of all peoples, including the group so commonly targeted by wokeness: "white" people. We must reject the false vision of monolithic "whiteness" urged upon us in schools, colleges, seminaries, congregations, businesses, and other organizations today. We should reject the mindset of judgmentalism and hatred so often practiced in our milieu. "White" people are not a different form of humanity. They are not better than anyone else nor are they worse than anyone else. Every "white" person is born in sin, benefits from God's common grace in untold ways, needs Jesus infinitely, and can become a born-again believer.

There is no special wickedness in "whiteness." To treat people as if there is based on their skin color and their community is, as stated above, "racist." It is, more technically, partiality.

Fourth, wokeness treats people as "oppressors" and "oppressed" due to skin color and power dynamics.

Scripture sees humanity in Adam. He is the first image-bearer, and we are all part of the race of which he is the first person. We all fall in him; we are not mere victims of his fall but are fellow criminals with him. His fall is our fall.[18] We would have done what he did if we walked in Eden beside him. This means that our natural unity is in Adam as (tragically) sinners, and our fundamental redeemed identity is in Christ. These are the two core groups of the human race. Are we in Adam, and thus lost and damned forever, or are we in Christ, and thus saved and bound for the New Jerusalem?

Coming to faith in Christ in no way entails erasing our background or ethnicity, as we have observed. But faith in Christ does necessarily involve seeing our purpose and identity as found in Christ and Christ alone. In practical terms, this means that there are not many humanities. There is Adamic humanity, such that we are *full image-bearers* in need of divine rescue, and there is Christic humanity, such that we are redeemed and remade in the image of the *true image-bearer* to look like Him.[19]

But wokeness overturns these truths. Its fundamental anthropological categories are not the biblical ones of believer or unbeliever, but oppressor or oppressed ("anthropology" means doctrine of humanity, or what makes us human). As we have seen, wokeness renders "white" people as oppressors and people of color as the oppressed. This is true racially, but as we saw in handling intersectionality, these categories apply much more broadly today to "underprivileged" peoples of all kinds. The Marxists first used this pairing of the rich and the poor, reading the former as evil and the latter as innocent. Today, these same

---

[18] Strachan, *Reenchanting Humanity*, 85.

[19] Ibid., 376–83.

identifiers apply along the lines of skin color, weight, the sexes, disability, the police, and more.

This is not a biblical approach. People of any background or ethnicity can oppress others—this is true. Furthermore, various people with "white" skin did create and benefit from a "racial" hierarchy in the American past (see Chapter 7). But in biblical terms, this invention was unfounded. It is not skin color that makes us either evil or righteous, nor is it one's heritage. Instead, we are all fallen in Adam. So too is it wrong to conclude per intersectionality that having more power or authority or influence than others ranks you as an "oppressor." This is the Marxist move; in his initial argument, the rich fundamentally wrong the poor. Wealthy people can wrong impoverished people, but it is not necessarily so. Scripture cautions the rich, yes, but it nowhere treats them as fundamentally evil (see 1 Timothy 6). Nor does it treat the financially poor as inherently pure.

We can extend this point. Men are not inherently abusers if they lead churches as pastors, exercising spiritual authority over the flock. Fathers and mothers are not evil for having God-given authority over children. Governors are not wicked for possessing civic leadership others do not have. Police officers are not warped as a consequence of administering the law on the street. Scripture teaches us that all authority figures must guard against sin and that every person must repent of it, but it nowhere encourages us to conclude that wielding authority makes you corrupt. Instead, throughout Scripture we see God expressly granting power and authority and influence to some and not others. This can be hard for us to swallow, admittedly, and leaders do not always lead well. But intersectionality (and wokeness more broadly) poisons our understanding of authority and leadership, a move we must reject. In general terms, unless a clear pattern of misdeeds exists, we must not identify "oppression" with any one group over others.

Fifth, wokeness traps us in a cycle of anger and victimhood.

As wokeness binds us, it drains us of compassion.[20] This is deeply ironic, because wokeness marches under the banner of tolerance,

---

[20] For example, Robin DiAngelo has a rather shocking chapter in her book in which she rails against white women who cry, either out of empathy for the suffering of

unity, and progress. But remember this: No ungodly system truly fosters such virtues. Ungodly systems have certain contact points with God's truth, yes, because of common grace. Yet you cannot embrace an un-Christian worldview and end up a Christian disciple. Only the Gospel of divine grace saves the soul. Only true Christianity, involving "teaching them to observe all I have commanded you" (Matthew 28:20), makes true disciples.

Though wokeness promises compassion, it bounces its check. The aforementioned stamp of guilt upon white people as racist means that wokeness produces all sorts of anger, rage, resentment, and hostility.[21] Wokeness does not create peace; it creates division, terrible division. This is true in its strictly academic form; this is true in its adapted activist form. The embrace of wokeness is not an embrace of biblical Christianity and, most significantly, the Christian Gospel. The embrace of wokeness means an embrace of grievance, anger, and hostility.

We can mention a related problem here: Different woke voices operate as if "black" people are powerless. Robin DiAngelo, for example, has made a thriving career for herself by giving seminars at which she alleges that "white" people have created deeply problematic situations by "white privilege," "white complicity," or "white tears." Understandably, numerous people react strongly to DiAngelo's claims.[22] But there is also a subtler form of division that wokeness like DiAngelo's creates. It suggests to "white" people that they need to help "black" people or else the former are trapped. This is not a new idea. Shelby Steele weighs in on it with potent words:

---

black people or out of conviction of their own prejudicial shortcomings. DiAngelo notes that if a black person sees a white person crying and wants to comfort that individual, the white person should not accept such a gesture and should seek to move on, since an emotional demonstration is simply taking up unnecessary space. DiAngelo, *White Fragility*, 131–38.

[21] Derrick A. Bell, *Faces at the Bottom of the Well: The Permanence of Racism* (New York: Basic Books, 2018), 29, 196; Coates, *Between the World and Me*, 83, 105.

[22] In my reading of *White Fragility*, I lost track of how frequently DiAngelo reported "white" people disliking her presentations.

There is at least a whisper of doubt over my entire generation of educated blacks—a whisper, frankly, of inferiority. Are we where we are because of merit, or because of jerrybuilt, white guilt concepts like affirmative action and "diversity"? How different, really, is diversity's stigmatization of us as "needy victims" from segregation's stigmatization of us as inferiors? In either case, we are put in service to the white American imagination.... In both cases we were a means to a white end.[23]

I do not doubt that woke leaders think they are helping minority voices. But as Steele attests, liberal and woke solutions to our societal conditions often hurt more than they help. They divide more than they unite. They service "white guilt" and cultivate dependence rather than creating biblical oneness. In addition, in a woke system, the individual person is displaced by a stereotypical cog in the machine.[24] One's own narrative, story, quirks, strengths, and weaknesses are easily lost in such a framework. Instead of taking agency, wokeness encourages people to embrace their victimhood.[25]

How counter this is to the Bible. Scripture does not encourage us to think of ourselves as victims but as criminals fully complicit in Adam's rebellion and deserving of eternal judgment as a result. Furthermore, whatever groups we may belong to by way of background, we must also say two truths:

---

[23] Shelby Steele, *Shame: How America's Past Sins Have Polarized Our Country* (New York: Basic, 2015), 138.

[24] See Bell, *Faces at the Bottom of the Well*, 196.

[25] Jason Riley critiques leftist thought on just this count: "Liberalism has also succeeded, tragically, in convincing blacks to see themselves first and foremost as victims. Today there is no greater impediment to black advancement than the self-pitying mindset that permeates black culture. White liberals think they are helping blacks by romanticizing miscreants. And black liberals are all too happy to hustle guilty whites. The result, manifest in everything from black studies programs to black media to black politics, is an obsession with racial slights real or imagined." Jason Riley, *Please Stop Helping Us: How Liberals Make It Harder for Blacks to Succeed* (New York: Encounter, 2015), 173.

1. Nothing comes above our identity as Christians.
2. We are not called to a life of grievance, victimhood, and anger, but are instead freed from such a life.

Once we hated God and one another. Now as Christians, we love God and love one another. Are there tough and tricky issues to sort out in a fallen realm? Yes, there are. We sort them out, though, knowing that God has made each individual person fearfully and wonderfully as a living reflection of His glory (Psalm 139:14). We must thus be very wary of any worldview that loses sight of the uniqueness and dignity of the individual and trains some to see themselves as victims. The call of Christ is to reject victimhood, take ownership of our sin, and find freedom in the Kingdom of God through the grace of God.

Sixth, wokeness gives approval to evil—both in the public square and in rejecting God's design for the sexes.

The intersectional worldview denies that there is such a thing as created order. Claiming what Scripture teaches—that God has made every person either a man or a woman for His glory and our joy—is seen as oppressive cisgender heteronormativity that does violence to sexual minorities and the genderqueer.[26] So we see an essential truth: Wokeness is not friendly to biblical complementarity. Wokeness reads difference as discrimination, traditional sexual distinctiveness as a hostile reality, and hierarchy of any kind as evil abuse. The Bible, by contrast, reads difference, sexual distinctiveness, and authority in different terms. We think here of 1 Corinthians 11:3, which states:

> But I want you to understand that the head of every man is Christ, the head of a wife is her husband, and the head of Christ is God.

---

[26] Patricia Hill Collins, *Intersectionality as Critical Social Theory* (Durham, North Carolina: Duke University Press, 2019), 102–3.

This teaching shows us that headship, though hated by a neo-pagan order, is an illustrious part of divine design.[27] The eternal Father is head of His eternal Son; the Son is head of His Church; the husband is head of his wife. This is a key part of what we call "creation order." Adam's being made first in the garden signals what God desires in the home and the Church: that men would lead, teach, and shepherd the whole flock of God (Genesis 2:7; 1 Timothy 2:9–15). A wife submitting to her husband is not demeaning or bad; it is doxological and reflects the marriage of Christ and His Church (Ephesians 5:22–33). Earthly covenants thus enflesh the heavenly covenant, the marriage of Christ and His blood-bought people.

There is a great deal more to say here, but we must lay this mark down: Christianity and intersectionality—and wokeness more broadly—have polar-opposite views of the sexes. There is no divine design in wokeness; there is only one's personal identity, following one's own heart, and expecting others to affirm one's chosen path. This is what love is in wokeness: not transformation, but affirmation. This value is found all throughout this ideology. For example, in a recent *Washington Post* article praising different proponents of "social justice," the reporter featured a "drag duo" based in Toronto. Alongside brief profiles of activists teaching three-year-olds about their inherent racial biases, journalist Natalie Jesionka wrote the following: "Kaleb Robertson and JP Kane are performance artists who have experience in early education and have been offering free drag story time in Toronto since 2016." What's the goal of drag queen story hour, in their words? "We want kids to have the tools and knowledge to accept all members of their community and celebrate their differences," according to Robertson. "So if they see someone with a beard wearing a dress, they are coming from a place of acceptance and understanding."[28]

---

[27] Owen Strachan and Gavin Peacock, *The Grand Design: Male and Female He Made Them* (Fearn, Scotland: Christian Focus, 2016), 75.

[28] Natalie Jesionka, "Social Justice for Toddlers: These New Books and Programs Start the Conversation Early," *Washington Post*, March 18, 2021,

Wokeness does indeed seek acceptance. But it does not want people to accept biblical complementarity. It pushes very hard against God's creation order and the reality and goodness of the sexes. It seeks to subvert God's design and overcome it. The social movement that most incarnates wokeness, Black Lives Matter, states just such an aim. As the BLM website has said, "Black Lives Matter is a radical social intervention."[19] Here are several quotations from past days that show what radical changes BLM seeks:

> We disrupt the Western-prescribed nuclear family structure requirement by supporting each other as extended families and "villages" that collectively care for one another, especially "our" children, to the degree that mothers, parents, and children are comfortable.

This involves transgender activism:

> We are committed to...doing the work required to dismantle cis-gender privilege and uplift Black trans folk.... We are committed to embracing and making space for trans brothers and sisters to participate and lead.

It includes wholesale approval of "queerness":

> We are committed to fostering a queer-affirming network. When we gather, we do so with the intention of freeing ourselves from the tight grip of heteronormative thinking or, rather, the belief that all in the world are heterosexual unless s/he or they disclose otherwise.

---

https://www.washingtonpost.com/lifestyle/2021/03/18/social-justice-antiracist-books-toddlers-kids.

[19] Alex Nitzberg, "Black Lives Matter's Agenda Is about More Than Race," *The Hill*, September 6, 2016, https://thehill.com/blogs/pundits-blog/civil-rights/2944 51-black-lives-matter-agenda-is-about-more-than-race.

The movement could not have been clearer in days past about its radical ambitions:

> Justice as imagined by its organizers is not only about ending anti-black racism. Visions of true justice must include freedom for black people who are queer, transgender, formerly or presently incarcerated, undocumented or facing any number of other challenges.

In supporting homosexuality, transgenderism, and the demise of the natural family, BLM aligns itself in the starkest terms against God's creation order. Scripture is clear that homosexuality and gender-bending are sins not only against God's will, but against God's design. God's judgment comes upon all who embrace such evil. See Romans 1 on this count:

> For this reason God gave them up to dishonorable passions. For their women exchanged natural relations for those that are contrary to nature; and the men likewise gave up natural relations with women and were consumed with passion for one another, men committing shameless acts with men and receiving in themselves the due penalty for their error.... Though they know God's righteous decree that those who practice such things deserve to die, they not only do them but give approval to those who practice them. (Romans 1:26–27, 32)

This is the resounding conclusion of God's appraisal: those who practice such things "deserve to die" (verse 32). This is true of every human person, for sin of every kind draws the wrath of God upon our head. Yet we must not miss that the Apostle Paul teaches that there is a special form of blasphemy in depraved sexuality. The body is made for *Creator worship* (as our whole person is), but fallen sexuality turns our bodies into vessels of *creation worship*. Much as people around us are encouraged to use their bodies any way they desire, we must warn people away from this ideology. In embracing sins of this kind (and any kind), we travel a downhill road to judgment. We who have been forgiven much must preach much about the wages of sin and the redemption found in Christ.

What we are warning people away from is not just bad behavior, but a disenchanted worldview. More simply, we are turning them away from *neopaganism*. Paganism is the anti-wisdom of the serpent which deconstructs ordered reality—the God-made world—and replaces it with a new order, an anti-order ruled by the devil. In this anti-order, there is no Creator; no divine design; no male or female; no script for sexuality; no God-designed family with a father, mother, and children; no need to protect and care for children at all; no Savior, Lord, or theistic end to the cosmos; and no judge of evil.[30]

The theologian Peter Jones calls this "the religion of one-ism." This contrasts with what Jones calls "two-ism," the biblical approach to reality, in which God fundamentally stands above and apart from His creation, grounding all distinctions, judging all the earth, placing His image in the earth under divine authority to live according to divine design. One-ism, by contrast, reduces the world to a dreary sameness: "there are no real distinctions, everything is made of the same stuff, matter is eternal, and it has this spark of divinity within it."

So it is that we must thus "invent gender and marriage," making each whatever we desire it to be, while expressing "tolerance for all religions" and "all lifestyles." Yet even as our neopagan age talks about tolerance, it does not practice it. As we noted in the introduction to this chapter, our pagan age actually has a hard edge to it, and it marches under the banner of forced affirmation. It urges us to approve of four major sexual movements: feminism, postmarital sexual libertinism,

---

[30] This material on neopaganism is adapted with permission from my book *Reenchanting Humanity*. See also my coauthored books *What Does the Bible Teach about Lust?*, *What Does the Bible Teach about Homosexuality?*, and *What Does the Bible Teach about Transgenderism?*, each an accessible resource for Christians written with Gavin Peacock and published by Christian Focus (2020).

transgenderism, and homosexuality. Each of these is a part of neopaganism.[31] Feminism overturns the biblical ideal of the woman, sexual libertinism severs sex from marriage and encourages men and women to act sexually without respect to morality, transgenderism revolts against the very concept of divine design in terms of identity and appearance, and homosexuality revolts against the sacred order in terms of sexual identity and practice.

These four ideologies are not just sub-biblical. They represent nothing less than an anti-order, a worldview that is in truth no worldview at all. If most modern people do not bow to stone deities, this in no way means that they are not cheerful participants in neopagan worship. They may not be directing their spiritual and bodily rebellion toward a given god, but they are nonetheless following the anti-wisdom of the serpent and denying God's design.

Neopaganism is no longer the exception in the West; more and more, it is the norm. The Church must see the spread of neopaganism in our time, for it is a crucial part of BLM's platform. If this seems like a new challenge, it is not. It has a new thrust—hence the "neo"—but it is actually the oldest competitor to the Christian faith there is. As Abraham Kuyper proclaimed over one hundred years ago at Princeton Seminary, we cannot "forget that the fundamental contrast has always been, is still, and will be until the end: Christianity and Paganism, the idols or the living God."[32] As in days of old, so today. It is ultimately either Christianity we will follow, or it is paganism.

---

[31] Yet we do not mean to indicate that these causes neatly align with one another. As Douglas Murray has observed, the LGBT movement and the broader "social justice" movement "do not in fact interact well with each other. The oppression matrix is not a great Rubik's cube waiting for every square to be lined up by social scientists. It consists of a set of demands which do not work together, and certainly not at this pitch." Douglas Murray, *The Madness of Crowds: Gender, Race, and Identity* (London: Bloomsbury, 2019), 233–34.

[32] Abraham Kuyper, *Lectures on Calvinism* (Grand Rapids, Michigan: Eerdmans, 1931), 199.

Stiff as the competition is, the Church has the truth of God. It knows the beauty of biblical manhood, biblical womanhood, biblical marriage, biblical sexuality, and biblical creation order. We are not playing from behind or with a weak hand. We have the very mind of Christ (1 Corinthians 2:16). Furthermore, as our culture and society grow increasingly evil, God will use that encroaching darkness to draw people to the light. He is a saving God, and He loves to turn evil purposes to divine ends. Even as the West embraces the absurd and the decadent, Christians should only preach and live out the truth even more. The solution to what we face is not to downplay biblical complementarity in order to avoid offending those pulled to paganism. The solution is to preach the truth in love and live according to the truth in joy and hope.

As noted earlier in these pages, we are not seeking to be *reasonable* Christians as defined by a sinful world. We do not calibrate Christianity to the specifications of unbelievers and present that sanitized, culturally approved form of it to them. Instead, we proclaim the whole counsel of God, and we live by it. We are not responsible for sanding off the edges of the biblical faith. We are not called to offer people a palatable religion that they naturally like and find inoffensive. We are called to preach the Gospel to fellow image-bearers who are drunk on their sin. We are tasked with teaching "all things" Christ commanded us to disciples (Matthew 28:20). We are those who confess not only that all of Scripture is inspired, inerrant, and authoritative, but that all of Scripture is *good* and good for us. This is true of God's design for the sexes and the family; this is true of all God lays before us in His perfect Word.

Seventh, wokeness overturns the Gospel's "no condemnation in Christ" promise.

The key evil wokeness addresses is the problem of "whiteness" and "white supremacy." As noted earlier in this chapter, we fall prey to unrighteousness per woke thought when we participate in and benefit from "whiteness," which cannot help but produce "white supremacy." Consequently, we overcome this condition not through justifying faith grounded in the person and work of Christ, but through performing acts of cultural repentance and by becoming "antiracist." This antiracist engagement must consist of concrete acts of secular penance.[33] It is in every sense a works-based system. Strangely, it is being adapted in our time by evangelicals. Sin undergoes serious redefinition in such a scheme, as Voddie Baucham Jr. has observed: "Not only are white Christians who fail to adopt antiracist theology and repent of racism in jeopardy of being alienated from God, but those who fail to elevate the preaching of the antiracist message to the same level as the preaching of the Gospel are apparently preaching another gospel," one that is not the true Gospel at all.[34]

In the woke system, we recall, racism is not primarily an attitude of the heart. It is an ineradicable element of "whiteness." It is baked into American society, and every "white" person (or person helped by it) is guilty of benefiting from racism because the "systemic injustice" of this public order privileges "whites" in all sorts of ways. The consequences of this view, especially when Christianized, could not be more momentous. In wokeness, we can be saved, be justified by faith in Christ, and yet still be guilty of our "white complicity" in "white supremacy." In reality, this sad state is not a *possibility* for those benefiting from "whiteness"; this is a *reality*. We see that there is thus a problem that the Gospel does not solve. In woke Christian thought, the Gospel can give us a new birth, but it does not overcome and defeat our inherent participation in "whiteness" (if we benefit from it). Here is where we see wokeness (and CRT) at its absolute deadliest. According to this system, there is a condition that Gospel faith does not make right. Only "antiracism," a regimen of ritual confession and penance on the individual side and political improvement and public policy on the communal side, makes our racist wrongs right.[35]

---

[33] Kendi, *How to Be an Antiracist*, 209.

[34] Voddie Baucham Jr., *Fault Lines: The Social Justice Movement and Evangelicalism's Looming Catastrophe* (Washington, D.C.: Salem Books, 2021), 87.

[35] We do well to remember that not only "white" people come up short for opposing "white supremacy," but at some level everyone of any skin color does. It is not enough to not be "white" in woke ideology; you must be actively seeking to tear

As a system, we conclude that wokeness both adds to and subtracts from the Gospel. There is more that must be done for "white" people than the simple Gospel does. Thus, "It is finished" is not technically correct; wokeness would have us correct Jesus in His dying breath at Calvary. There is more for sinners to do than *just* believe and repent. So wokeness adds to the Gospel. But it also subtracts; it takes away the transforming power that is in the blood of Christ. We may get our ticket punched to Heaven, but if we have bought into "whiteness" (whether personally or as a system), we are not transformed. We need human ideology—CRT—for this. We need "antiracism." We need, even as born-again believers, to go further and overcome our condition of "oppressor." Wokeness adds to the Gospel; therefore, wokeness subtracts from it. The end result is a gospel that is thoroughly unlike the biblical Gospel. Stronger still, the end result is a gospel that is *anti-Gospel*.

We are now equipped to understand what so few do today: that wokeness violates what the Apostle Paul expressly teaches. In Romans 8:1, we read, "There is therefore now no condemnation for those who are in Christ Jesus." This status is due to God's judicial verdict pronounced on the basis of our faith in the atoning work of the Son. As Christians, God has regenerated us and given us saving faith; as a result, God has removed His own just sentence of condemnation from us. In His courtroom, all who trust Christ are not only *not guilty*, but *innocent*. This is not a feeling; it is a fact. It does not owe to us; it owes to God. It does not come and go; it is stable, purchased, and our possession—now and for all time. It is God's courtroom pronouncement, and no one can

---

down the supremacist order to be an antiracist, fully and totally committed to the cause, as Kendi and others argue. It is still true that "white" people are objectively guilty for their "whiteness" and that this is the single greatest social ill targeted by wokeness. But it is also true that groups like Asian Americans that enthusiastically engage and use white societal structures to advance without challenging them fail at some level as well. This is why in some woke breakdowns of privilege, Asian Americans no longer are treated as "people of color." There is considerable tension here within the woke system, we note, and different woke voices land in different places on this matter.

edit it, reverse it, or refute it. This is true of every Christian without exception in biblical terms (see Romans 5:12–21).

If this sounds miraculous, this is because it is indeed a miracle. Yet wokeness dares tell us that even if a "white" person becomes a Christian, we are actually *still* condemned. There is fine print we apparently did not read. If we are "white" or benefit from the system of "whiteness," we have an extra layer of sinful guilt that the Gospel does not innately overcome. We are guilty of complicity in "white supremacy," whether "white" or not. Unless we are thoroughly antiracist, we are on the wrong side of history. As Christians, we may have thought it was enough to repent of our individual sins; it turns out it was not enough. Even after coming to faith, by not opposing "white privilege" and "white supremacy," we have participated in ongoing injustice. We have done so not through intentional unjust words and deeds in some cases, but simply by virtue of being "white" (or by not opposing "whiteness" if we are not "white"). We therefore must repent of our participation in "systemic injustice," a condition our conversion to Christ did not overcome.

Not long ago, Ibram Kendi—the leading woke voice in America today—encapsulated the ideas just covered. Speaking on how "whiteness" is "killing" white people, he said this to a packed room in Manhattan:

> More white people are finally beginning to realize how white supremacy and how even whiteness itself is killing them.... It literally is posing an existential threat to humanity. It always has. And so fundamentally, antiracism is life. It literally is, it can save humanity.[36]

---

[36] Judson Memorial Church, "How To Be Anti-Racist: Ibram X. Kendi in Conversation with Molly Crabapple," YouTube, filmed on August 15, 2019, https://www.youtube.com/watch?v=BhbbmjqcRvY. I saw this video through the "Woke Preacher Clips" Twitter account (@WokePreacherTV): https://twitter.com/WokePreacherTV/status/1374345130925260801.

Kendi said this while chuckling several times, but his open attack on image-bearers is anything but humorous. Actual "white supremacy" is unquestionably evil, but Kendi is not speaking of that. He is explicitly targeting mainstream "whiteness" and traditionally non-racist "white people." He does so with spiritual language, reminding us that wokeness is religious—it is a religion. It carries us like a tide, causing us to see "whiteness" as our societal original sin and "antiracism" as our new secular gospel.

Wokeness is not, as we have been at pains to say, benign. It is not atheological. It is a direct attack on the Gospel itself, and it is a replacement gospel. There is no room for merging such teaching with the teaching of Scripture. You choose one, or you choose the other. This is not a system compatible with Christian faith. It is the antithesis of the Christian faith, and it is definitely "an existential threat to humanity," to use Kendi's line.

In Kendi's pronouncements, as well as other "woke Christian" arguments, we can never truly overcome the evil of "whiteness." Even if born again, the person benefiting from "whiteness" is effectively trapped—trapped by past American history, trapped by shared guilt, and trapped by an utter inability to overcome their inherent racism.[37] Wokeness reads

---

[37] It is true that if we were born in slavery-supporting regions in past centuries, we would have had some involvement in wicked social structures, even unintentional and unknowing involvement. Switching the example, if we grew up in Nazi Germany and were indoctrinated to hate Jews in the Hitler Youth, we would undoubtedly have picked up sinful habits and patterns of thought that would demand repentance in the name of Christ. But in these examples, there is a clear and discernable body of evil ideology and actions that would be influencing and affecting us, manifesting in our own discrete sins against God. Indeed, being German even in such an evil era would not make us more lost than an unregenerate person in any area of the world; it would mean that evil would encroach upon us such that we would have definite temptations offered us by our majority culture. Even in such instances, though, we would not be guilty of *society's sin*, but would always and only be guilty of our *own personal involvement in sin*.

It is not impossible that our own modern context could fall prey to similar patterns of sin that would then reach into our lives and tempt us personally. Our sexually depraved twenty-first-century culture, for example, could be softening our morality in ways we do not fully comprehend. But our own guilt before God will always be for "whiteness" of any form as definitively and uniquely condemned, though there is no biblical support for such a view, and though in Scripture a given people's past crimes in no way render their descendants culpable for their actions. In doing so, it leaves a distinct group of people without real hope of change, let alone transformation.

The Gospel announces forgiveness and resulting innocence; wokeness announces guilt and unending condemnation. God's good news is the ministry of freedom; wokeness is the ministry of imprisonment. It tells "white" people and those who benefit from "whiteness" that they are indeed guilty of participation, even unwitting participation, in "white supremacy." It calls people back to the altar to confess sins they never knew they committed simply because of the color of their skin. It restores the status of condemned—"racist"—to men and women who thought they were justified by faith and not only free of guilt, but innocent in the sight of God.

This is why we need the Gospel: because ungodly systems like wokeness seek to take us captive. They even seek to take the Gospel itself captive. But God speaks a better word. The Gospel does not condemn

---

our *own* discrete thoughts, desires, actions, and words, not *society's*. If this were not true, then the Corinthian Christians—as one example—would have been guilty of sins simply by virtue of living in a wicked locale like Corinth. But the Corinthians were not guilty of sins simply because they *lived in Corinth*; they were guilty on different counts, as 1–2 Corinthians show, because they *embraced Corinthian debauchery*. Said differently, Corinth pressed in on the Church and threatened to affect the Church, but Corinth could not make the Church sin against God. The Corinthians were accountable for their own sin before the Lord. All this helps us understand why we must be exceedingly discerning about the concept of "systemic injustice" and our involvement in it. It is easy for us all to be imprecise in these matters.

Even if our context does have real failings that present us with real temptations, we should still be very careful about equating our modern public order with that of slave-supporting America (as diverse woke voices do). This is a stretch that defies sound thinking for numerous (stated) reasons. Making this connection actually makes it *harder* to fight patterned sins of partiality, because if everything is "white supremacist," then nothing is. Where such a claim is made, there must be abundant, evidence-driven proof to back it up. I write this even as I confess that we are always more sinful than we know and always fail to confess our sins to God as we should—which means God is infinitely more gracious than we comprehend.

you as a "white" person for having "white" skin. Do we all have tendencies and failings to watch and be aware of as Christians hailing from a given family and context? Yes. If you show partiality or find pride in your natural state (whatever it may be), then that is sinful. Having noted that real temptation, though, we are all sinners by birth. As such, we are all in the same condition with no person of any background or skin color being fundamentally better or worse off than any other due to their skin color. "Whiteness" does not make you extra-condemned compared to the normally condemned sinners. No natural trait or identity marker can do this.

Our skin color is not a barrier to the kingdom; praise God, Jesus has died for people of every color, every background, and every people group. No matter what our past is, no matter what our family or ethnic group's past is, no matter what our church's tradition is, if we ourselves have repented of our sins and trusted Christ as our Savior, we *objectively* cannot be condemned (Romans 8:1). God has pronounced us innocent in His sight, thanks to the imputed righteousness of Jesus Christ. This is His verdict, not man's. No one can overcome it.

We do sin, yes, and even fall into patterns of sin as a believer, necessitating spiritual carefulness and regular repentance (James 3:2). But no one can reverse the decision of God anchored in the death of His Son and realized in justifying faith. If in Christ we are not legally condemned, we cannot *be* legally condemned (Romans 8:33–34). We are innocent in God's sight. No ideology can change this. While fighting *situational sin* until we die, our *judicial status* is unchanged and unchanging: "innocent" in Christ. This is our standing now, and it will be our standing until the end of the age, when we are acquitted by divine grace before the Great White Throne.

All this helps us see that "Christian wokeness" is preaching "another Jesus," a Jesus who does not end up much of a savior at all (2 Corinthians 11:4). We may follow Him in faith as believers, but according to woke ideology, doing so does not overcome our inherent "white supremacy." This bears repeating: To overcome that condition, we need wokeness;

we need human ideology driven by the Marxist tool of the oppressor and oppressed framework. As naïve evangelicals, we might have thought we were only sinners; it turns out per woke thinking that "white" evangelicals are sinners and oppressors. Even after coming to faith in Christ they have supported and participated in a system of "white supremacy."

Remember once more that in woke thinking this is not *conscious and intentional* "white supremacy" of the kind we rightly decry in the Ku Klux Klan. It is *participational* or *ontological* "white supremacy" derived simply from our skin color (or our failure to challenge such systemic evil, whatever color we may be).[38] Because of our skin color or failure to dismantle "whiteness," we have a condition to address (for we cannot repent and decisively put it behind us in woke ideology) that we did not know we had. Beyond this, we have a whole set of "antiracist" actions to perform, even as they will never take away the stain on our soul.

In comparison to the good news of the Gospel, what *bad news* this is. We Christians who thought we were not condemned are in fact very much condemned. In woke ideology, we are condemned for our complicity in "structural oppression." Jesus died, it seems, and destroyed the power of every sin—except the sins of being "white" or benefiting from "whiteness." These wrongs only Marxism can address. Even if we buy such a framework, though, take note: According to wokeness, we will never overcome our complicity in "systemic injustice" driven by "white supremacy." Unlike in biblical salvation, we'll never put our guilt behind us, its power crucified with Christ (Romans 6:6). No, "woke Christianity" tells us that we can only name our racism, oppose it by action, and continually lament it until we die.

Neither can we free our children or grandchildren from this system, notably. If they participate in "whiteness," they too are condemned. Like us, they can never outrun their guilt, but only identify it and try their hardest to work against it. But mark it: The Gospel won't be enough for them. They won't overcome their natural condition; they'll only be able

---

[38] By "ontological," I mean inherent, or fixed. It is our natural condition irrespective of our actions, deeds, thoughts, or words.

to undertake ritual self-denunciation, penance, and self-loathing in trying to meet a standard they never will achieve.

Conclusion

We must sit up and take notice here: This is not God's Gospel. This is a worse gospel, infinitely worse. This is man's gospel; legalism is what comes out of the heart of man, not divine grace. This is in truth an *anti-gospel*. It is anathema. This unbiblical system will not save you. Following wokeness all the way through means that you will be in eternal peril, trapped in your works even as you trust them to make you more "anti-racist," striving for social salvation but never attaining it. You will hear the beat of the "tell-tale heart," and you will feel tremendous guilt for your participation in "structural evil," but you will have no way to change your situation. You will be trapped; in that hour, you will be what the Scripture says: *taken captive*.

DISCUSSION QUESTIONS

1. What does it mean for the Christian to "take every thought captive" to obey Christ (2 Corinthians 10:5)?
2. How do wokeness and CRT commit the sin of bearing false witness?
3. How does wokeness detract from God's design for humanity?
4. In what ways does wokeness end up committing the very sin that it critiques?
5. If the Gospel can be summed up as "God—sin—redemption," how does CRT redefine each of these three categories?

CHAPTER 4

Why Is Wokeness an Ungodly System?

Part Two: Cultural Issues

*Without justice what are kingdoms but great
bands of robbers?*

—*Augustine*

The Maginot Line, built in France shortly before World War II, was designed to keep Nazi (German) troops from entering the country. This defense system was constructed in several phases starting in 1930 by the Service Technique du Génie (STG), which was overseen by Commission d'Organisation des Régions Fortifiées (CORF). The main construction was largely completed by 1939 at a cost of around three billion French francs. The Maginot Line represented a system of strong points, fortifications and military facilities, and more. These structures reinforced a principal line of resistance made up of the most heavily armed *ouvrages*, which were essentially fortresses.[1]

These fortresses were something to behold. They included at least six "forward bunker systems," two entrances, and were connected via a network of tunnels. The blocks contained infrastructure such as power stations, independent ventilating systems, barracks and mess halls, kitchens, and water storage and distribution systems. Their crews ranged from

---

[1]   J. E. Kaufmann et al., *The Maginot Line: History and Guide* (Barnsley, United Kingdom: Pen & Sword Military, 2011), 3–45. For information about the STG and CORF, see ibid., 54, 64.

five hundred to a thousand men.[2] In these and other details, the Maginot Line was impressive.[3] It bristled with military power. There was just one problem: It was not suited to modern warfare, which, as pioneered by the Nazis, featured rapid tank movement, relatively little attention to the maintenance of captured territories when in battle, and coordinated strikes. The Maginot Line was fitted for a different challenge and a different age.

Why consider military history in a book on wokeness? Because, like the ill-fated French defenses of yesteryear, our theology is not adapted to the major challenge of our day. We are prepared for what you could call "soft postmodernism"—the belief that there is no objective truth, no "ought" in life, and that science tells us the meaning of the cosmos. We are not prepared for the "hard postmodernism" that is now dominant in our culture. Unlike the earlier form of ten to thirty years ago, hard postmodernism presents a very carefully framed argument, many oughts, a clear good group and bad group, and maintains that science—like all disciplines—is shot through with Western rationalism borne of white supremacy.[4] If you do not know this, however good your intentions may be, you are equipped for a different struggle than the one that is knocking on your door. Wokeness is not soft postmodernism; wokeness is hard postmodernism.[5]

---

[2]   Ibid., 14–26.

[3]   See the entry on "Maginot Line" on Wikipedia: https://en.wikipedia.org/wiki/Maginot_Line#:~:text=The%20Maginot%20Line%20(French%3A%20Ligne,to%20move%20around%20the%20fortifications.

[4]   CRT advocate Thandeka Chapman writes, "Critical race theory is rooted in critical studies, ethnic studies, and women's studies. To expand intersections of race, class, and gender, CRT has borrowed theoretical concepts from postmodernists, poststructuralists, and postcolonial thought." Thandeka K. Chapman, "Origins of and Connections to Social Justice in Critical Race Theory in Education," in *Handbook of Critical Race Theory in Education*, eds. Marvin Lynn and Adrienne D. Dixson (New York: Routledge, 2013), 104.

[5]   See Helen Pluckrose and James A. Lindsay, *Cynical Theories* (Durham, North Carolina: Pitchstone Publishing, 2020), 207–9. They use the term "reified" postmodernity, but I think it works as well to use the hard and soft distinctions.

In this chapter, I will continue my critique of wokeness. My analysis here shows us that the postmodern thought we now deal with is not the postmodern thought of days past. It is hard-edged, exclusivist (in a sense), and built for war. It has major consequences for theology (as our previous chapter showed), and it has major consequences for society, institutions, and the Christian worldview. The stakes are high here, and we must be like the men of Issachar, knowing the Word and the times in which we live (1 Chronicles 12:32).

First, wokeness corrupts true justice, making it distributive and not retributive.

According to Critical Race Theory and intersectional thought, civil law and basic institutional structures throughout society need to be re-envisioned. The law has heretofore supported inequity, so the argument goes. Thus, the law (and hiring practices and admissions policies and other sorting elements) needs reformulating such that it is not a tool of retributive justice (rendering to each what they deserve), but a tool of distributive justice (reapportioning privilege to those without it).[6] Equality of outcome, not equality of opportunity, is the desired result. Said differently, in CRT thinking, the fundamental concern of civil law is not to apply justice proportionate to human actions, but to enact "social justice" based on cultural considerations.

We can quickly note that minority groups have been discriminated against in many cases in history, in some cases to a terrible degree. Furthermore, law enforcement officers must be held accountable for their actions, and police officers who err should be disciplined like any other person. Nonetheless, if we relinquish the law, demonize law enforcement, and defund the police, we descend into anarchy. We create an unstable society. We wrong many who would then live without justice and who would be preyed upon by evildoers.

On this matter of the proper design of law, we must consider Romans 13:3–4:

---

[6] Richard Delgado and Jean Stefancic, *Critical Race Theory: An Introduction*, 2nd edition (New York and London: New York University Press, 2012), 28.

For rulers are not a terror to good conduct, but to bad. Would you have no fear of the one who is in authority? Then do what is good, and you will receive his approval, for he is God's servant for your good. But if you do wrong, be afraid, for he does not bear the sword in vain. For he is the servant of God, an avenger who carries out God's wrath on the wrongdoer.

Government, and thus the law by extension, has claimed many duties unto itself in our time. Note, however, what Paul says rulers exist to do:

1. To be a terror to bad conduct
2. To put evildoers in fear
3. To stimulate good
4. To be God's servant for public good
5. To bear the sword
6. To avenge God's wrath on the wrongdoer

What a consequential program for government this is. Clearly, Christians have a strong place for justice and mercy in society. This is no new idea; it was a key component of the life of God's people in the Old Testament, much as they failed to live up to God's standards (for example, Amos 5:11–15; Micah 3:1–3). Of course, times have changed. Followers of God in the Old Testament centered their identity in Israel, a geopolitical and spiritual nation ruled by God. This unique historical regime was expected to dispense both punitive justice and grace-filled mercy at times, depending upon the situation, to its citizens—even while it promoted true religion under the guidance of the Torah.[8] In the New Testament, however, Church and state are distinct, with each possessing a unique

---

[7] Wayne A. Grudem, *Christian Ethics: An Introduction to Biblical Moral Reasoning* (Wheaton, Illinois: Crossway, 2018), 429–31.

[8] Geerhardus Vos notes, "The union of the religious lordship and the national kingship in the one Person of Jehovah involved that among Israel civil and religious life were inextricably interwoven." Geerhardus Vos, *Biblical Theology: Old and New Testaments* (Carlisle, Pennsylvania: Banner of Truth Trust, 2000), 125.

function and particular mission (Matthew 22:21). The Church proclaims the Gospel and provides order to its disciples (Matthew 28:18–20), while the state promotes civil law and provides order to society (1 Peter 2:13–14). It is not the job of the Church to police society, nor is it the job of the state to win souls.

Even with this change in the situation of God's people, the New Testament points to government as the instrument of common human justice in the world. The institutions formed by God have real authority, and humanity is called to obey them: rulers, police, military, and so on. Romans 13 reveals that civil law matters tremendously. It is a gift of God to all the earth, in fact. But justice in the biblical mind is distinct from earthly justice. Man talks much about justice, but he knows not of what he speaks. In this passage and others, justice is not a means of *redistributing* privilege (per the narratives of the underprivileged). Biblical justice is *retributive* in nature, recompensing people for their deeds.

If there are real imbalances in a society and people are being wronged, then the law corrects that. But civil law, as instituted by God and reflecting the very character of God Himself, is not designed to administer therapeutic justice nor to heal society. The government is given by God to function as a protector, not a custodian, of its citizens. The state is to defend the rights of its people—not to tell them where to live, what to eat, how to be educated, or to remove every hardship from their existence.[9] Said simply, civil rulership is given to us by God to restrain evil and to promote public good.

This material on justice speaks to the proposal for "reparations" that has gained some traction in our time. Because of past American evils, the argument goes, we should pay money and grant privilege to the descendants of slaves and others who suffered (genuinely) from racial injustice.[10] This case is being framed in distinctively Christian ways today, and some commentators draw on this passage to make it:

---

[9]   Robert L. Woodson Sr., *The Triumphs of Joseph: How Today's Community Healers Are Reviving Our Streets and Neighborhoods* (New York: Free Press, 1998), 118.

[10]   See, for example, Ta-Nehisi Coates, "The Case for Reparations," *The Atlantic*, June 2014, https://www.theatlantic.com/magazine/archive/2014/06/the-case-for-reparations/361631.

You shall not bow down to them or serve them; for I the LORD your God am a jealous God, visiting the iniquity of the fathers on the children to the third and fourth generation of those who hate me, but showing steadfast love to thousands of those who love me and keep my commandments. (Deuteronomy 5:9–10)

The argument made by some is that this passage teaches us that successive generations bear guilt for the sins of their ancestors. At first blush, this passage could seem to teach such a concept. But on closer analysis, we must distinguish here between the *long-term* effects of sin and the *judicial guilt* for sin. This passage does not teach that future generations are judicially guilty for ancestral sin. Instead, it teaches us that pursuing idolatry will yield long-term effects. Descendants will not bear guilt for ancestral idolatry as if they committed it, but they will feel the effects of it. We see this happen in vivid form after David commits adultery with Bathsheba and has her husband, Uriah, placed in a battlefield killing zone. He loses his kingdom, and the loss of the kingdom affects many people for a good long time. Yet though his children suffer the *effects* of David's sin, they are not *judicially guilty* for it.[11]

However, this is what some voices argue today. They claim that "white" people are in fact complicit in past evils and should "repent" for them. This is what Thabiti Anyabwile communicated when he wrote the following in 2018: "My white neighbors and Christian brethren can start by at least saying their parents and grandparents and this country are complicit in murdering a man who only preached love and justice.... I'm

---

[11] We understand this personally. If a husband wrongs his wife—God forbid—by committing adultery as David did (or vice versa), then his actions will affect his children in many ways. But though his children would bear the effects of his actions, they would not in any way be *responsible* for his sin. They did not cause it, they are not on the hook for it, and they cannot be held accountable for it. No doubt they would feel the weight of his failing keenly, and hopefully they would learn from his transgressions, but at no point would they be held guilty for what he did.

saying the entire society killed Dr. King."[12] When Anyabwile's article released, it caused a major stir, for many evangelicals protested their lack of direct involvement in the assassination of Dr. Martin Luther King Jr. Most did not know the broader ideological context of this indictment. Anyabwile's call to "repentance" came from a structuralist conception of evil—a woke one in which all participate in "systemic" sin. He did not speak out of passion alone, as some might have initially thought, but out of the overflow of woke thinking. In wokeness, we really are *judicially guilty* of ancestral sin, and we really must "repent" of those sins, it seems.

This is an unbiblical idea. It might sound right when we first hear it, for Christianity does indeed call for humility and much searching of soul. Yet we must always be precise with our categories and precise with our doctrinal terms.[13] Neither the Old nor New Testament teaches ancestral guilt. Neither Testament institutes payment of reparations for sin. Of course, Scripture encourages us to fear God and walk humbly with Him at all times (Micah 6:8). This entails, I believe, the truth that it is right to reckon with the past in a spirit of humility and to pay the lessons of history forward in one's own days. Furthermore, where we have wronged one another situationally, we make restitution (see Exodus 22; Numbers 5). Yet the New Testament nowhere teaches ancestral guilt. Nor does it institute a system of payment (in monetary form or otherwise) for wrongs

---

[12] Thabiti Anyabwile, "We Await Repentance for Assassinating Dr. King," the Gospel Coalition, April 4, 2018, https://www.thegospelcoalition.org/blogs/thabiti-anyabwile/await-repentance-assassinating-dr-king.

[13] You can make the case; in fact, that this is what theology *is*. This is what sound doctrine is. It is an undertaking that depends on precision, care, discernment, and fine-tuning. Though a good number of sheep hear the faith presented weekly as a largely non-intellectual enterprise, the Christian faith is staked upon theological carefulness. The difference between soundness and unsoundness, life and death, truth and falsehood, Heaven and Hell is often slight. This is why we need—desperately— sound men who are well-trained in handling the Scriptures (Nehemiah 8:8; 1 Timothy 3:2; Titus 1:9; 2 Timothy 2:15, 24). Though it may be presented otherwise, the Christian ministry is a ministry necessitating serious precision, great watchfulness, careful training, and considerable labor. All this work is motivated by love for God and love for God's people. We do not commend learning for its own sake, but rather learning and thinking and labor to make disciples who obey *all* that Christ taught (Matthew 28:16–20).

done by one people group to another. Instead, the blood of Christ unifies across all lines, as we shall see in Chapter 6.

In the blood of Christ, hostility and division die. People who have nothing in common covenantally or otherwise end up having Christ in common by faith, and that fact is so grand and gripping that it means that these diverse peoples truly share everything. They are not reduced to indistinguishable sameness, of course, but they are united in the only thing that ultimately matters: the forgiveness of sins. This truth pushes Christians away from embracing a system of fiscal payment to those descended from people who suffered in past days. If ever there were people who should have made some kind of restitution to one another, after all, it would have been both sides of the hot-blooded Jew-Gentile divide. Furthermore, given that the Apostle Paul was a former persecutor of Christians, and a prolific one, he would have had the highest repara-tions bill of anyone. Yet Paul nowhere taught that justly aggrieved peoples (including people of different ethnicities) should recompense one another for past wrongs in a reparational scheme.[14] Instead, they were told to realize their union with Christ, to embrace being one body, to overlook wrongs, and to forgive one another (Ephesians 4:32).

Wokeness tells us differently. It says that justice must take distributive form, giving everyone the same living conditions and advantages. This is what "equity" looks like, alongside "inclusion" and "diversity." But we need to test these ubiquitous phrases, at once so undefined and so loaded with weight. As I stated in an earlier chapter, I have always loved basketball. I took to the game from my earliest days (I've since become

---

[14] There is a profound difference between making *restitution* for material wrongs done and paying *reparations* for past injustices. If I take something tangible from you, I should definitely compensate you as much as I can. But this is because there is a real material deficit involved. Nowhere does the New Testament lay out a system for emotional, psychological, or physical reparations. If we break the law, we suffer tangible consequences; if we wrong a believer (outside of restitution), we repent and seek forgiveness—or grant it. But we do not go on from there to exact from the sinner therapeutic repayment; there is no emotional *stigmata* we require. If we owe a material debt, we pay it to the fullest extent; if we have done real wrong, we repent and ask forgiveness. Then, assuming forgiveness can happen, we move on, entrusting final sorting out of all earthly matters to God.

a major Premier League fan as well). In playing basketball, I was treated equably—I had the same shot at a Division 1 college program that other kids had. No one put a law or policy or teaching in place that barred Owen Strachan, a five-foot-seven kid from rural Maine weighing 150 pounds dripping wet, from Duke or North Carolina or Gonzaga. However, though I enjoyed equality of opportunity (which *is* equality, traditionally defined), I sadly but justly did not experience equality of outcome. No recruiter from major basketball programs called me. This is because I was not "owed" a basketball scholarship. I had a shot at such an attainment like any kid, but I had no "right" or just claim to play in the Atlantic Coast Conference (ACC).

This is part of what makes our society's push for equity, inclusion, and diversity ironic. The same people who call for these oft-undefined ideals to become realities are not infrequently those who won their place in the world not by *equality of outcome* (where they were handed their platform) but by earning their spot through *equality of opportunity*. No one barred them from becoming an athlete, movie star, writer, director, musician, or intellectual. They won their place on the team, whether literal or figurative; they climbed, scraped, hustled, and earned their spot. This is as it should be, harsh as that sounds in a performance-trophy age. Yet there is good, tremendous good, in the struggle.

Not everyone will have the same precise conditions for their pursuit, of course; there is no way to level society such that everyone starts from the same base and experiences the same conditions of life. (Socialism has tried, over and over again, with miserable results as the norm.)[15] The just society focuses instead on removing barriers of access per biblical law and sound reasoning.[16] Biblical justice is not *distributive*, we see. It is

[15] See Kristian Niemietz, *Socialism: The Failed Idea That Never Dies* (London: London Publishing, 2019); Rand Paul, *The Case against Socialism* (Northampton, Massachusetts: Broadside Books, 2019); and Arthur Brooks, *The Conservative Heart: How to Build a Fairer, Happier, and More Prosperous America* (Northampton, Massachusetts: Broadside Books, 2015).

[16] In the public square (not evangelicalism directly), Shelby Steele speaks to his discovery that conservatives advocated for real justice, against the stereotypes of the same: "Conservatives didn't want to take you over, make you a pawn in some

fundamentally *retributive*, focused not on creating equal outcomes, but rather righting past wrongs and removing unfair impediments.[17] It is anchored in the justice of God. It is aimed at present evils. It is closely connected to the state and divinely instituted authorities like rulers and those who police evildoers. It is never utopian on this side of eternity, but it is conducted under the awareness that earthly justice is often proximate and never perfect.

Furthermore, biblical justice is not mercy. It is sometimes conflated with mercy, but it should not be. Justice is distinct from mercy. Let me explain: while justice is God *giving us* what we surely deserve, mercy is God *not giving us* what we deserve (in spiritual terms, the full force of His holy wrath). Our neopagan world, denying the Creator-creature distinction, wants to collapse mercy and justice, making them the same thing. But this will not do. Justice points to the righteous character of God and reminds us all that outside of Christ, we will pay the just penalty of our sins. It is a comfort, therefore, to the believer. But to the unbeliever, justice is a rightful terror. It cannot be otherwise; indeed, it must be so. Yet the fact of divine justice is not a defeater for our witness to unbelievers; rather, the justice of God fills us with urgency, and by the Spirit's leading, it wakes unbelievers up to own their desperate condition so they can cast themselves on the mercy of God.

Though it is a kindness of God for men and women to live in a generally just society, justice is not salvific, personally transformative, or ultimately a comfort to the unbeliever. Praise God, the same God who

---

abstract policy goal, like 'integration' or 'diversity.' They wanted to apply the discipline of freedom to problems of race and poverty, and even to the problems of the great middle class. They understood that freedom was equal opportunity in itself. What had to end were the evils of persecution and discrimination, the eternal enemies of freedom." Steele, *Shame*, 185.

17   To clarify, an unfair impediment would be—to use my basketball analogy—the state of Maine passing a law barring young men below five-foot-eight from playing high school basketball. An unfair impediment is *not*, for example, my being short, not having access to my own skills trainer, or not having the money to send a highlight video to college coaches. But our socialistic culture confuses this point, with all manner of bad policies resulting. Remember: Life in general terms is hard, not easy. Accepting this truth helps us greatly.

is perfectly just is also perfectly merciful. Still, we must not make the common mistake of mingling these two attributes of God, nor of choosing one over the other. The God of justice is the God of mercy, and we see this in the cross of Christ. But the justice executed at Calvary means the legal condemnation of the Son; it is the mercy poured out at Calvary that purchases our pardon. These are high and holy realities, but we must not miss this: The cross of Christ gives us God's ultimate resolution of the justice-mercy conundrum. The same cross satisfies divine justice and secures divine mercy. This shows us that justice is retributive, not distributive, even as it reveals that the satisfaction of justice enables the experience of mercy. God does not set aside His justice in the death of His Son; He meets the full terms of His holy nature through the cross.

If the preceding section seems like a theological tangent, it is not. Only when we understand divine justice will we rightly frame earthly justice, and thus avoid utopian versions of it that in truth yield no justice at all. Proposals for reparations, we note here, actually yield no justice at all in the end, for the people who suffered in past days see no satisfaction from them, and people living today must thus chip in to pay for crimes they did not commit. Here we see that much of what is called "justice" today is actually injustice and does not do anything to make wrongs right. While honoring the emperor (1 Peter 2:17), we Christians remember this: if you truly want wrongs made right, you cannot look to any earthly decision or civic body, but only to a holy God.

Second, wokeness greatly complicates interracial adoption, marriage, and even friendship.

Wokeness, and "social justice" like it, are tools of division. Speaking of "social justice," Roger Scruton has identified "resentment of those who control things" as its "emotional source."[18] "Social justice" is not impartial and equable; as we have seen at some length, it is all too often driven by resentment and the desire to reframe society so that "white" oppressors—and majority groups more generally, per intersectionality—are unseated

---

[18] Roger Scruton, *Fools, Frauds, and Firebrands: Thinkers of the New Left* (London: Bloomsbury, 2015 [1985]), 13.

and dethroned. The consequences of such a worldview—a secular religion—are momentous for personal connections and relationships. Cherished realities like interracial adoption, marriage, friendship, and certainly church membership all come into question. Where wokeness is embraced, suspicion, hostility, and eventually division will follow.

This is especially poignant when one thinks about social fragmentation. So-called "interracial" adoption is a lovely thing in basic human terms. Yet not long ago, Ibram Kendi tweeted this amid media coverage of Supreme Court Justice nominee Amy Coney Barrett's adoption of "black" children (two from Haiti):

> Some White colonizers "adopted" Black children. They "civilized" these "savage" children in the "superior" ways of White people, while using them as props in their lifelong pictures of denial, while cutting the biological parents of these children out of the picture of humanity.[19]

Kendi then argued that adopting such children in no way makes someone "not a racist":

> And whether this is Barrett or not is not the point. It is a belief too many White people have: if they have or adopt a child of color, then they can't be racist.[20]

A writer for *Christianity Today*, Sitara Roden, spoke of her own adoptive background in a positive way, but also agreed with Kendi's perspective on bias:

---

19   Ibram X. Kendi (@DrIbram), Twitter, September 26, 2020, as cited in Jason Lemon, "Why Ibram Kendi Is Facing a Backlash over a Tweet about Amy Coney Barrett's Adopted Haitian Children," *Newsweek*, September 27, 2020, https://www.newsweek.com/why-ibram-kendi-facing-backlash-over-tweet-about-amy-coney-barretts-adopted-haitian-children-1534507.

20   Ibid.

This is a conversation I've had with my own white family. Just because I am not white and a part of their family does not mean their implicit biases are any less real. How you view the nonwhite person in your family, that you might have raised, is bound to be a different valuation than the person of color you see on the street.[21]

It is of course true that "transracial" adoptive parents could be racist or ethnocentric. Adoption is good, after all, but it does not cleanse your sins. Nonetheless, in these comments, we witnessed what wokeness yields. The belief that "white" people are inherently racist means that even good-hearted acts—acts that involve tremendous self-sacrifice, financial commitment, and the changing of an entire pattern of life to welcome an adopted child—are seen as racist.[22] Barrett and her husband were not generous-hearted human beings in natural terms but were portrayed as "white colonizers" with evil motives. Even adoptive parents should be faulted for their "implicit biases."

This commentary shows us the untamed resentment at the heart of wokeness. What is commendable in scriptural terms is interpreted as evil in ideological terms. Adoption is not driven by human generosity; it is driven by oppressive instincts. In response, we need to be clear: Such ideology is anti-human and anti-Gospel. What Ibram Kendi is selling, no believer should buy. This is an all-too-clear illustration of what wokeness leads to: it corrupts your worldview, causing you to see the world

---

[21] Sitara Roden, "Dr. Ibram Kendi, Amy Coney Barrett and Evangelical Adoption: Transracial Adoption Doesn't Make You Non-Racist; But It Doesn't Make You Racist Either," *The Exchange with Ed Stetzer*, September 30, 2020, https://www.christianitytoday.com/edstetzer/2020/september/kendi-barrett-adoption.html. Roden is the managing editor of Stetzer's media platform, *The Exchange*.

[22] What's more, a good number of Christians adopt children who have considerable physical, mental, and psychological challenges. The motive in such instances is the total opposite of "colonization"; it is Christlike mercy and kindness, as I have seen firsthand, and such expensive acts of love often stretch adoptive families to their limits as they help the helpless and welcome the abandoned. God will hold accountable, fully accountable, all who slander adoptive couples in these evil ways. Not a stray comment or a careless tweet will escape God's perfect justice.

wrongly, with "white" people being effectively evil, their actions being necessarily poisonous, and the lines between "races" being uncrossable, effectively.

Many evangelicals have done what Barrett did. These people are not perfect; they have their flaws; some of them may even need to grow in their handling of diversity. But to adopt a child, including one that looks different from you, is the very essence of true religion, according to James 1:27. James asserts:

> Religion that is pure and undefiled before God the Father is this: to visit orphans and widows in their affliction, and to keep oneself unstained from the world.

Wokeness takes a biblical desire (adopting children in difficult circumstances) and reads it as malformed. Instead of encouraging families to adopt, including "white" families, such a mentality stimulates false guilt, teaching people that they do not want to adopt out of love, but out of a "colonizing" mentality. This assertion may play well among those who condemn "white" people, but it is against the nature of the kingdom of Christ, where Christians love their neighbor without respect to skin color, background, class, or any other marker.[23]

Wokeness causes similar problems with regard to marriage, friendship, and church membership. In March 2021, social media activist Kyle Howard showed as much when he tweeted: "It's no coincidence that the black men who are used as tokens to promote & enable white supremacy are almost ALWAYS married to white women. That's how exoticism works. They sacrifice their blackness to have white & the white receives them so long as blackness is merely their body."[24] This is a "racialized"

---

[23] For a compelling account of an interracial friendship founded upon faith in Christ, see Raleigh Washington and Glen Kehrein, *Breaking Down Walls: A Model for Reconciliation in an Age of Racial Strife* (Chicago, Illinois: Moody Press, 1993).

[24] Kyle J. Howard (@KyleJamesHoward), "Full transparency: 1. I think the biggest theological battle I've had to do is regarding my doctrine of the church & role of Faith. I've endured so much church related abuse & trauma alongside my family &

vision of marriage. In this framing, a "black man" does not marry a "white woman" because of genuine love, let alone Christian calling. He does so because he lionizes "white supremacy" and sees "whiteness" as exotic. He is nothing more than a "token" and is used as such by "white" people. According to Howard, he effectively sacrifices his "blackness" in marrying a woman of a different skin color.

What a false and destructive vision of marriage across skin color this is. It is not only tragic to read such words, though. This kind of ungodly ideology will have real effects on spouses. If we buy the lie that "white" people are inherently and inescapably oppressors, what will this do to marriages where one spouse is not "white"? How will such ideology affect our group of friends if that group is composed of people of different skin colors and backgrounds, including some "white" people? What will this teaching do to church membership in congregations that are diverse because people have found a common home due not to shared heritage, but to shared love of the proclamation of God's Word?

We already know the answer. Some of us have seen this play out. We've watched as wokeness has taken a friend, family member, or church member captive. Suddenly, all this person talks about is racial evil and white supremacy. Their friendships fracture; the captive thinks it's not them, but the wicked people around them. I have even heard reports of this occurring in marriages. One spouse is taken captive by wokeness and turns on the person who has covenantally loved them, forgiven them, been forgiven by them, and made a life together. Wokeness even divides parents from children. This is true in the case of adopted children who do not share their adoptive parents' skin color; it is also true of children who come to different conclusions than their father and mother. Though they were well-loved, they now feel great anger against their "oppressor" parents. They have been trained by wokeness to despise, and so they do.

_____

I've had to work thru a ton of guilt. 'Kyle, why the hell did you stay?',", Twitter, March 27, 2021, 12:00 p.m., https://twitter.com/KyleJamesHoward/status/1375840051985313794.

All this grieves us deeply. But let us not merely shake our head at such instances, multiplying as they are in our time. Let us resolve to do all we can to stop wokeness from winning more captives. Let us play offense and defense against it in our homes, churches, schools, communities, and networks. Let us remember that marriage of people from different backgrounds is beautiful and that the Word of God nowhere teaches that spouses should consider one another guilty or righteous along "racial" lines. Let us never forget that the diverse Church is a testimony to the power of the Gospel; Christians must not structure the Church intentionally to exclude any natural group of any kind. Skin color is not our unifying point, background is not our unifying point, and finances are not our unifying point. The Church is for repentant people— period. By believing this and holding fast to it in a fractured world, let us pursue friendship across backgrounds of all kinds, giving the world a beautiful testimony of the saving—and uniting—cross of Christ.

We also must point out that these are not theoretical possibilities we are addressing. Many marriages already cross dividing lines of background and ethnicity. Many thriving friendships across natural differences exist. Many churches draw people of diverse backgrounds as they preach the Gospel and welcome all to fellowship. But wokeness would have us forget all this, or else ignore it. Instead of emphasizing the real unity we already have, this ideology tells us that we have no hope of real unity (for it is based in this belief).[25] Yet in common grace terms and especially special grace terms, our age is not nearly as divided as certain activists and ideologues say it is. They are actually the ones creating the division they say is everywhere. They will not admit this, but it is true, nonetheless.

The dark magic behind wokeness despises all this. It tells us that unity is impossible. But this is a lie, and a vicious one. In reality, it is

---

[25] This is a crucial point: Wokeness does not believe in any grace-driven form of unity, whether we speak of common grace or special grace. The point of the system is not true unity of the kind shared among friends; the point of the system is removing "privilege" and "oppression" from society by dethroning some and elevating others. As Marx intended, this is a system built to divide, not unite.

wokeness that makes unity impossible, not Christianity. It is wokeness that divides the true Church, not the Gospel. It is wokeness that seeks nothing less than the destruction of creation order, marriage, family, church, and society, not God's Word. In love and in hope, we must reject this system; we must do nothing less than spit its poison out of our mouths.

Third, wokeness destabilizes truth, making it narrative-driven rather than absolute.

Wokeness advocates typically embrace what is called "standpoint epistemology," meaning that our social location and possession of privilege will shape our handling of truth.[26] Minority interpreters who have enjoyed less privilege (which per CRT blinds us from seeing truth) are able to "see" things in texts that others cannot. This hermeneutical commitment is based on the idea that "whiteness" as a privileged construct hinders interpreters from grasping dimensions of the text that underprivileged people can see. This commitment relativizes interpretation, whether of the Bible or of other books. It makes exegesis a culture-driven practice. Minority exegetes can see things that "white" exegetes cannot.[27]

Such a system leads many troubling ways. One application of standpoint epistemology is the promotion of different perspectives as distinct personal or communal "truths." We're familiar with this concept from "soft postmodernity," but it has purchase in "hard postmodernity" as well. If employed, this means that Christians will be justified in coming to altogether different conclusions about the meaning of biblical texts. A woke hermeneutic will contend that there is not one meaning of a given text, or perhaps two dimensions of the one meaning of the text, the original and the canonical (whether the fuller meaning is expressed primarily in direct citations, as some Christians believe, or also along

---

26 Delgado and Stefancic, *Critical Race Theory*, 43–56.

27 The work of Neil Shenvi and Pat Sawyer is insightful on this count. See *Engaging Critical Theory and the Social Justice Movement*, accessible online at https://ratio-christi.org/engaging-critical-theory-and-the-social-justice-movement.

typological lines, as I and other Christians believe).[28] Instead, there is an array of meanings in any given biblical passage, for we all bring our own "standpoint" to the task. Furthermore, the more underprivileged we are, the more purchase on the truth we have, and the more privileged, the more we are prevented from seeing the truth.[29]

Wokeness's epistemology is deeply damaging to the pursuit of truth. Can we bring our biases and background into our work to its detriment? We surely can. Is it healthy to read a wide range of voices? It is. Does this possibility of bias, however, undermine the very nature of our theological work, rendering our sermons and writings and claims merely the "racialized" words of one representative of a group? It does not, and it must not. Yet wokeness pushes even harder on this point, and as presented by some advocates insists that reason itself is racist. This claim ends up being nonsensical, however, for unless one commits oneself to communicating in gibberish, one has to use reason.[30] Clearly, it is not reason itself that woke thinkers critique as Western (for they publish lengthy books that make numerous reason-based arguments), but rather the use of reason to support un-woke precepts and worldviews that they dislike.

A statement, claim, proposition, or story is not true because of our background, cultural standing, or lack of privilege; our teaching is true because it accords with truth, with the Word of God above all. As H. B.

---

[28] The disagreement referenced here is a good-faith disagreement, and like eschatological matters and some other fine points of theology, is a conversation had among trusted brothers and friends. On this hermeneutical matter, the two camps are very close to one another when compared to liberal interpreters, for each believes in a defined meaning of biblical texts. For strong cases from these camps, see Abner Chou, *The Hermeneutics of the Biblical Writers: Learning to Interpret Scripture from the Prophets and Apostles* (Grand Rapids, Michigan: Kregel, 2018) and Dennis Johnson, *Him We Proclaim: Proclaiming Christ from All the Scriptures* (Phillipsburg, New Jersey: P&R, 2007).

[29] Delgado and Stefancic openly admit their epistemological stance, stating: "For the critical race theorist, objective truth, like merit, does not exist, at least in social science and politics. In these realms, truth is a social construct created to suit the purposes of the dominant group." Ibid., 104.

[30] Reason for biblical Christians is not magisterial, but ministerial. It does not rule the text but serves our understanding of God and his Word.

Charles insightfully states, "[T]ruth is truth, whether I experience it or not. The Lord does not need my experience to validate His Word.... The Word of God speaks for itself."[31] Charles is quite right. In biblical Christianity, the truth is the very Word of God. Our doctrine, therefore, is grounded in the text, but ultimately in the *God who has authored the text* through human writers. In wokeness, however, there is no deeper ontological grounding for truth; rather, wokeness simply asserts its commitments without foundation beyond our own narratives. Human narratives *are* the grounding of truth in a woke system.

It is difficult to underplay how significant this point is. If in practice we make truth narrative-driven and relative rather than theistic and absolute, we lose truth. If we lose truth—true truth, normative and norming truth derived from the meaning of biblical texts—then we lose the superstructure of the Gospel and the Christian faith.[32] Christianity depends upon propositional truthfulness; truthfulness is grounded in the character and identity of God. To personalize and relativize truth according to social location is to take truth out of God and ground it in us and our world. Truth *is* personal, but it is grounded in our personal God, not in our fallen stories and experiences.

We encounter similar trouble when we carve up exegesis and doctrinal formation according to skin color or community. In *Reading While Black*, for example, Esau McCaulley issues a strong indictment of conservative evangelicals: "Talking of reading critically is a slightly dangerous thing because Black traditional voices are often weaponized in evangelical spaces against Black progressive voices."[33] What McCaulley wrote could be true, but this is an ungenerous reading of conservative evangelicals. It makes the nature of the conversation over sound doctrine *racial* rather than *theological*. It reads evangelicals, including many

---

[31] H. B. Charles, *On Pastoring: A Short Guide to Living, Leading, and Ministering as a Pastor* (Chicago, Illinois: Moody Publishers, 2016), 130.

[32] David F. Wells, *The Courage to Be Protestant: Reformation Faith in Today's World,* 2nd edition (Grand Rapids, Michigan: Eerdmans, 2017), 47–51.

[33] Esau McCaulley, *Reading While Black* (Downers Grove, Illinois: IVP Academic, 2020), 15.

"whites," as weaponizing interpretation against "blacks." This kind of argument is quite common today. But it has serious problems. Let's think about a few of them.

First, "white" evangelicals are right to disagree with anyone of any background who does not rightly interpret the Word. What was it the Apostle Paul said to young Timothy?

> Do your best to present yourself to God as one approved, a worker who has no need to be ashamed, rightly handling the word of truth. (2 Timothy 2:15)

This is not, contra the stereotypes, a Western "white" man writing this. This is a Middle Eastern Jew urging an inexperienced pastor to handle the Word rightly. This indicates that there are right and wrong ways to preach biblical texts. It is not Eurocentric hermeneutics that champions this principle, but a redeemed Jew (by background) from the Middle East. Following Paul's logic, we must do all we can not to be "ashamed" by doing what comes naturally to us all: interpreting passages according to our own standards, our own views, our own biases, and our own background. Yes, our personal experiences factor into our theological work, but never in such a way as to affect a text's meaning; instead, they help us appreciate the depth of biblical truth, and they open our eyes to ways to *apply* (not *interpret*) the Word.

Second, evangelicals disagree with people of every skin color and background. The same conservative Christians who rightly critique the liberation theology of James Cone, for example, also critique in no uncertain terms the neo-orthodox theology of Karl Barth, the prosperity gospel of Kenneth Copeland, the emergent church theology of Brian McLaren, the postmodern universalism of Rob Bell, the feminist theology of Rosemary Ruether, and the "gay Christian" theology of Matthew Vines. What do all these figures have in common? They could all be grouped as "white." This is just a sampling of "white" theologians or activists who conservative evangelicals rightly teach against. This goes back to the Reformation, at least. Martin Luther, John Calvin, Ulrich Zwingli, and the English Baptists all went toe to toe with "white" Catholic thinkers and disagreed in the strongest possible way over the most important matters. They did not do so because of "race" (though some evangelicals have held unsound views of this concept, to be sure), but because of God's truth. Yet this important reality is missing from McCaulley's presentation and others like it. It is not "race" that motivates rejection of liberation theology, but love of the Body—the Body that spans all tribes, tongues, nations, and peoples.

Third, McCaulley's framing is in grave danger of reading "black" Christians who identify as conservative as outliers. McCaulley's case is not uncommon today in its reading of a common "black theology." Yet this overlooks the reality that many "black" people love conservative evangelical doctrine. They are not in any way outliers. They are children of God. They have rightly interpreted the Scriptures. Their voice is not the "white man's voice" speaking through them. Their voice is their own, and they are wronged—grievously wronged—when they are presented as custodians of "white evangelicalism." They are no such thing. If they are allowed to speak, and if their experience is valid for debate and consideration as the more progressive "black" experience is valid, then they will bring their own background to the table, their own life story, and their own reasons for coming to conservative doctrinal conclusions.

It is the strangest thing today. Personal experience matters and is validated when you come to progressive conclusions, but not when you arrive at conservative convictions. Your voice *must* be heard when it speaks leftism, but not when it declares conservatism. You are true to your "heritage" when you embrace "social justice" but not when you hold to retributive biblical justice. When you are a progressive, you are a prophet; when you are a conservative, either doctrinally or politically, you are a pawn. As with other tenets of woke ideology and secular thinking, reading people in these ways is wrong. Embracing such ideology will deconstruct, stone by stone, a theological worldview from Scripture, and replace it with a "racialized" worldview from unbiblical sources.

Woke epistemology begins by saying something realistic—that everybody has their own perspective. But it loses sight of the fact that God's truth is true for everyone, regardless of their background or past experience. God's truth is true at all times and in all places. We should not pursue a system of truth that molds to *us*; if we are to know God, we need a system of truth that molds to *God*.[34] God defines truth, in other words, not us—not our race, our experience of oppression, or our own views. This is what Jesus voices in His high priestly prayer to the Father:

> Sanctify them in the truth; your word is truth. As you sent me
> into the world, so I have sent them into the world. And for
> their sake I consecrate myself, that they also may be sanctified
> in truth. (John 17:17–19)

As we have observed, only in Christian epistemology anchored in God Himself do the one and the many cohere, and only in this divine system do we have unity in diversity.[35] Wokeness, however, gives us only diversity, for its dependence upon standpoint epistemology ends up collapsing the world into radical multiperspectivalism and a resulting contest for power. Instead of unity in diversity, we are consigned to diversity without unity, and out of that disunified mess will inevitably come estrangement and even hostility.

The narrativizing drift urged by wokeness will have effects in broader society beyond matters of Christian hermeneutics. Part of what occurs when wokeness advances is that speech is both racialized and chilled.

---

[34] Francis Schaeffer famously spoke in his day of "the God who is there." He had these powerful words to say in an age that denied the personal God: "The historic Christian answer concerning verifiable facts and knowing depends on who God is, on who is there. The God who is there according to the Scriptures is the personal-infinite God. There is no other God like this God." It is not that we "know God exhaustively" as believers," Schaeffer rightly notes, but we "can know God truly." Francis Schaeffer, *The God Who Is There*, Book One in *The Francis Schaeffer Trilogy* (Wheaton, Illinois: Crossway, 1990), 101–2.

[35] Cornelius Van Til, *The Defense of the Faith*, 3rd edition (Philadelphia, Pennsylvania: Presbyterian and Reformed, 1955), 26.

Free speech suffers, for as Henry Louis Gates Jr. observed some years back, "speech codes kill critique," squelching dissent.[36] But it is not just that dissent is squelched; dissent is racialized (as all speech is), making debate "racial" rather than intellectual. This is not a negative outcome, however, but a positive one, for in woke thought it is right that we prioritize the promotion of underprivileged voices over the prerogative of free speech.[37] The voices we need to hear, after all, are not all voices, but minority voices.[38] In fact, much dissent—as with much free speech today—is called "hate speech." Free speech in truth has little purchase in a woke system, for wokeness reads traditional legal documents like the Constitution and Bill of Rights as outmoded, having been formed in unjust eras of history.[39] In the end, wokeness leaves only one side with the ability to speak. All others must close their mouths, "do the work" of an antiracist, and accept the new social order.

All this shows us that we should resist the racialization of biblical interpretation—and of speech more broadly. In closing this point, we should not miss the opportunity to point out what the preceding shows

[36] Gates went on to note, "[Y]ou cannot begin to conduct [rational discussion of opposing viewpoints]...when you outlaw the expression of the view that you would criticize." Henry Louis Gates Jr., "Let Them Talk: Why Civil Liberties Pose No Threat to Civil Rights," *New Republic*, September 20, 1993, https://newrepublic.com/article/149558/let-talk.

[37] This so-called "solution" is rooted in standpoint epistemology, a concept introduced in Chapter 1. Craig Mitchell describes such a mindset as it appears in the field of biblical interpretation, specifically in the thought world of black liberation theology: "It is the reader who places his values and meanings upon the text. This means that only poor blacks, the Ghettocracy, can have an understanding of the Bible. Only those who can see through the lens of poverty and oppression can understand the truth of the Bible, because the Bible was largely written by and to poor, oppressed people." But Mitchell rightly notes that such a mindset is hostile to biblical Christianity and to an affirmation of the divine authorial intent of Scripture. Craig Mitchell, "Rev. Michael Eric Dyson: An Analysis," in *Keep Your Head Up: America's New Black Christian Leaders, Social Consciousness, and the Cosby Conversation*, ed. Anthony B. Bradley (Wheaton, Illinois: Crossway, 2012), 212–13.

[38] Delgado and Stefancic assert: "Minority status...brings with it a presumed competence to speak about race and racism." Delgado and Stefancic, *Critical Race Theory*, 10.

[39] Ibid., 3, 26.

we need in the Church (the foremost burden of this book). We do not need preachers who share our background, skin color, class, sex, and experience to minister grace to us in a meaningful way. This is how the world thinks: *I need a church that fits me and my profile. I can only really learn Christian truth when it comes to me from someone similar to me and my lived reality.* But this is not true in two senses: First, this is in no way what the Bible directly commends. We don't need personalized preachers, but rather men of God who stand on the Word and speak the truth in love to us, shepherding the flock by the rule of Scripture.

Second, this defies what the apostles did in missionary activity and what Christians have done for centuries to proclaim Christ. We don't necessarily send missionaries to cultures that reflect their own background; we may, but we may well not. In many cases, missionaries go to countries that are entirely different from their own country and their own heritage. They do so because they love image-bearers enough to preach Christ to them, seeking their rescue from everlasting damnation. This proclamatory love is true love, whether heard through an American pulpit, a clandestine gathering in a secret room, a mountain lodge, an apartment in a megacity, or anywhere else. True love is not "you look like me, so we're united." True love is Christological love, and Christ left Heaven, being not like us, to become one of us in order to save us.

We are all saved by this man. He is the God-man, the true human, the Middle Eastern Jewish Messiah who died for us. We do not have a customizable Savior. We do not choose one who looks like us and thinks like us—this is what the natural man does, striving to match his natural partiality with his spiritual desires. Christians do the opposite. We submit to a King who is like us in our humanity but different from us in many respects. Yet we do not protest the exclusive Lordship of the man Christ Jesus, but bow the knee to Him, find our identity in Him, and join together in loving fellowship with all who, like us, are desperate sinners saved by Him.

Fourth, wokeness errs in seeing societal disparities as injustices.

Woke thinkers and activists frequently cite societal disparities as proof of racism. They will point to differing levels of health, literacy, or access to services among diverse races, and where people of color have less help in statistical terms, they will conclude that racism is to blame. This argument is frequently not traced to any actual policy and legal measure that is provably "racist." Instead, the claim goes, where we find disparities between "races," we are seeing evidence that America is shot through with "systemic injustice" and "systemic oppression" propelled by "white supremacy" as practiced (intentionally or not) by "white" people. So it is that "white supremacy" is employed to explain every discrepancy, every difference, and our broader societal problems.

This is problematic in two major ways. First, unless you truly believe that having "white" skin really is evil in fundamental terms, you will eventually find yourself struggling to substantiate how "white supremacy" creates "structural racism." Such rhetoric may play well in a tweet or hashtag; it may draw applause when shouted through a bullhorn or preached from a music stand. But as scholar Glenn Loury has shown, this language is problematically vague as often employed:

> The invocation of "structural racism" in political argument
> is both a bluff and a bludgeon. It is a bluff in the sense that it
> offers an "explanation" that is not an explanation at all and,
> in effect, dares the listener to come back. So, for example, if
> someone says, "There are too many blacks in prison in the
> U.S. and that's due to structural racism," what you're being
> dared to say is, "No. Blacks are so many among criminals,
> and that's why there are so many in prison. It's their fault, not
> the system's fault." And it is a bludgeon in the sense that use
> of the phrase is mainly a rhetorical move. Users don't even
> pretend to offer evidence-based arguments beyond citing the
> fact of the racial disparity itself. The "structural racism" argu-
> ment seldom goes into cause and effect. Rather, it asserts
> shadowy causes that are never fully specified, let alone

demonstrated. We are all just supposed to know that it's the fault of something called "structural racism," abetted by an environment of "white privilege," furthered by an ideology of "white supremacy" that purportedly characterizes our society. It explains everything. Confronted with any racial disparity, the cause is "structural racism."[40]

Loury's words land—and with a bang. As he captures, the claim of "structural racism" not only explains some things; it is used by some in such a manner that it "explains everything." If you see a problem, it owes to this. If you watch a troubling video on the internet, it is caused by this. If you hear of communal differences, it proceeds from this. You don't have to prove your claim; the claim is so big, so all-encompassing, that all you need to say are the words "structural racism," and the conversation is over.

But our antenna as Christians should be up at this point. Why? Because believers are not a people of fuzzy generalities and sloppy thinking. We are a people of truth. The truth is so strong that it sets us free (John 8:32). This is true from the roots to the branches of our lives. We depend on the truth for our eternal salvation, and we depend on the truth for balancing our checkbooks. Propositional truth is not lesser than experience; it tests and norms our experience. This matters greatly for handling societal disparities. Statistics about differences between "racial" groups could be showing us evidence of present racism in the form of tangible policies, yes. We know all too well from American history that the law matters. But such data may yield far more complex conclusions than the monocausal explanation of racism. This is not only true of matters of different "races"; in many areas of a fallen world, you'll find significantly more complexity in wrongdoing, suffering, injustice, and evil than a single overarching cause like "white supremacy."

[40] Glenn Loury, "Unspeakable Truths about Racial Inequality in America," Quillette, February 10, 2021, https://quillette.com/2021/02/10/unspeakable-truths-about-racial-inequality-in-america.

Thomas Sowell addressed all this years ago in his definitive handling of disparities. "The crucial question is not whether evils exist but whether the evils of the past or present are automatically the cause of major economic, educational and other social disparities today." According to Sowell, we should question the assumption that "disparities are automatically somebody's fault, so that our choices are either to blame society or to 'blame the victim.'…[for] whose fault are demographic differences, geographic differences, birth order differences or cultural differences that evolved over the centuries before any of us were born?"[41]

Sowell's analysis is air-clearing. If your eyes are genuinely open to the world before you, you'll see that while color-based partiality is a real sin that occurs among us, there are many other factors in our individual and collective differences.[42] For example, though whiteness is seemingly said to grant people societal privilege, the data tell a far more complex story than we have been told. As one example that runs contrary to what one might expect from media coverage, "white" men rank behind Asian men, Asian women, Pacific Islander men, and American Indian men in terms of "controlled lifetime wage per hour."[43] We see a similar incongruity between the narrative of "white privilege" and suicide rates. In 2018, the last year reported as of the writing of this book, "white" people committed suicide at the rate of about 17 people per 100,000 of their group. This rate was about 10 people per 100,000 higher than "black," "Hispanic," and "Asian/Pacific Highlander."[44] If "white privilege" is such a strong force, what accounts for this surprising finding?

Do these data singlehandedly dispel the possibility of "systemic injustices" in America that directly cause disparities? No, they do not. That possibility always exists for fair-minded thinkers. But even these

---

[41] Thomas Sowell, *Discrimination and Disparities* (New York: Basic Books, 2018), 117.

[42] For more on this, see Baucham, *Fault Lines*, 153–57.

[43] "The Racial Wage Gap Persists in 2020," Payscale, https://www.payscale.com/data/racial-wage-gap.

[44] "Racial and Ethnic Disparities," Suicide Prevention Resource Center, https://sprc.org/scope/racial-ethnic-disparities.

limited citations reveal the flaw in reading statistics in one or even several categories and then drawing a monocausal explanation from them. Could there be such a thing as "white privilege?" Yes, that is possible. But if there is, we must substantiate the concept.

As one further example, we think of a matter like "redlining," commonly presented in woke circles as clear evidence of structural evil. This occurs when neighborhoods populated by people of color are "redlined" as problematic by real-estate leaders. As one source has noted, "redlining," as just one example, may well happen, but is "hard to prove."[45] When it does happen, it can happen along "racial" lines, yes, and this is clearly wrong and should be opposed as such. But what is called "redlining" and condemned as unequivocally evil may well be more complex. For example, if crime rises in a neighborhood, realtors or officials may steer clients away from it.[46] This may be due solely to concerns—justified concerns—over safety. Such a decision may be read as clear and present evidence of "racism" when it may or may not fit that bill. On "redlining" and other such claimed instances of injustice, there may be some material and statistics that could be read to back up the conclusion of "racism" or partiality. In numerous cases, however, there will be other factors that complicate such a diagnosis.[47]

---

[45] See Willis L. Krumholz, "Bloomberg's Plan for Black Americans Doubles Down on the Left's Failures," The Federalist, January 22, 2020, https://thefederalist.com/2020/01/22/bloombergs-plan-for-black-americans-doubles-down-on-the-lefts-failures.

[46] Sowell treats this matter helpfully—see Discrimination and Disparities, 31–35.

[47] People may enjoy privileges of various kinds—this is possible. But we should be careful about making too much of these supposed benefits, and we should always be clear that the greatest blessing anyone can receive is saving faith. Scripture nowhere trains us to despise or dislike people who have earthly advantages we do not have. If wickedness is occurring around us, then we oppose it, but in ordinary terms, we are called to live lives of quiet contentment, knowing that ultimately it is not any human person's failing or succeeding that accounts for our life situation, but our Father's sovereign will and "plan" (οἰκονομίαν in the Greek, per Ephesians 1:10). You will not hear this in the public square today, but we are in spiritually dangerous territory if we let ourselves grow angry over the station God has given us. Our culture trains us to resent and encourages us to be vengeful, but this is not the teaching of God's Word. Whatever other sins wokeness entraps us in, it clearly

Leaving societal matters for a moment, we ultimately know why our culture is fractured. In the simplest biblical terms, "white" skin is not our core problem. Sin is. In the biblical mind, sin does not affect and inhabit one group more than others. One group is not thus more guilty than any other group in foundational terms. We are all equally guilty in Adam, for sin is the universal problem of the human race. But not generic sin—actual sin. Sin committed by individual people—people of every tribe, tongue, nation, and background. People who have a great education or no education. People raised in a Christian home or an atheistic one. People from the left or the right. People from privilege or no privilege (socially speaking). The biblical diagnosis has not changed. It is the best one for what ails one; it is the very truth itself. Sin is not found in one group; it festers in every human heart and expresses itself in ungodly thoughts, desires, feelings, words, and actions. It takes concrete societal forms, yes; but when it does so, there is proof of its presence in the form of laws, policy, measures, enforced postures, and the like.

Where there is no such proof, we should avoid generalizing. In doing so, ironically, in rejecting huge but vague explanations of our foremost problems, we will actually set ourselves up to address those failings. Remember: Sin is concrete, terrifyingly real, and tangible, according to God. As a result, addressing sin in this world is also a matter of real action. Where sin is hazy and fuzzy, though, solutions can only be the same—or else misdirected and devastatingly uncalibrated, such that retribution does not fit or redress the crime, but only worsens the situation.

Fifth, wokeness reads cultural events in search of its dominant narrative, omitting many nuances and outright counter-truths.

As traced above, our culture and society are falling prey to what we call "monocausality." This means that we trace very complex realities to just one simple factor. For example, income and employment disparities, infant mortality rates, and overall health statistics are said today to

---

militates against the call to "be content with whatever you have" of Hebrews 13:5 (see also Philippians 4:11–12; 2 Corinthians 12:10; 1 Timothy 6:6–11, among many other passages). It breeds anything but contentment, peace, calm, and gentleness.

reflect racism; quote a percentage showing a difference between "races" and you've proven racism.[48] Such data could reflect racism, sure. But we need to be wary of monocausality and recognize that in many instances there are numerous factors at work.

This is true as well with police shootings. We need a data-driven approach characterized by thoughtfulness and reasonableness. Honest brokers can see that there is a tragic stream of violence in different communities. Nationally, African Americans between the ages of ten and thirty-four die from homicide at thirteen times the rate of white Americans, according to researchers from the Centers for Disease Control and Prevention and the Justice Department.[49] This kind of statistic, correlated closely with the breakdown of the family, itself a complex reality, should cause us to yearn and work for stronger communities.

In recent years, citizen deaths in the course of police encounters have inflamed our country. According to Manhattan Institute senior fellow Heather Mac Donald, for the last five years, the police have fatally shot about one thousand civilians annually, the vast majority of whom were armed or otherwise dangerous. Black people account for about 23 percent of those shot and killed by police; they are about 13 percent of the U.S. population. However, for the year 2019, the *Washington Post's* database of fatal police shootings showed fourteen unarmed "black" victims and twenty-five unarmed "white" victims.[50] These numbers are incongruent with descriptors often employed such as black "genocide"

---

[48] For an argument that racism is the primary factor causing employment and income inequality, see Beverly Daniel Tatum, *Why Are All the Black Kids Sitting Together in the Cafeteria? And Other Conversations about Race* (New York: Basic Books, 2017); 211–12; Richard Delgado and Jean Stefancic, *Critical Race Theory: An Introduction*, 2nd edition (New York and London: New York University Press, 2012), 47; and Derrick A. Bell, *Faces at the Bottom of the Well: The Permanence of Racism* (New York: Basic Books, 1992), 3–7.

[49] Heather Mac Donald, "There Is No Epidemic of Fatal Police Shootings against Unarmed Black Americans," *USA Today*, July 3, 2020, https://www.usatoday.com/story/opinion/ 2020/07/03/police-black-killings-homicide-rates-race-injustice-column/3235072001.

[50] Ibid.

or "epidemic." Certainly, there are more stats and matters to handle. We never want to dismiss easily the role of corruption and flagrant sin in any area of life. But in the case of our society and culture, we do well to avoid simple answers to complex questions.

This reasoning holds up in different examples of purported racist killings. No two deaths are the same, and it is entirely possible that sin would factor into the death of citizens and that racism would be a factor. But to use just three recent instances, our culture did not frame the shootings of George Floyd, Jacob Blake, and Breonna Taylor in a careful manner, recognizing the need for judicial process, the rule of law, and courtroom proceedings to play out. Instead, the initial response to the tragic deaths of these individuals was that racism and systemic injustice caused them. Though the Bible commands us to be slow to speak, slow to anger, and quick to listen, many Christians followed the culture in this way. They issued pronouncements, proclamations, and communiques that judged these tragic deaths as owing to "racism" and unchecked police brutality.

No sane person wanted these image-bearers dead; these deaths hit all of us hard, for they reminded us how evil and fallen the world is. The death of just one man or woman made in God's image is a terrible thing. Yet details soon emerged that complicated the narrative that racist cops gunned these individuals down in cold blood. In Floyd's case, fentanyl was at the least affecting him physically even before a Minneapolis police officer knelt on him to subdue him.[51] I concur with what Voddie Baucham Jr. said in his overview of this sad story: "The George Floyd case was indeed tragic. However, it was not unique. Nor does it represent clear evidence of a particular pattern of police brutality regarding black men."[52]

In Blake's case, police officers first tried to subdue him by brute strength, then used tasers on him, and then—as he went for a knife in

---

[51] Lou Raguse, "New Court Docs Say George Floyd Had 'Fatal Level' of Fentanyl in His System," KARE11, August 26, 2020, https://www.kare11.com/article/news/local/george-floyd/new-court-docs-say-george-floyd-had-fatal-level-of-fentanyl-in-his-system/89-ed69d09d-a9ec-481c-90fe-7acd4ead3d04.

[52] Voddie Baucham Jr., *Fault Lines: The Social Justice Movement and Evangelicalism's Looming Catastrophe* (Washington, D.C.: Salem Books, 2021), 56.

his car—shot him multiple times.[53] In Taylor's case, police fired into the apartment where Taylor slept only after being fired upon.[54] There is more to each case than what I have covered, yet even these details show that the popular narrative around each of these deaths was more complicated than it initially seemed.

It was not just that there was more to the story than first reports indicated; it was that a portion of people used the initial narrative of racist police brutality to torch, destroy, and burn American cities. Whether affiliated with Black Lives Matter, Antifa, or no group at all, rioters set this country ablaze with few public forces to stop them. Total damage to the country is estimated in the billions upon billions of dollars; in Minneapolis, the site of Floyd's death, the cost rings in around $550 million—the most expensive instance of public destruction in American history.

As we have observed, shootings of citizens must always be taken seriously. Cops can be racist, as anyone can be; in general, they are imperfect people as we all are, and they are frequently put in difficult situations that require rapid responses and split-second decisions. Each case should be considered for its own particulars, and it should never be a light thing that people die at the hands of police. Yet here we cannot fail to remember that the government does not bear the sword in vain (Romans 13). God Himself has instituted the state, and thus state authority. It is a common grace blessing to have police, and in actual experience, many people across backgrounds and ethnicities prefer to have more police protection in their communities rather than less. This is especially true in troubled areas of whatever kind.

---

[53] Margot Cleveland, "Why Kenosha Police Officers' Use of Force on Jacob Blake Was Justified," The Federalist, August 31, 2020, https://thefederalist. com/2020/08/31/why-kenosha-police-officers-use-of-force-on-jacob-blake-was-justified.

[54] Kelsey Bolar, "Justice for Breonna Taylor Isn't Indicting Police Officers for Acting in Self-Defense," The Federalist, September 25, 2020, https://thefederalist. com/2020/09/25/justice-for-breonna-taylor-isnt-indicting-police-officers-for-acting-in-self-defense.

The police are not above scrutiny; no public official is. But Scripture would have us see police as a gift from God to humanity. Fathers and mothers should train their children to honor police officers (and military members and others in similar roles). In many communities, police officers restrain wickedness and do so at tremendous personal risk. In fact, according to PragerU, a police officer is eighteen times more likely to be shot than a "black" man is.[55] Our culture is shaping and promoting a narrative that is seriously flawed—and flawed in the anti-institutional form that fits wokeness more broadly. We recall here Marx's hatred of God-ordained elements of society, and we note that it is alive and well today. We must reject such a mindset.

Though America has surely had major problems with "racism" and ethnocentrism and must always stay vigilant about such evils, we should steer clear of woke narratives. We should always test secular ideologies, secular claims, and narratives that form at warp speed on social media. We should be slow to speak, slow to anger, and quick to listen (James 1:19–20). Wokeness purports to have all the explanatory power for our societal chaos. As I am at pains to say, it does not. In actuality, it biases us and leaves us with overly simple answers to complex questions.

Sixth, wokeness destabilizes the free market and attacks limited government, rejecting what Scripture commends in principle while practicing it in theory.

Wokeness is scorching against "capitalism." As one of many examples, Delgado and Stefancic query this: "If racism is largely economic in nature—a search for profits—and hypercapitalism is increasingly showing itself as a flawed system, what follows for a theory of civil rights?"[56] There's a lot baked in here: racism is economic and "hypercapitalism" is

---

[55] "Are the Police Racist?," PragerU, August 22, 2016, accessible at https://www.prageru.com/video/are-the-police-racist/?fbclid=IwAR0a7lBv5v57-Cp6TRmtdmpV71Mvd6FgyzbhDjRYJ-CzZopKjkbQobfsoMQ.

[56] Delgado and Stefancic, *Critical Race Theory*, 107. See also Ibram X. Kendi, *How to Be an Antiracist* (New York: One World, 2019), 156–63; Robin DiAngelo, *White Fragility: Why It's So Hard for White People to Talk about Racism* (Boston, Massachusetts: Beacon Press, 2018), 21.

flawed. It is, of course, true that in a fallen world, there are only "flawed systems." Every system will thus contain evils and crimes and misdeeds. It is also true that the free market absolutely can be used for racist and wicked ends; it surely was at times in days past. This is one of the major claims of wokeness, including one voiced by an organization called the New History of Capitalism (NHC), a scholarly movement that seeks to discredit capitalism as racist. Similarly, the 1619 Project, a historical collaborative overseen by the *New York Times* (released in 2019), also views capitalism as an inherently racist economic system.[57]

Wokeness despises the free market. It distrusts it. As one example, various woke voices have argued that the origins of the American "capitalist" system are racist. For instance, at a congressional hearing in the summer of 2020, journalist Ta-Nehisi Coates enlisted one of Cornell University historian Edward Baptist's claims to argue for reparations. Coates said, "By 1836 more than $600 million, almost half of the economic activity in the United States, derived directly or indirectly from the cotton produced by the million-odd slaves."[58] But according to economist Art Carden of the American Institute for Economic Research, this stunning statistic is unambiguously false. It's worth taking a moment to show why, given how frequently we hear these kinds of arguments today.

---

[57] Recent published monographs which depict capitalism as racist include Sven Beckert, *Empire of Cotton: A Global History* (New York: Alfred A. Knopf, 2015) and Edward E. Baptist, *The Half Has Never Been Told: Slavery and the Making of American Capitalism* (New York: Basic Books, 2017). The 1619 Project's main contention is its assertion that the real founding of the United States happened in the year 1619 when slaves from Africa arrived in Virginia. According to economic historian Philip Magness: "The 1619 Project's editors relied almost entirely on NHC scholars for its treatment of slavery's economics, which appeared in a feature article by sociologist Matthew Desmond." Phillip W. Magness, "The New History of Capitalism Has a 'Whiteness' Problem," American Institute for Economic Research, December 10, 2019, https://www.aier.org/article/slavery-did-not-enrich-americans.

[58] "Here's What Ta-Nehisi Coates Told Congress about Reparations," *New York Times*, June 19, 2019, https://www.nytimes.com/2019/06/19/us/ta-nehisi-coates-reparations.html. Coates's numbers come from Edward Baptist's *The Half Has Never Been Told*, 322.

The economics get technical (as economic matters do), but essentially, Coates's data depend upon a major statistical error from Baptist. Through an accounting blunder, Edward Baptist inflated the actual size of the cotton sector by almost tenfold. Carden has noted that cotton was a major output of the antebellum Southern economy, comprising approximately 5–6 percent of it. It was not, however, the commercial engine of either Confederate fantasy or modern revisionism.[59] In addition, slavery actually handcuffed the market by artificially restraining the labor, ingenuity, and ability of slaves; it did not aid "capitalism," but was rather a wicked brake on the free market.

On this last point, Carden has concluded insightfully:

> The American economy would have grown had cotton—or something else—been cultivated by free labor rather than slave labor.... Slavery was not necessary for cotton, and cotton was not necessary for industrialization. Had chattel slavery never taken hold in the United States, we would very likely be richer than we are today. The "slavery➔cotton➔industrialization➔ modern prosperity" argument seems to condemn American capitalism, but it is wrong.[60]

Slavery did not build the American economy, then. As Carden shows, slavery *hampered* the American economy. This is not what you'll hear in many classrooms today, but it's true—slavery slowed the free market down, made terrible use of American resources, and impeded human flourishing not only for slaves, but for the entire society. Much as the stereotype of the leering slaveowner is used today to represent the heart of the American free market, the reverse is true. The slaveowner was a part of the American economy, but in no way a positive, driving force.

---

[59] Art Carden, "Slavery Did Not Enrich Americans," American Institute for Economic Research, June 25, 2020, https://www.aier.org/article/slavery-did-not-enrich-americans.

[60] Ibid.

The slaveowner may have gotten wealthy in some cases, but he did so while inhibiting—not strengthening—the broader social order.[61]

Yet this is not the only problem with wokeness and its relation to "capitalism."[62] Though woke leaders seek to replace the free market with state-controlled systems that will yield "equity" as they see it, the free market is actually a tremendous engine for good for all peoples. While not impervious to manipulation (nothing is in this world contra utopianism), the free market has fundamentally changed the world, lifting people across the world out of serfdom into freedom. Economist Walter Williams explains why: "The relative color blindness of the market accounts for much of the hostility towards it. Markets have a notorious lack of respect for privilege, race, and class structures."[63] If woke leaders truly wanted "fairness" and "equity," they would be unabashed supporters of the free market.

In actuality, many are—but on a personal level only. There is, in general, a double-mindedness about the free market among woke leaders. On the one hand, it is seen as wicked and inherently corrupt. On the other hand, woke scholars and activists do well by it—in some cases, obscenely well. Robin DiAngelo charges fifteen thousand dollars per speaking event and has earned over two million dollars from her book *White Fragility*, even while castigating capitalism as a racist economic system.[64] Ibram Kendi and Ta-Nehisi Coates have even higher price tags:

[61] Part of what we need to understand here is the difference between American slavery and biblical forms of the same (which included far more opportunity for mobility and agency than did race-based chattel slavery). For that material, see Chapter 7.

[62] "Capitalism" is Marx's term; it's better to use "free market" or some equivalent.

[63] Walter E. Williams, *Race & Economics: How Much Can Be Blamed on Discrimination?* (Stanford, California: Hoover Institution Press, 2011), 29.

[64] Charles Fain Lehman, "The Wages of Woke: How Robin DiAngelo Got Rich Peddling 'White Fragility,'" Washington Free Beacon, July 25, 2020, https://freebeacon.com/culture/ the-wages-of-woke-2. If it is true, according to DiAngelo's worldview, that all whites are motivated by unconscious and unintentional racial bias, the thoughtful reader must ask: Could DiAngelo herself be blind to ways in which her own unconscious racism might be fueling a career in which she profits off of the subject of race?

Kendi's speaking fee is twenty-five thousand dollars, while Coates's fee is between thirty thousand and forty thousand dollars per event.[65] Even as these leaders decry "capitalism," they make more in a day than many Americans make in a year.

Here we are in familiar territory with leftist and secular thinking. The behavior described above is deeply hypocritical, and disturbingly so. If "capitalism" is deeply flawed, as many woke voices argue, then leading lights of the movement should not be making a mint off of it. They should reject the free market. They should genuinely own their Marxist principles. But they show no desire to do so. They want to torch the system that feeds them, and that feeds them well, funding their huge salaries, their flush speaking gigs, and their creature comforts. On this point, we are reminded that wokeness is not only contradictory to sound thinking, but is contradictory to its own principles. It is truly a house divided.

Seventh, in general terms, wokeness represents a different system of thought than Christianity, one we should carefully study but ultimately reject.

As we have seen, wokeness overlaps with Christianity in that it expresses concern for those who seek to navigate a world divided over racial and ethnic reasons. But even the way wokeness construes this problem is decidedly different from the biblical vision, and the solution offered by wokeness to the problem it frames is radically opposed to Gospel redemption. Wokeness is a system we do well to study, think about, analyze, and critique; but it is not a system we should endorse, adopt, or embrace.

In the final analysis, wokeness as taught by many is less a direct response to the Gospel and more a reworking of justice and equity to form a this-worldly religion. Wokeness is akin to the Protestant liberalism of roughly one hundred years ago, but with a less supernatural frame. Wokeness sits loose in a philosophical sense but is connected to the following modern ideologies:

---

[65] Ibid.

- Wokeness has little grounding in a theistic system; it is this-worldly from the start.
- Wokeness uses the categories of Marxism, with people being either oppressor or oppressed.
- Wokeness champions the neo-pagan sexual ethic, one distinct from biblical sexuality.
- Wokeness is a utopian justice movement at its base; it syncs with both Enlightenment revolutionary movements and liberationist theological camps and connects in different ways to each.

Beyond these observations, it is appropriate to conclude that wokeness is a new religion. This is increasingly becoming clear. Ibram Kendi, for example, tweeted in 2019 that "Racism is death. Antiracism is life."[66] Whatever else Kendi may mean, his framing of "antiracism" as "life" signals that this concept has essentially salvific status for him. This is conversion for Kendi and others of his ilk (and increasingly, many thought leaders in American schools, corporations, HR departments, sports teams, and the list goes on). To be a "racist" (remember that he means this structurally) is to be dead. But to take up the cause of "antiracism" is life itself. This is religious and spiritual language.

A more technical description of this new religion, in my view, is "Utopian Judicial Paganism." Here are the basic commitments that run behind and through wokeness (or UJP more descriptively):

- Anthropology: Neo-paganism (no Creator, no creation order, we are our own rulers)
- Sexual ethics: Compulsive libertinism (we express our desires, and all should approve)

---

[66] Ibram Kendi (@DrIbram), "Racism is death. Antiracism is life," Twitter, August 4, 2019, 9:45 a.m., https://twitter.com/DrIbram/status/1158011047451811842.

- Political theology: Marxist Statism (we trust the state to rule us and make things right)
- Metaphysics: Postmodern Darwinism (evolution explains life with no absolute truth)
- Theology Proper: Mystic Selfism (we should follow our hearts, not any authority)
- Soteriology: Therapeuticism/Ritualism (we become our best self by doing the work)
- Eschatology: Utopian Earth-Centrism (we'll make the earth right through social justice)

What does all this mean? It means that the worldview of wokeness is not a Christian one where God is Creator and Ruler, but an atheistic one where man is divinized. Though the categories mentioned above blur and bleed over in some respects, the tenets of the system that opposes Christianity in our time nonetheless stand out in certain respects. Humanity thus has no script for sexuality; we may all follow the lusts of the flesh, and in fact must be ironically compelled toward a libertine sexuality, such that sexual wildness becomes the law of the land. The world is not made up of different institutions that embody and correspond to divine creation order; instead, the world should and must become a globalist whole, a divinized secular kingdom where utopian statism rules. Fairness and equity define the public order, with equality of outcome guaranteed. Social justice reigns supreme.[67]

Yet much as the state supplies all we need, so too does wokeness/UJP have a mystical and therapeutic streak in it. All things must be ordered according to man-centered social justice, necessitating government control. But at the same time, people (at least some people)

---

[67] With regard to the public elements of this religion, see the incisive breakdown by Daniel J. Mahoney, *The Idol of Our Age: How the Religion of Humanity Subverts Christianity* (New York: Encounter Books, 2018). One need not be a Catholic to track with this eloquent critique; in reality, Mahoney's criticism of Pope Francis is telling, for it shows just how much humanism has invaded traditional Catholicism today. Evangelicals do well to pay attention here; the same invasion is happening in our circles.

must be free to find and publicly celebrate their true selves. When this union of statism and selfism breaks free of the traditional constraints of Judeo-Christian religion, fundamentalist creationism, free markets, democratic government, personal responsibility, and strong local church presence in communities, then the earth will be made right, rescued from global warming, intolerant dogmatism, political liberty, and communalism. We will not live forever in a world made right by God, what Christians call "escalated re-creation." Instead, we will live in a world governed by science, technology, and justice. Wokeness does not do away with eschatology; it immanentizes it in a distinctly humanist form, but not live-and-let-live humanism—hard-edged judicial and statist humanism.

UJP dethrones God and makes man the measure of all things. In this sense, it is a successor to the Protestant liberalism that so reshaped American Protestantism one hundred years ago.[68] It is a justice movement, but one connected to numerous other unbiblical and ungodly ideologies. Not every person pulled to wokeness buys all this, of course. Some do, to be sure; the leaders of wokeness definitely do. But many have little idea of the truly sinister nature of this movement, nor of the fact that in hard-to-spot ways, it is truly a new religion—or, if one prefers, a different, new worldview that is in reality a strange and frequently contradictory blend. Wokeness is both authoritarian and libertine; both utopian and nihilistic; both state-worshipping and self-exalting. It is not internally consistent, like many worldviews, especially those developed in a post-truth age. Yet it is no minor competitor for the Western heart, the Western mind, and the Western soul.

---

[68] It is also the successor to "Moral Therapeutic Deism" (MTD). While sharing some elements with MTD, UJP is harder-edged and more society-focused. MTD asserts, basically, that God exists for me, and if I do what I should, I'll be who I want to be; UJP asserts that the world is not at all right, that we must make it right, and that we can do so by overhauling the social order.

Conclusion

As is clear, wokeness is no trifling matter, no passing fancy. It is not "soft postmodernism"; it is *hard postmodernism*, and an intellectual Maginot Line will not repel it. We cannot treat this ideology with kid gloves. We cannot treat any ungodly system in that way. Instead, we must "demolish strongholds" by subjecting unbiblical systems to thorough biblical, theological, and ethical critique, emulating the Apostle Paul as we do so (2 Corinthians 10:4). While recognizing certain limited points of contact with biblical Christianity, we do not embrace part of Marxism, or part of Epicureanism, or part of existentialism, or part of homosexuality, or part of transgenderism, or part of postmodernity as believers. We learn about these worldviews, we compassionately engage those following them, and we refute them. Using the apostle's language, we go to war against them, in order that we may live and that the influence of unbelief may be overcome.

DISCUSSION QUESTIONS

1. What are some statistics that run counter to the wokeness narrative?
2. Why does wokeness condemn capitalism (i.e., free market enterprise) as an economic system?
3. If you viewed life from a CRT lens, how would it affect your interracial friendships?
4. How does CRT's push for subjective experience clash with Christianity's view of truth?
5. How is the Bible's view of justice different from wokeness's definition of justice?

CHAPTER 5

What Does the Bible Teach about Identity and Ethnicity?

Part One: Old Testament

*I will make you as a light for the nations, that my salva-
tion may reach to the end of the earth.*
—Yahweh to Israel (Isaiah 49:6)

Though our postmodern age tells us that identity is fully malleable,
occasionally an event occurs that destabilizes this view. The woman
born as Rachel Dolezal was born to white parents and grew up near
Troy, Montana. She had grown up in a home with multiple adopted
African American children. According to Dolezal, she publicly decided
to become "black" years later.

Dolezal prospered in her new identity, teaching African studies at
Eastern Washington University. She also served as head of the Spokane
chapter of the National Association for the Advancement of Colored
People (NAACP). However, reality intruded. In 2015, her parents told
reporters that their daughter was white and was presenting herself as a
black activist in the Spokane region. The story went viral. Dolezal lost
her job, though she wrote a memoir: *In Full Color: Finding My Place in
a Black and White World.*[1]

Recently, a similar event took place. Jessica Krug grew up in subur-
ban Kansas City as a member of a Jewish family. Later she adopted the

---

[1]   Rachel Dolezal with Storms Reback, *In Full Color: Finding My Place in a Black
and White World* (Dallas, Texas: BenBella Books), 2017.

name "Jess La Bombalera" and presented herself as "Afro-Latina." One of her online bios described her as "an unrepentant and unreformed child of the hood."[2] She became a professor at George Washington University, and like Dolezal worked as an activist. At June 2020 hearings to speak about police brutality, Krug publicly said this:

> I'm Jessa Bombalera. I'm here in El Barrio, East Harlem—you probably have heard about it because you sold my [expletive] neighborhood to developers and gentrifiers...I wanna call out all these white New Yorkers who waited four hours with us to be able to speak and then did not yield their time for Black and Brown indigenous New Yorkers.[3]

Some media outlets reported that after Krug said this, several white people gave up their speaking spots. It turns out, however, that Jessica Krug was an unrepentant and unreformed child of the suburbs. Like Dolezal, La Bombalera was recently exposed as pretending to be something she was not. Why do these cultural occurrences matter to us? They matter because they show us two key realities of our age:

1. Identity is said to be personally constructed (until it's not).
2. There is a very lively conversation over what race is at all.

We could say much about the first point, but we need to zero in on the second. Is race real? Is it something clear and definable? While many of us would not accept the category of "trans-black" as Dolezal claims

---

[2]   Lauren Lumpkin and Susan Svrluga, "White GWU Professor Admits She Falsely Claimed Black Identity," *Washington Post*, September 3, 2020, https://www.washingtonpost.com/ education/2020/09/03/white-gwu-professor-admits-she-falsely-claimed-black-identity.

[3] \ "East Harlem Resident and Professor Jessica Krug Admits She Is Not Black (Update)," *Harlem World Magazine*, September 8, 2020, https://www.harlemworldmagazine.com/east-harlem-resident-and-professor-jessica-krug-admits-she-admits -she-is-not-black.

for herself, should we not think more deeply about this matter? What is race, and is it a Christian category?

As Christians, such questions drive us to one source: the Bible. In what follows, we look at five insights from Scripture—in this chapter, the Old Testament in particular—that help us form a biblical understanding of the human person with regard to identity and ethnicity. In sum, we will see in this chapter that "race" is not a defined biblical reality, and that instead Scripture drives us to see all humanity as one race, one given an identity by God through the *imago Dei* and offered God's mercy even in the face of our shared depravity.[4]

First Truth: God Creates One Human Race of Image-Bearers

The Bible begins with the oneness of humanity. In the Garden of Eden, there is no enmity and strife in the God-made world. God makes the man and the woman in his image, as Genesis 1 shows:

> Then God said, "Let us make man in our image, after our likeness. And let them have dominion over the fish of the sea and over the birds of the heavens and over the livestock and over all the earth and over every creeping thing that creeps on the earth."
> So God created man in his own image,
>   in the image of God he created him;
>   male and female he created them.
> And God blessed them. And God said to them, "Be fruitful and multiply and fill the earth and subdue it, and have dominion over the fish of the sea and over the birds of the heavens and over every living thing that moves on the earth." (Genesis 1:26–28)

---

4   John Piper, *Bloodlines: Race, Cross, and the Christian* (Wheaton, Illinois: Crossway, 2011), 206–7.

This passage teaches us the basic truths of humanity. We see that there is both unity and distinction in this passage. There is one human race here. Yet there is also male and female.[5] There is only the first couple at this point, but it is apparent that there are not multiple forms of humanity. Men are not from Mars, and women are not from Venus. The distinctive sexes are one race. Thus, we can make this theological point: oneness is not sameness in Eden. God loves the diversity of his creation. He made a spectacular pluriformity of living things—tiny fish and diving birds and huge redwoods—but the apex of His work was the human person. From time immemorial, the Lord had planned this moment, the moment when He would produce His greatest creation, His masterwork, the only being made in the "image" (*tselem*) and carrying the "likeness" (*demuth*) of God Himself.[6] This was not true of the animals, marvelous as they are; it was not true of the celestial bodies, brilliant as they are; it was not true of the oceans, much as they roar. Humanity is the *pièce de résistance* of the holy work of God.[7]

It is the speech of God that begets the man and the woman, not a cosmic accident. The text focuses our attention on the nobility and beauty of the human race. The Lord already has given the call to "multiply" to the living creatures on the fifth day, and He calls His image-bearers to the same task. But the man's charge is unique: he must "have dominion over" the living creatures, a commission that extends to the whole "earth," and one which advances as his seed multiplies. Mankind is not God; he is a mere creature, but a creature with a limitless charter. He is made by God to display God to the world God has formed. To look at man is to confront the reality of the Almighty: *imago Dei*, "image of God."

---

[5]   Derek Kidner, *Genesis: An Introduction and Commentary*, Tyndale Old Testament Commentaries (Carol Stream, Illinois: Tyndale, 1967), 52.

[6]   See John F. Kilner, *Dignity and Destiny: Humanity in the Image of God* (Grand Rapids, Michigan: Eerdmans, 2015), 128. I concur that we should not draw a strong distinction between the Hebrew terms for "image" and "likeness" in this text.

[7]   Some of this material is adapted with permission from my book *Reenchanting Humanity*.

The first biblical words about the human race define the first man and woman in undeniably theological terms. Humanity is the creation of God; man is not an evolved product of the other creatures but is made by God Himself (Genesis 2:7, 22). The Genesis account draws a clear and unmistakable line between the beasts of the field, the birds of the air, and the fish of the sea on the one hand and mankind on the other. Genesis 1 distinguishes between God-made creatures and does not draw genetic linkage of any kind between animals and mankind. It is true, though, that all beings have a common origin of existence: God's speech. We are right to teach creation *ex nihilo*, "from nothing," but we must also teach of creation *in verbo*, "by word."

In this text, the created order is brimming with vitality and exploding with possibility. Creation forms one symphonic sound of praise—the song of life and freedom—in its overflowing diversity.[8] From the start, we cannot miss the fact that the God of the Bible loves diversity, difference, and the many-splendored beauty of a world that operates in perfect harmony yet contains too many creatures and living beings to count. The God of Genesis 1 and 2 clearly does not wish to populate this realm with a blurry sameness. He is the God who makes one human race but two sexes. Every last person is *made in God's image*; every single person, extending the point further, *is the image of God*.

The foregoing emphasizes what we call the *ontological* nature of the image. (This fancy word means, effectively, being or essence.) The image in which we are made is a matter of our being, we might say. The image is not fundamentally something we *do*; it is something we *are*. We are *fully* the image of God, we say in theological terms, but only Christ is *truly* the image of God. Every person is an image-bearer, but no one is an end unto themselves; the end of the human race is Jesus Christ. He is the one who shows us what humanity is at its summit, when the person in question is impeccable, without sin, wholly devoted to the Father, and

---

[8]   In keeping with this theme, the psalmist exhorts all of creation to give collective praise to the Creator in Psalm 148. Allen P. Ross, "Psalms" in *Bible Knowledge Commentary*, eds. John F. Walvoord and Roy B. Zuck (Wheaton, Illinois: Victor Books, 1985), 897–98.

perfectly righteous in every way (see 1 Corinthians 15:42–49; 2 Corinthians 3:18, 4:4). That is *true* humanity, not the humanity that uses our God-given capacities for idolatry, selfishness, and creature-worship.

In Eden, there is just one human race, not many races. Our skin color is part of the beautiful diversity of the God-made world, as are numerous elements of our person. We are not the same person, but we are the same race. Humanity as made by God is not divided into many species but is one. Many different worldviews and religions tell us differently, but biblical Christianity begins in a place of absolute human unity. It also shows us the wonder and beauty of every human life. We are not mere specs on a chart somewhere, we are not dust in the wind, and we are not participants in societal archetypes that render us embodiments of stereotypes. Every person is a God-made being. Every person has God-given dignity and worth. Every person *is* the image of God.[9]

What radical teaching this is. Against what many ideologies teach, some humans are not more human than others, to riff off of *Animal Farm*. Because every person is made in God's image, every man and woman is *fully* human. In biblical teaching, you are not less human if you have less ability and functioning in various categories.[10] No, every person is a fully human being, and no one can erase this reality. No one can alter it. We who know Scripture know this truth. Every person is an individual, created by God to display His glory in some natural way. The doctrine of human image-bearing means that we must never despise a person for their skin color, background, traits, abilities (or lack thereof),

---

[9]　See 1 Corinthians 11:7, which identifies "man" (husbands in marital terms) in this way; by extension, we reasonably conclude that the woman (women more broadly) are image-bearers, with men having the leadership role—headship—in creation order, and thus in marriage and church leadership.

[10]　Thankfully, this is not true, for we all have our deficiencies. I would be in trouble, for example, if human value was dependent on height, mathematical abilities, culinary abilities, and many other areas. More seriously, it is common for sinful groups to see some people as more human than others based on certain traits or abilities. Mark this: Scripture *never* does this. Every person has God-given dignity, even post-fall: "Of how much more value is a man than a sheep!," says Christ in Matthew 12:12. Man is not a beast or animal following the Fall; he may act like one, but he is not one.

or heritage. Instead, we must treat all people with honor and dignity. Even human sinfulness (see our next section) does nothing—and I mean nothing—to change this truth.

C. S. Lewis captured the truths we are contemplating some years ago:

> There are no ordinary people. You have never talked to a mere mortal. Nations, cultures, arts, civilizations—these are mortal, and their life is to ours as the life of a gnat. But it is immortals whom we joke with, work with, marry, snub and exploit—immortal horrors or everlasting splendors. This does not mean that we are to be perpetually solemn. We must play. But our merriment must be of that kind (and it is, in fact, the merriest kind) which exists between people who have, from the outset, taken each other seriously—no flippancy, no superiority, no presumption.[11]

Second Truth: The Fall Introduces Enmity between God and Man—and Humanity Beyond

To understand humanity, we need to understand not only God's making, but man's undoing. Genesis 3:1–13 gives us the true story of the real historical Fall of the human race. We examine this chapter now to understand what has gone wrong with mankind, a matter that requires careful attention if we are to grasp afresh how we can find unity and forgiveness in God. The account of the origin of human evil begins with the subversion of the created order. In Genesis 1:26 and 1:28, the man and woman are called to "have dominion over…the creatures that crawl on the earth." The serpent, one of the wild animals made by God, was formed on the sixth day, just as humanity was. The Lord had taken pains to provide for such creatures, having given them "every green plant" for their sustenance (Genesis 1:30). The serpent was not made by God to

---

11 C. S. Lewis, *The Weight of Glory* (San Francisco, California: HarperOne, 2001 [1941]), 45–46.

stalk and devour fellow animals, but to enjoy the good gift of the Creator who revealed Himself to be Sustainer as well. But this is just what the snake did on the day when Adam fell: he hunted the man who was made to rule over him.

Adam and Eve would not have been confused about God and His desires. The first words of the Lord spoken to humanity in Genesis 2 express God's moral law. Before the woman came into being, the Lord gave the man the following command and prohibition: "You are free to eat from any tree of the garden, but you must not eat from the tree of the knowledge of good and evil, for on the day you eat from it, you will certainly die" (Genesis 2:16–17). Adam first learned that he was "free" to consume food from any tree; the Lord's communication to him centered in the bounty spread before him.[11] With this boundless gifting noted, the Lord prohibited Adam from eating the forbidden tree's fruit. Here was blessing and also limitation placed before Adam, each within arm's reach in Eden.

We return to Genesis 3:1–5. The serpent, we learn here, was "cunning." Without any explanation or backstory, the evil animal speaks to the woman. The serpent's words matter, but so too does this conversation itself. The man was called to lead his wife; she was made from his body, and he named her. But the man did not keep his charge, nor protect his wife. At this point in the story, Adam should have crushed the serpent's skull. The Lord had called him, after all, to "work" and "guard" the garden (Genesis 2:15). This was his priestly commission from God, given before the woman was made from his flesh. The Lord held the man responsible for the state of his home, in other words. But in the Fall, the man failed to obey God, and he failed to hold back the serpent from his wife.

---

[11] R. Kent Hughes nicely sums up these dimensions of God's words to Adam: "God's word to him was first *permissive*: 'And the LORD God commanded the man, saying, "You may surely eat of every tree of the garden"' (v. 16). Adam was to partake of everything in the garden to his heart's content, which included the tree of life. This is lavish, extravagant abundance, and Adam could take from the tree of life if he wanted it. Everything was there for him—everything he could possibly want." R. Kent Hughes, *Genesis: Beginning and Blessing*, Preaching the Word (Wheaton, Illinois: Crossway Books, 2004), 54–55.

At this point, Eve had taken the leadership role in the marriage, betraying God's design. With her husband doing nothing to stop her, she obeyed the serpent and ate the forbidden fruit:

> So when the woman saw that the tree was good for food, and that it was a delight to the eyes, and that the tree was to be desired to make one wise, she took of its fruit and ate, and she also gave some to her husband who was with her, and he ate. Then the eyes of both were opened, and they knew that they were naked. And they sewed fig leaves together and made themselves loincloths.
>
> And they heard the sound of the LORD God walking in the garden in the cool of the day, and the man and his wife hid themselves from the presence of the LORD God among the trees of the garden. But the LORD God called to the man and said to him, "Where are you?" And he said, "I heard the sound of you in the garden, and I was afraid, because I was naked, and I hid myself." He said, "Who told you that you were naked? Have you eaten of the tree of which I commanded you not to eat?" The man said, "The woman whom you gave to be with me, she gave me fruit of the tree, and I ate." Then the LORD God said to the woman, "What is this that you have done?" The woman said, "The serpent deceived me, and I ate." (Genesis 3:6–13)

How telling this passage is, and how tragic. The woman took the tree's food, ironically, to gain wisdom. But she had rejected wisdom itself in making this decision. So did Adam, who allowed himself to be led by his wife, reversing the rightful order of the marital relationship.[13] The man, we learn in verse 6, was not far off from this interaction; he was

---

[13] John Calvin minces no words on this point, which is so often soft-pedaled in our day: "Indeed, it was not only for the sake of complying with the wishes of his wife, that he transgressed the law laid down for him; but being drawn by her into fatal ambition, he became partaker of the same defection with her." John Calvin,

"with her," and she gave him the food. Adam acquiesced. He raised no hand against the Satanic serpent attacking his wife. The one created to rule the serpent was thoroughly ruled by the serpent.

We ought not to think that Adam did something we would not have done. Instead, what Adam did is what we ourselves would have done. In historical terms, the sin of Adam is the sin of all humanity; the death of Adam is the death of all humanity. In 1 Corinthians, the Apostle Paul connects Adam to all people: "For since death came through a man, the resurrection of the dead also comes through a man. For just as in Adam all die, so also in Christ all will be made alive" (1 Corinthians 15:21–22). Through Adam, all die—all without exception. There is no one who can opt out of this condition, this sorry state. It is where we all are. It explains every single act of human evildoing and tribal hatred, past, present, and future. This is why people show partiality—sinful favoritism—to one another. This is why we discriminate against one another. This is why we use image-bearers for our own purposes. It owes not to government, or lack of education, or too much TV-watching. It owes to the real historical fall of the real historical Adam. We sinned in him; we died when he died.

The overarching term for our spiritual condition is this: *total depravity*. This potent phrase means that sin reaches into every aspect of the human person. Before the Fall, we had an innocent (but not perfect) nature. Following the Fall, we had a sinful nature. This signifies that evil comes naturally to us. Even without teaching or coaching, we sin against God through idolatrous and impure thoughts, desires, words, and actions. Our minds, hearts, souls, bodies, and entire beings are oriented toward wickedness; we are not as bad as we could be, left without any moral intuition or instinct whatsoever, but we are totally ruined by sin, and as such are comprehensively evil. The human heart is "desperately wicked" in the words of Jeremiah 17:9 (KJV). Though we all like to think we are better than others, in biblical terms, there is no one who should

---

Commentaries of the First Book of Moses Called Genesis, vol. 1, ed. Anthony Uyl, trans. John King (Ontario, Canada: Devoted, 2018), 60.

think he is superior to any other person. We are all equally condemned before a holy God. Some heap up greater damnation than others through their pursuit of sin, yes, but we are all lost in sin by nature.

The letter to the Ephesians brings these threads together into convulsive summation of human depravity:

> And you were dead in your trespasses and sins in which you previously lived according to the ways of this world, according to the ruler of the power of the air, the spirit now working in the disobedient. We too all previously lived among them in our fleshly desires, carrying out the inclinations of our flesh and thoughts, and we were by nature children under wrath as the others were also. (Ephesians 2:1–3)

What a head-spinning rebuke of human pride. We are not inherently righteous; instead, Christians once lived according to trespasses and sins that left us dead in spiritual terms. We were not *children of light*. We were *children of wrath*. Again, this is not because we had a high-level indoctrination campaign in "Methods of Evildoing." Our wrath-deserving selves manifested sin from day one. Nothing in natural terms could change this reality. No one can overcome it by human means. No one can undo it. This is who we are from birth, and this is who we are until God saves us. Because of this condition, the Scripture puts no hope and no confidence in anything related to the natural man. We are not encouraged in a utopian direction, as if the world will magically make itself right. We are not told to hope that any earthly ruler or institution will overcome evil in our time. Christians seek to be "salt and light," absolutely, but we are never directed by the Word of God to find a molecule of hope in this cursed place (Matthew 5:13–16). All our hope is trained on God, all our confidence is located in God, and all our trust is deposited in God. Not an atom of such things belongs to man, or the world of men.

This confession goes against how we are trained to think today. We often hear that we are fundamentally good and beautiful and perfect just as we are. We should update this: In wokeness, some are fundamentally good and beautiful and right just as they are, but others are definitively not. Those who participate in "whiteness," as we have covered already, are in no way right as they are. Wokeness is thus a new unbiblical Manichaeism. It reads some people as naturally good and others as naturally bad. The Bible teaches the opposite: It teaches that we are *all* sinful and lost. We are inestimably valuable as those made by God, but in Adam we have plunged into death and sin and evil. We cannot come to God; we cannot savingly know the Lord by natural means. We cannot even please the Lord: "A good tree can't produce bad fruit; neither can a bad tree produce good fruit" (Matthew 7:18). We neither want nor follow God's will. In our fallenness, though we know truths about God in a basic form, we can't think in a God-glorifying way with a redeemed mind: "The natural person does not accept the things of the Spirit of God, for they are folly to him, and he is not able to understand them because they are spiritually discerned" (1 Corinthians 2:14). We are totally depraved and thus totally unable to come to God.

The real historical Fall of a real historical Adam tells us why things go wrong in our world. This is truly the explanation of explanations. Every evil thing traces back to this: the Fall of Adam. Here is why we show partiality to one another. Here is why we allow our hearts to judge one another. Here is why we do terrible things to fellow image-bearers. It is not because there is a good and justifiable reason. It is because we are sinners. As stated earlier in this book, in our natural condition we are not victims—we are criminals. We may be wronged by others; we surely will. But we are not innocent by nature, as we have established. We committed Adam's sin with him, effectively. We are no better than him, and we have no excuses for our sin.

Here is where we need to go to comprehend why centuries, even millennia, of societal violence and evil confront us when we study history. It is because of the inherent depravity of the human heart. Every person without exception is a sinner by nature. Our sin manifests in different ways and takes different forms in different eras, yes, but all human people have a perverse commonality on this count. We who are made to be one human race and dwell together as grateful worshippers of the living God instead separate ourselves, judge others, and commit idolatry by exalting ourselves. Made to take dominion of the earth, we instead take dominion over one another.

This, again, is not only a prehistoric problem. This is a present-day problem. It is the central predicament faced by every person. In any discussion of identity, "race," ethnicity, justice, evil, and change, the personal evildoing of sinful humanity must take first place. When you deny personal human sinfulness (for sin is always personal, committed by people against God and man), you close yourself off from understanding what ails us. Conversely, when you affirm human sinfulness at the personal level, you set yourself up to not only understand our present travail, but to address it rightly through the wisdom of God.

We face disunity and commit partiality of many kinds for one reason and one reason alone: our sin. It is not that society is flawed, and we are innocent. It is that we are sinful, and so our world is polluted with our sin. This does not mean that Christ died (see Chapter 6) for society in general; it means that if things are to be made right here, we must be made right. We are the issue at hand. We are not *victims*, though we may have suffered due to the sin of others. We ourselves are *criminals*. We have no rescue in ourselves. We have no hope of self-rehabilitation. We cannot focus our bitterness on others and so make our own problems vanish. We are the problem. Christ, as we shall see, is the only solution.

Third Truth: God Scatters the People Because of Pride

Following the Fall of the human race in Genesis 3, things take a terrible turn. The children of Adam take different paths. Seth's line is faithful to God, but Ham's line is not. Yet even as God uses the house of Seth to preserve a people for himself, no person or tribe is untouched by sin. In fact, things get so bad that even after the flood of Genesis 6, God issues a scattering judgment at Babel. This event explains why there are such spread-out, disconnected people groups on Planet Earth. Genesis 11 gives us the story:

> Now the whole earth had one language and the same words. And as people migrated from the east, they found a plain in the land of Shinar and settled there. And they said to one another, "Come, let us make bricks, and burn them thoroughly." And they had brick for stone, and bitumen for mortar. Then they said, "Come, let us build ourselves a city and a tower with its top in the heavens, and let us make a name for ourselves, lest we be dispersed over the face of the whole earth." And the LORD came down to see the city and the tower, which the children of man had built. And the LORD said, "Behold, they are one people, and they have all one language, and this is only the beginning of what they will do. And nothing that they propose to do will now be impossible for them. Come, let us go down and there confuse their language, so that they may not understand one another's speech." So the LORD dispersed them from there over the face of all the earth, and they left off building the city. Therefore its name was called Babel, because there the LORD confused the language of all the earth. And from there the LORD dispersed them over the face of all the earth. (Genesis 11:1–9)

This is an act of judgment by God. Self-idolatry drove the building of the tower. In response, the people's "language" (verse 7) was confused, and the Lord Himself "dispersed" or "scattered" the peoples across the earth (verse 8). The people should have used their intellects and technical skills to praise the Lord. Instead, they sought to praise themselves, to stand out. They went so far—literally—as to try and establish their greatness as on par with God's. The human heart truly knows no bounds in its ability to exalt itself over God. As a result, both geography but also speech—which was given for the worship of God and the unity of the race—separated the peoples.

So it was that God sent the peoples out, splitting them in an unalterable way. No human person, however idealistic and well-intentioned, can undo what the necessary work of God's judgment wrought. If the flood meant that the earth essentially shrank to the population of the ark of Noah, then Babel means that the earth essentially expanded to an unprecedented degree. The first act of judgment made the earth small; the second act of judgment made it impossibly big. Unity was no longer possible in natural terms.

None of this material indicates that human distinctiveness is an outworking of judgment. As we saw earlier in this chapter, God had always planned for humanity to multiply and take dominion of all the earth. This dominion would be shared by all peoples. The image of God would be displayed by all peoples, and those people would naturally have spread across the earth and formed their own enclaves and groups.[14] As we noted above, God's plan was unity for His image-bearers but not uniformity; distinction and difference and diversity are not viewed negatively, but positively, in the biblical worldview. What happened at Babel is that instead of the one human race honoring God in its own place and distinctive form, God forcibly split it apart. People meant to dwell in unity would instead distrust, wrong, and try to rule one another for their own purposes. The markers of distinctiveness that should have turned the human heart to thankfulness and praise will instead be read negatively. People would not love one another for their God-given uniqueness but would hate one another for it.

This, again, makes no sense. It is not right. It is not the pure wisdom of humanity's Maker. It is the product of the fallen heart. Though diversity should prompt praise, it instead provokes jealousy, fear, tribalism,

---

[14] J. Daniel Hays, *From Every People and Nation: A Biblical Theology of Race*, New Studies in Biblical Theology, vol. 14 (Downers Grove, Illinois: Apollos, 2003), 50.

distrust, and hatred. All this owes to humanity's sin at Babel. All of it is the experience and expression of God's judgment on that sin.

Fourth Truth: God Welcomes the Stranger into Israel

Yet from this wreckage a covenant people will emerge and endure. In the midst of this terrible dissolution, the Lord calls Israel—founded in Abraham—to be a light among the nations. For example, His holy law necessitates kindness and hospitality to aliens, as He declares:

> When an alien resides with you in your land, you must not oppress him. You will regard the alien who resides with you as the native-born among you. You are to love him as yourself, for you were aliens in the land of Egypt; I am the Lord your God. (Leviticus 19:33–34)

God nowhere endorses nativism. His people are called to be distinct from the world, but they are never justified in wearing their Israelite status as a badge of pride. They were, in fact, to reach beyond their own kin, their own family, and show mercy to others. If anything, being an Israelite entailed a life of utter humility. For those to whom much mercy had been given, mercy was expected.

We glean one powerful illustration of hospitality to the stranger in the story of Ruth. Ruth's mother-in-law, Naomi, found herself a foreigner in the land of Moab after her hometown of Bethlehem was beset with famine. While in Moab, Naomi suffered the loss of her husband—her primary source of protection, provision, and companionship (Ruth 1:3).[15] Naomi's two daughters-in-law, Ruth included, soon experienced the deaths of their own husbands. Naomi urged these young women to go back to their own people, the people of Moab, to make a better life for

---

[15] Naomi's husband has been "buried in an unclean land," Daniel Block notes, which, according to some Jews, was "considered the ultimate punishment." Daniel I. Block, *Judges, Ruth*, vol. 6 of New American Commentary (Nashville, Tennessee: B&H, 1999), 628.

themselves (Ruth 1:15). But Ruth had other plans. She responded to her mother-in-law with these poignant words:

> "Do not urge me to leave you or to return from following you. For where you go I will go, and where you lodge I will lodge. Your people shall be my people, and your God my God. Where you die I will die, and there will I be buried. May the LORD do so to me and more also if anything but death parts me from you." And when Naomi saw that she was determined to go with her, she said no more. (Ruth 1:16–18)

Ruth was not swayed by the promise of a better life in her home country of Moab. She rejected the chance to go back "to her people and to her gods" (verse 15); she did not want to return. She is an example of a woman who presses in to know the Lord and His people. In this true story, we are getting a little preview of a resonant biblical melody. Though God loved Israel, He loved others from outside the nation as well. Israel was God's covenant people; yet Israel could not rightly conclude that God loved only Israelites. His people were bigger and broader than this chosen nation, vital as it was to God's plan; indeed, as the story went on, figures like Ruth and Rahab show us that many who were not of Israel by birth were actually more "of Israel" spiritually than many Jews by birth.[16] God had a people for Himself, but this people was not ethnically locked; instead, this people would stream to God from all the earth, ultimately being numbered as the stars in the sky.

The story of Ruth shows us this glorious truth in her own situation. But Ruth's bloodline unveiled it in even more dramatic fashion. Just a few generations after she lived, David was born. David did not initially rank as a likely candidate for Israel's kingship; he was short, anonymous, and relatively unvalued in his own home. But God had big plans for

---

[16] This emphasis on multiethnic inclusion, even in the Old Testament, becomes especially evident in Matthew's backward-looking genealogy at the beginning of his Gospel (Matthew 1:5). Hays, *From Every People and Nation*, 158–59.

David. Amidst all the warriors of Israel, David alone had the courage to go up against evil Goliath (1 Samuel 17). God strengthened him in doing so and gave David the head of the Philistine giant. David, it turns out, is the king who prefigures the greater King, Jesus Christ. All this from the bloodline of a Moabite woman.

Conclusion

This biblical material is faith-building. It shows us that God is doing a work in biblical history that no one would have expected, and no one but God could have orchestrated. The human people involved did not know what God was doing in their day. They knew nothing of the Father's perfect will and all-wise plan (Ephesians 1:3–14). Yet the Father was indeed bringing all things to their rightful end. He had bigger plans than it initially seemed; the story of Ruth, it turns out, was not a rarity, but was typical of where the story of God's people would go. Not only would occasional individuals like Ruth come to worship Yahweh, the covenant God of Israel. God had actually planned for people from every corner of the earth, people scattered due to Babel, to come back to Him, to be saved by Him, and to form part of His household. This was not a plan God scrambled to come up with; this was His purpose from the beginning. The people chosen by God would not have to pretend they were His nor fake their identity; they would be genuinely welcomed and genuinely accepted.

But all this resolution lay in the future in terms of the Old Testament story. Despite hints and foreshadowing, the Old Testament does not ultimately give us the climax to the story of God's people. We close the first major section of Scripture not knowing how the plotline resolves. I am reminded at this point of what sometimes happens when I read *The Chronicles of Narnia* to my children. The plot resolution is just around the corner, but I am asked at that precise moment, "What's going to happen, Daddy?" I have to shake my head and laugh, for that's our common instinct. Outside of the Narnian world, the same is true: in the New Testament, God's answer to man's sinful disunity is just around the corner. Indeed, it is in a real sense on the very next page.

DISCUSSION QUESTIONS

1. According to the Bible, is there one race (singular) or multiple races (plural)?
2. How does wokeness's categorization of "the fundamental human problem" differ from the Bible's categorization?
3. If human beings came together in unity in the building of the tower of Babel, why did God choose to disperse the peoples?
4. Did God extend His grace only to the nation of Israel in the Old Testament? How does the story of Ruth factor into your answer?

CHAPTER 6

What Does the Bible Teach about Identity and Ethnicity?

Part Two: New Testament

There is no peace to be found anywhere else or in anyone else. It is Jesus only and only Jesus.
—*H. B. Charles Jr.*

Some years ago, the Christian songwriter Michael Card told a heartbreaking story through song. Card's father, whom he loved very much, was a doctor and had to perform complex acts of surgery that would take hours and hours to complete. When his father would return home after a long day, Michael would try to connect with his dad. His father—feeling, no doubt, the weight of lives hanging in the balance before him—would go to his study and shut the door and even lock it in order to get his wits back after a hard day's work. Young Michael, in an attempt to connect with his dad, would slide pictures under the door—attempting, by any means, to get his father's attention.[1]

We all naturally want a father who loves us. We all deeply desire a father who brings us safety and security and blessing and belonging. But in a world that is fallen and shot through with sin, the reality is this: finding such comforts is difficult indeed. Scripture tells us, however, how we may finally and lastingly come home to the heavenly Father. We are told how

---

[1] Michael Card, "Underneath the Door," from the album *Scribbling in the Sand: The Best of Michael Card—Live*, Word Entertainment, 2002, compact disc.

we may find what we were designed for. It is not through might, or pedigree, or works, or human ingenuity. It is all through the blood of Christ.

In the previous chapter, we saw the fundamental unity of humanity in the image of God, but also the terrible reasons for our sinful divisiveness. Now in this chapter, we examine from the New Testament exactly how God gathers a people for Himself. We see in this chapter how, in the New Testament, Paul taught both Jews and Gentiles of the Ephesian church that they were dramatically and supernaturally one in Christ. Their sin and alienation were overcome by Him and realized through justifying faith. Though knowing this truth does not brush away every hard question we face today about identity, "race," justice, and ethnicity, the Bible centers all our hopes for humanity not in *many people*, but in just *one person*: Jesus Christ.

In the pages that follow, we look first at Paul's words to the Ephesians on human sinfulness, covering in brief what we laid out in the previous chapter. We then look at length at the unifying power of the cross of Christ. From there, we consider several other passages in the New Testament that shape a properly biblical understanding of identity, ethnicity, and oneness. It turns out that we as believers have what the world most needs: the blood of Christ.

First Truth: The Peoples of the Earth Are Alienated by Sin

> Therefore remember that at one time you Gentiles in the flesh, called "the uncircumcision" by what is called the circumcision, which is made in the flesh by hands—remember that you were at that time separated from Christ, alienated from the commonwealth of Israel and strangers to the covenants of promise, having no hope and without God in the world. (Ephesians 2:11-12)

In Ephesians, the Apostle Paul has a burden to reveal where true unity is found. His letter is addressed to the Ephesian Christians, who were Gentiles by background. He points to the stark covenantal division between the Gentiles and the Jews: The Gentiles were "separated from Christ," "alienated" from Israel, and "strangers" to the grace of God mediated through the covenants with creation, Noah, Abraham, Moses, and David (verse 12). The condition of the Gentiles expresses the natural problem of the human race. Apart from divine grace, we are all "separated from Christ." Theologian John Stott notes,

> Long before Feuerbach and Marx, the Bible spoke of human alienation. It describes two other and even more radical alienations than the economic and the political. One is alienation from God our Creator, and the other alienation from one another, our fellow creatures.[2]

Ephesians 2:1–3 pointedly declares that no one is a natural-born participant in the covenants of promise since everyone is born dead in his trespasses and sins. But the problem for the Gentiles was still worse—they did not even know about the covenants.[3] The term Paul uses, "covenants of promise," reminds us of the entire narrative-driven sweep of Scripture. Sin brought death, but the covenants came with the promise of life—spiritual life unto everlasting life. Yet outside of the covenants, the human and Gentilic condition is stark indeed. There is "no hope" in our natural state. Furthermore, we still divide from one another, as Stott notes:

---

[2] John R. W. Stott, *God's New Society: The Message of Ephesians. Bible Speaks Today* (Downers Grove, Illinois: InterVarsity Press, 1979), 90.

[3] Harold Hoehner observes that the Gentiles lacked five privileges enjoyed by Israelites, namely, that they were: (1) "separate from (literally 'without') Christ"; (2) "excluded from citizenship in Israel"; (3) "foreigners to the covenants of the promise"; (4) "without hope"; and (5) "without God (*atheoi*, 'apart from God') in the world." Harold W. Hoehner, "Ephesians," in *Bible Knowledge Commentary: New Testament Edition*, eds. John F. Walvoord and Roy B. Zuck (Wheaton, Illinois: Victor Books, 1985), 625.

Men still build walls of partition and division like the terrible Berlin wall, or erect invisible curtains of iron or bamboo, or construct barriers of race, colour, caste, tribe or class. Divisiveness is a constant characteristic of every community without Christ.[4]

Stott is right to apply Paul's words to other forms of division. This passage, Ephesians 2:11–22, deals contextually with Jew-Gentile covenantal relations. But it applies beyond that to the widest possible extent. In Christ, we learn here, every exclusionary boundary marker falls. This is because the most significant wall dividing humanity has toppled—the covenant wall between Jew and Gentile. If this can fall, so can every other barrier between peoples of every kind.

But we are running ahead of ourselves here. The natural state of the Gentiles is that they are "without God" (verse 12). It is important that we be reminded of this today. We are encouraged to look much to the world for encouragement and help and wisdom. But to be without Christ is to be without hope. The people around us who act and live and move are not only *emotionally hopeless*; outside of Christ, they are *objectively hopeless*. They truly cannot do anything in themselves to change this state. With such teaching, Paul is laying the groundwork for his next section, which will be covered in our following chapter. With the Ephesian church, he is telling us, effectively, "Whatever you do, do not look to the Gentiles for hope, for solutions, for the antidote to what ails us. The Gentiles do not have the solution. Only those who have God can find hope and all that hope yields."

Second Truth: The Two Peoples Are United in Christ

In the next section of Ephesians 2, Paul transitions from problem to solution. The answer to what ails us is bound up in one word, one glorious title: Christ.

---

4   Stott, *God's New Society*, 96.

But now in Christ Jesus you who once were far off have been brought near by the blood of Christ. For he himself is our peace, who has made us both one and has broken down in his flesh the dividing wall of hostility by abolishing the law of commandments expressed in ordinances, that he might create in himself one new man in place of the two, so making peace, and might reconcile us both to God in one body through the cross, thereby killing the hostility. And he came and preached peace to you who were far off and peace to those who were near. For through him we both have access in one Spirit to the Father. (Ephesians 2:13–18)

There is no more desperate condition than that of the Gentiles in Paul's mind. In their natural state, the Gentiles were "far off" from God. As mentioned earlier, this meant they were without hope. But all this changed with the coming of Jesus. Through faith in Him, the Gentiles may draw near to God. Note the expressly Christocentric answer Paul gives to our conundrum: "the blood of Christ" (verse 13). The blood of Christ is the solution humanity needs for our alienation, estrangement, anger, hatred, and hopelessness. The blood of Christ washes us clean; it functions as the very εἰρήνη, "peace," between God and man and between man and man (verse 14).

The blood of Christ, Paul teaches, is effectual and powerful (verse 14):

1. It makes Jew and Gentile "one."
2. It breaks down to ashes the "dividing wall of hostility."
3. This is accomplished by the flesh of Christ, the atoning sacrifice that is the Son of God, which brings the Old Covenant law to perfect fulfillment.

The Old Covenant law is so perfectly met and fulfilled and consummated in Christ that Paul can use the language of its being "abolish[ed]" (verse 15). Harold Hoehner observes that, according to the apostle, Christ "rendered the Law 'inoperative' (*katargēsas*) in believers' lives."[5] Therefore, there is not one form of Christianity for the Gentiles and another for the Jews. There is just Christianity, driven by the blood of Christ, such that "one new man" now exists (verse 15). This in turn means that there are not two groups any longer in terms of divided identity. While Jews and Gentiles each have their own background, Christ has become their *primary* identity, their *ultimate* identity.

Verse 15 declares that there is "peace" between Jew and Gentile. Note that peace is not prepared for us as a future possibility; peace has been made and offered. Peace is in Christ and Christ alone. Outside of Christ, the covenantal "hostility" (*eckthran*) spoken of in verse 16 between Jew and Gentile persists (so too with all other peoples of whatever kind). But in Christ, we are reconciled to God (verse 16). Reconciliation between those hailing from the covenant people and those born outside the covenant community does not for Paul come in positive feelings *about Jesus*. It does not flow from merely trying to do *what Jesus did*. It certainly is not found in *wanting things from Jesus*. Reconciliation is anchored in *what God has done in Christ*. This reconciliation comes "through the cross" (verse 16). It is finished. Reconciliation, therefore, is *objective*. No sinful person can accomplish it; neither can any sinner undo it. God has done it.

The wrath of God is propitiated at the cross. Jesus becomes the wrath-bearing sacrifice for sinners. John Calvin rightly asserts,

> Sin is the cause of enmity between God and us; and, until it is removed, we shall not be restored to the Divine favor. It has been blotted out by the death of Christ, in which he offered himself to the Father as an expiatory victim.[6]

The cross is so powerful that it kills hostility (verse 16) and reconciles both Jews and Gentiles to God. John Chrysostom comments on the

---

[5] Hoehner, "Ephesians," 626.

[6] John Calvin, *Commentaries on the Epistles of Paul to the Galatians and Ephesians*, trans. William Pringle, vol. 21 of Calvin's Commentaries (Grand Rapids, Michigan: Baker Books, 1999), 239.

importance of Paul's use of the word *apokteinas*, "kill," in verse 16: "[Paul] did not say that [Christ] dissolved it; he did not say that he put an end to it, but he used the much more forceful expression: He killed! This shows that [the enmity] need not ever rise again. How then does it rise again? From our great wickedness. So long as we remain in the body of Christ, so long as we are one with him it does not rise again but lies dead."[7] We have a terrible problem, one of double alienation, for sinful man is estranged from God (vertical alienation) and from his fellow neighbor (horizontal alienation).[8] As Chrysostom captures, the remedy for this problem is so great that it solves both dimensions.

Of course, we must get the priority right here: our reconciliation is first *vertical* and secondarily *horizontal*. John Piper says it well: "Vertical and horizontal reconciliation happen together and inseparably through faith in Christ."[9] All the anger and alienation and division between Jews and Gentiles have collapsed. There is no more hostility. What wondrous words these are; in such evil days as ours, they might sound too good to be true. But they are not. The power of Christ's cross, and Christ's cross alone, is such that for those who are born again, hostility as a state of being, a natural condition, or a habit of mind has ceased.

This is not because we have adopted cultural ideology. It is not because of a secular system of thought. No, hostility has *objectively* ceased. It ceased in the first century, and it thus has no power over us in the Church in the twenty-first century. Hostility is undone by the cross-work of the King. So comments nineteenth-century theologian Charles Hodge:

> When Christ is said to reconcile people to God, it means that he propitiated God, satisfied the demands of his justice, and

---

[7] John Chrysostom, "Homily on Ephesians 5.2.16," as quoted in M. J. Edwards, ed. *Galatians, Ephesians, Philippians*, vol. 8 of Ancient Christian Commentary on Scripture: New Testament (Downers Grove, Illinois: InterVarsity, 1999), 141.

[8] Stott, *God's New Society*, 90.

[9] John Piper, *Bloodlines: Race, Cross, and the Christian* (Wheaton, Illinois: Crossway, 2011), 125.

thus rendered it possible that he might be just and yet justify the ungodly.[10]

There is nothing left to be done, because Christ has done it all. God's wrath is satisfied, for it was poured out on the Son at the cross. Because of this, now there is "peace" between the "far off" and the "near" (verse 17). How important this point is! Unlike in woke ideology, Christians know that we can never find lasting peace in natural terms and through natural means. This is because disunity, injustice, and hostility flow from our alienation to God, and secondly from our resulting alienation with one another. But if the vertical problem is resolved, then the horizontal is as well. Accordingly, Jesus is the only true hope of those who desire unity of any kind in the world. Human harmony is a good desire, one common to humanity beyond the Church. But there is truly no hope of peace outside of Jesus, for only Jesus solves our foremost problem: separation from God.

Our solution to disunity, injustice, and division is anchored in Christ and Christ alone. On this count, Calvin proclaims:

> If the Jews wish to enjoy peace with God, they must have Christ as their Mediator. But Christ will not be their peace in any other way than by making them one body with the Gentiles.[11]

What impactful words these are. In Paul's day, Jew and Gentile alike could point to a catalogue of alienation with one another. Though they were of "one blood" in creational terms per Acts 17:26, in situational terms the two groups were as far apart as they could be. They had no hope of unity. Perhaps they technically shared citizenship within the

---

[10]   Charles Hodge, *Ephesians*, Crossway Classic Commentaries (Wheaton, Illinois: Crossway, 1994), 89. This word "propitiated" means that Christ bore the Father's wrath on the cross and satisfied it. To understand this biblical doctrine, see J. I. Packer and Mark Dever, *In My Place Condemned He Stood: Celebrating the Glory of the Atonement* (Wheaton, Illinois: Crossway, 2008).

[11]   Calvin, *Galatians and Ephesians*, 236.

broader bounds of a given nation, but they had no means of lasting uni-fication. Hostility dominated. Hatred proliferated. Tension boiled as it does among people of varying backgrounds in the modern world. But Christ made an end of this separation. By "the blood of Christ," Jew and Gentile became one through repentance and faith.

The "wall" of hatred (verse 14) had, in a similar way, affected and even imprisoned the two sides in a condition of implacable bitterness. There was only one force that could tear down such a wall: the cross of Christ. Jesus, Paul straightforwardly asserts, "is our peace" (verse 14). What a memorable phrase this is.[12] We have no peace in ourselves; we bring only hostility to our interactions. The peace that Jesus gives us is not momentary peace, peace from a drug, peace from a pill, peace from a happy day, peace from a meditation session, or peace stemming from our good works. Peace of the lasting, enduring, uniting kind comes from— and truly in—only one Person on Earth: Jesus Christ.[13] It is precious, hard-won, blood-bought peace. By His death and through His resurrection, Jesus brings together what Satan has driven apart. Jesus has not only made it possible for Jew and Gentile to unite; Paul's language is iron-strong in its description of achieved effect: Jesus "made both groups one" and "tore down" the wall of division.

Accordingly, now there is "access" to the Father through the Son by the Spirit (verse 18).[14] Verse 18 states, "For through him we both have access in one Spirit to the Father." The Father is forgotten in many evan-gelical circles today. It is a little odd to talk much about the Father.[15]

---

[12] To quote Calvin: "If Christ is our peace, all who are out of him must be at vari-ance with God. What a beautiful title is this which Christ possesses—the peace between God and men! Let no one who dwells in Christ entertain a doubt that he is reconciled to God." Ibid., 235. Emphasis in original.

[13] H. B. Charles Jr. puts it succinctly: "There is peace in the person of Christ.... He himself is our peace." Charles, "The Peaceful Solution to Racial Unity," in *A Biblical Answer for Racial Unity*, ed. Richard Caldwell (Houston, Texas: Kress, 2017), 36.

[14] Hoehner, "Ephesians," 626.

[15] One happy exception is Ryan Rippee, *That God May Be All in All: A Paterology Demonstrating That the Father Is the Initiator of All Divine Activity* (Eugene, Oregon: Pickwick, 2018).

Though the Father is not referenced multiple times in Ephesians 2:11–22, the Father stands in back of all of this saving work (see Ephesians 1:3–14). The Son carried out what the Father planned and set in motion in sending the Son to Earth. How corrective this is of common liberal Christian portrayals of the Father as bloodthirsty and the Son as loving. The Father is wrathful against sin, yes. But the Father is the one who in love sets up the entire work of redemption, sends the Son, and pours out His anger against sin at the cross. The Father initiates a holy work of love that meets the terms of His holy justice.[16] How we need to recover a doctrine of biblical fatherhood! As believers, we have access to Him, and He is no longer far from us.

Recall the story of Michael Card as a boy trying to get his father's attention. Now, because of Christ, we do not have to try. We have the full attention and the full adoration of the Father. We are reconciled to God and reconciled to one another under the Father's loving leadership. We are not distant strangers in God's eyes; we are, as our next section shows, one body in Christ.

Third Truth: The Church Is the Multiethnic Household of God

In our third and final treatment of Ephesians 2, we see how Paul brings theological resolution to his treatment of blood-bought unity. It is not merely that redeemed people are saved; it is that God is joining them together.

> So then you are no longer strangers and aliens, but you are
> fellow citizens with the saints and members of the house-
> hold of God, built on the foundation of the apostles and
> prophets, Christ Jesus himself being the cornerstone, in
> whom the whole structure, being joined together, grows
> into a holy temple in the Lord. In him you also are being

---

[16] Matthew Henry, *A Commentary upon the Holy Bible*, 6 vols. (London: Religious Tract Society, 1888), 6:559.

built together into a dwelling place for God by the Spirit.
(Ephesians 2:19–22)

We should close our eyes and savor this passage afresh. We should
not let it bounce off us lightly. Paul teaches here that the result of the
work of Christ, His atonement for us, is that we are one family. The
blood of Christ washes us clean of all sin. When we have faith in God,
we are joined formally to the family. Once we were strangers and aliens;
now we are fellow citizens and family members.[17] Just as Jesus came alive
after death, so we come alive in Him (Romans 6:4). Though Paul does
not treat the resurrection extensively in the above passage, we do well to
point out—from other texts that speak with one biblical voice—that the
resurrection is the vindication and realization of all the atoning work
Christ accomplished at Calvary. Our sins are not cleansed through the
resurrection, but the cleansing of our sins carried out at the cross is rati-
fied in Jesus's triumph over the grave. His triumph, we recall, is the triumph of all who trust in Him.[18]

Jesus is the King, and the King is victorious in all His aims. His blood
has brought together believers as the "household of God," for by His
Spirit-empowered cross-work the Father has brought us into His fellowship (verse 19). We have a Father, a heavenly Father, and we have access
to Him. He is not far off but is near to all who love Christ. Christ is the
cornerstone (akrogōniaiou) of the household of God (verse 20). He comes
in fulfillment. He builds on the foundation laid by the apostles and
prophets (verse 20). The cornerstone is the unit that calibrates the entire
structure. As Hoehner comments:

---

[17] F. F. Bruce, *The Epistles to the Colossians, to Philemon and to the Ephesians,
New International Commentary on the New Testament* (Grand Rapids, Michigan:
Eerdmans, 1984), 302.

[18] We are reminded at this point that we must never choose between the cross and
the empty tomb. The cross secures; the resurrection realizes what the cross secured.
Without the cross, the resurrection has no meaning, for our sins are uncleansed,
and the Father's wrath remains on us. Without the resurrection, the cross is impressive but unrealized, its world-shaking power untapped. Praise God, the resurrection
ratifies what the cross realized.

In ancient building practices "the chief cornerstone" was carefully placed. It was crucial because the entire building was lined up with it. The church's foundation, that is, the apostles and prophets, needed to be correctly aligned with Christ. All other believers are built on that foundation, measuring their lives with Christ.[19]

Christ is the one in whom the whole structure joins together (verse 21). How practical this teaching is for us. We may have nothing in common with other Christians in terms of background, but we have this: Christ. We have Christ, and, as a result, we belong to one another, the Church.[20] Our membership in Christ's body is not first ecclesiological and then soteriological. Our belonging is through the cross alone. Through the cross, we are members of one another. Paul's metaphors here are textured and interwoven. We are "citizens" of God's Kingdom (verse 19), so we are royal subjects under divine rule. We are members of God's household (verse 19), so we are a family with a loving Father. We are growing "into a holy temple" (verse 21), so we are a living center of worship.[21]

We should all take heart from this portrait: God is molding us, making us, forming us, growing us—not in an isolated way, but as His Church, His people. At the same time individually, yes, God is working in us. But this is the opposite of "do it yourself" Christianity. As mentioned earlier, before the foundation of the world, the Father chose us in the Son (Ephesians 1:3–14). This is the context in which Paul states that we are created in Christ Jesus for good works (Ephesians 2:10). God has now knit us into the fabric of His Church. We have been brought into the family. The

---

[19] Hoehner, "Ephesians," 627.

[20] My comments here intentionally do not attempt to answer every eschatological matter that needs attention regarding the future plight of natural Jews, Israel, the Kingdom of Christ, the millennium, and so on. To learn more about these issues, which matter but should not cause hostility among God's people, see Timothy Paul Jones, *Four Views of the End Times* (Peabody, Massachusetts: Rose Publishing, 2006).

[21] Stott, *God's New Society*, 104.

whole structure is growing into a living temple. God is forming us as His dwelling place.

None of this, we note, is according to human wisdom. None of it is according to human design. None of it is dependent on human effort. All of it is dependent on and driven by God. All of it is intensely countercultural, then and now. To a watching world that asks us what our answer is for alienation and hostility, we say two things: (1) the cross, and (2) the Church. The cross alone has the power to create a new humanity, a new people, a new race birthed by God.[22] We do not most need to find peace within ourselves or *from ourselves*. We need neither "self-forgiveness" nor "peace from within." We need forgiveness *from God* and the peace that comes through faith in Christ. This heavenly peace will seep into all our relationships. Jesus has died; Jesus is risen. As the living Messiah, Jesus has triumphed over sin and death. He has reconciled God and man, and man and man. Jesus has taken two estranged peoples and has created "one new man" from them.[23] Coming to faith in Christ does not cancel our God-given identities, but rather refashions our identities around Christ. He is our center; He is our all.

God has not *tried* to reconcile us through the cross. Calvary is not His best shot at unification, with later needed boosts from Marxism and other ideologies. God *has* reconciled us through the cross. It is sadly true that we can play down and try to squelch this divine accomplishment. We can oppose it and try to frustrate it. But even such wicked actions cannot undo what God has done through his Son's death and resurrection. No other figure can do this. No one else can unify hostile peoples. Jesus is the only true hope of those who desire unity of any kind in the world. Anyone who wants true peace must look to Jesus and Jesus alone. The Gospel, and only the Gospel, is the way to unity in this fallen world. The Gospel does not solve the "spiritual aspect" of our natural divisions, leaving human philosophies and ideological "tools" to solve the other

---

[22] Owen Strachan, *Reenchanting Humanity: A Theology of Mankind* (Fearn, Scotland: Mentor, 2019), 238.

[23] Frank Thielman, *Ephesians, Baker Exegetical Commentary on the New Testament* (Grand Rapids, Michigan: Baker Academic, 2010), 170–71.

elements. The Gospel *is* God's solution to our divisions, our partiality, our inborn hatred, and our sins of every kind.

Beware any system—like wokeness, including wokeness adapted to Christianity—that tells you otherwise. It is now common to reject CRT and claim the Gospel, but to insist that the Gospel deals with the spiritual dimensions of our problem, leaving other dimensions unaddressed. This is not a sound view in biblical terms. It simply does not match what Paul teaches us about the cross. Just as Jesus is *the* way to God, the cross is *the* way to unity.²⁴ There is no other way. Christ is the only way. The cross is our only hope here.

This truth does not cancel the fact that image-bearers have natural affinities. Faith in Christ does not render us indiscrete beings without any human distinctiveness. Nor does it cancel out our own backgrounds and ethnicities. As we have stressed already, not all aspects of human culture are evil; not every word out of an unbeliever's mouth is heresy. Though unbelievers live a life of comprehensive sin and lack of glorification of God, in the Creator's common grace they can love their children, serve their community, enjoy sports, make beautiful art, promote justice where it is hindered, and eat good food. The natural man does not do so to God's glory, sadly. But this does not mean that the natural man is closed off from God's common grace. He is not. Nor is human society more broadly. Common grace is a lovely thing. It gives human life depth, and enjoyment, and a little taste of how good God is.

---

²⁴ This is a deceptively simple formulation. I sense that scores of professing Christians would nod their head to it, but the implications of it escape many today. If Jesus is exclusively the way to God per John 14:6 and the witness of the New Testament, then Jesus is also exclusively the way to any divine blessing and gift. The exclusivity of Christ applies not only to "getting our soul saved," then, but to the lasting possession of any good thing. Said differently, there simply is no true peace, hope, love, goodness, mercy, unity, equity, and justice outside of Christ. We may taste some measure of these things in temporal form in this life—we all will, and we all do. This is *common grace*. But it is nonetheless impossible to lay hold of these blessings lastingly outside of Christ—outside of *special grace*. It is not uncommon in our time, sadly, to collapse these two dimensions of the unitary grace of God.

But mark this: There is no salvation in common grace, and there is no ultimate unity in common grace. There is no new humanity in it. All such blessings are found only in Christ, and they become ours only when we trust in Christ as our Savior. As the Gospel is preached to us, God regenerates our hearts through the Spirit's quickening. This awakens faith in the finished work of Christ in us, and so we both trust in Christ and turn from all our sins. This is biblical salvation. It owes not to common grace, but to what we call "special grace." Special grace is delivered and announced only in the Gospel of Jesus Christ. You cannot find it anywhere else. The Gospel is the exclusive way to God, and so trusting in it is the only way to join the family of God. There is no other Savior but Christ, there is no other message of salvation but the Gospel, and there is no true family of God but the blood-bought, Gospel-trusting Church.

There is no family like the family of God in human history. There is no movement that crosses boundaries like the Christian mission. Christianity cannot be painted into a corner as the exclusive faith of one ethnicity or region; it is a global faith, a movement united by repentant belief in the atoning death and vicarious resurrection of Christ, yet diverse in terms of its reach, scope, and ultimate ingathering of people from every tribe and tongue. We who are a diverse people have Gospel unity. We are "one."[25]

Fourth Truth: The Church Is Made One Family as the Gospel Spreads

As the New Testament narrative unfolds following the cross, it seems proper to conclude that ethnicity is a vehicle by which God communicates in visible form the uniqueness and brilliance of the Gospel. His people have unity in diversity. Their unity does not compromise or foreclose diversity; their unity is a unity of many tribes, many peoples, and

---

[25] Hoehner notes that this word "one" is repeated in verses 14, 15, 16, and 18 of Ephesians 2. Harold W. Hoehner, "Ephesians," 626.

many groups joining together in worship of David's true successor and Abraham's true heir.

We can go further here. To be sure, the restored people of God is a group made up of Jews and Gentiles. This righteous remnant is populated by those of very different backgrounds, very different cultures, very different languages, and very different appearances. This collective is marked by tremendous diversity on the outside. But this group is essentially one on the inside, since each member of this community is born again and indwelt by the Holy Spirit of God (1 Corinthians 3:16).[26] These are people of Holy Spirit stock, a breed set apart, a clan separated from the power and control of sin.

This newfound unity is tested, however. In the Book of Acts, the Church's exploding in growth runs up against an ethnic dispute. Acts 6 tells the story:

> Now in these days when the disciples were increasing in number, a complaint by the Hellenists arose against the Hebrews because their widows were being neglected in the daily distribution. And the twelve summoned the full number of the disciples and said, "It is not right that we should give up preaching the word of God to serve tables. Therefore, brothers, pick out from among you seven men of good repute, full of the Spirit and of wisdom, whom we will appoint to this duty. But we will devote ourselves to prayer and to the ministry of the word." And what they said pleased the whole gathering, and they chose Stephen, a man full of faith and of the Holy Spirit, and Philip, and Prochorus, and Nicanor, and Timon, and Parmenas, and Nicolaus, a proselyte of Antioch. These they set before the apostles, and they prayed and laid their hands on them.

---

[26]   Paul Barnett, *1 Corinthians: Holiness and Hope of a Rescued People, Focus on the Bible* (Fearn, Scotland: Christian Focus, 2011), 57.

> And the word of God continued to increase, and the
> number of the disciples multiplied greatly in Jerusalem, and
> a great many of the priests became obedient to the faith.
> (Acts 6:1–7)

This is a noteworthy passage in the New Testament, for it shows us that the early Church was not immune to tension along ethnic lines. Though this passage does not go on to give us information about the later engagement of the Hellenists and the Hebrews in the context of the Church, it is clear that familiar divisions came to the surface in Jerusalem. The Greek Christians felt unfairly treated by the Jewish Christians. Wrongs that one ethnic group said were being committed by another threatened to upset the unity of the body of Christ. So the apostles took action. They appointed deacons, seven godly men to serve the body. (Several of the deacons were Hellenistic, showing that the apostles sought an equitable solution.)

This action did the trick. There were no reparations involved. There were no struggle sessions alleging fundamental ethnic guilt on either side. There was no further treatment of the issue. It was assumed by the early Church that the situation had been handled, and indeed the blessing of God came down from Heaven as a result. The Word "increased," the disciples "multiplied," and numerous "priests" came to faith in Christ (verse 7). The contrast between this handling of conflict and many twenty-first-century measures could not be starker. The Church had a problem to address; the leaders addressed it, and the body moved on.

There is valuable material here for a Church threatened by worldly division in our time. We too may well confront real problems in our congregations and institutions. Some of these problems may run along ethnic or personal lines. Instead of going nuclear, instead of embracing worldly resentment and grievance culture, instead of pursuing secular sociological means to address our challenges, we should go to texts like this. Our elders and statesmen should seek just and swift answers for what troubles the body. Neither side should demonize the other. Instead, the body should embrace a godly response and then move on in order to keep pushing back the forces of darkness together.

This is not merely because in church "we all just get along." This is because we are truly *one body* in Christ. We are united to Christ, and as a result, we have real spiritual union with one another. This union is far deeper than any worldly affinity or connection, meaningful as those can be. Our birth family matters, our ethnicity is a part of us, and our background is the providentially written story that we inhabit. Faith in Christ does not mean disowning any of these factors that shape us and help to form who we are. But our union with Christ—and thus our union with all Christ's people—is stronger than anything in this world. It is *spiritual* unity. It comes from Heaven, it defies the devil, and it is more powerful than hate. Spiritual union is ultimate. It is defining. It doesn't try to bring us together; it decisively makes Christians a family in objective terms. As stated previously, this isn't because we *feel* this way. It is because of God's action. We may not always get along well as a household, but we are one regardless.

This is what the church in Jerusalem had to learn. Becoming a Christian was not a temporary decision. It was a lifetime reality. It meant that people who had little in common in terms of their background now had everything in common in terms of Christ. It was just this sort of church that the world needed to see. The New Covenant was realized. The blood of Christ was effectual. There was no people like the people of God, a body unified not by shared affinity for anything worldly, but only for the crucified and resurrected Messiah.

This family is *still* just what the world needs to see. Humanity is naturally divided and tribal, but by the Gospel of grace, men and women from every background become the very Bride of Christ. We do this not by engineering "diversity" and "inclusion" through man-centered formulas, but simply by evangelizing and discipling everyone we can, everyone who will listen, and everyone who will come as the Spirit moves to hear the Word preached and the Gospel proclaimed.

Praise God, this is what many of us *have* seen. I do not set myself up as the foremost human witness of God-given diversity. However, in my brief time on this earth, I have seen God's Gospel bring people together in the Church. I've shared membership with people who have nothing in common with me in terms of background. I've watched as marriages across skin color are forged out of common love for Christ. I've met people from all across the world in the context of the local church and learned much about cultures distinct from my own. I know of many couples who adopted children out of desperate circumstances and have done so because God gave them love for fellow image-bearers—not from any evil motive. My experience is not uncommon; it is not unique. It is what God has been doing for a long time in too many local churches to count. Wokeness tells us all this cannot happen or should not happen or will not happen; but what my limited testimony shows is that such unitive work *is happening*. In fact, no one can stop it from happening, much as the devil tries to do so.

The Gospel unites people. This sounds simple, at least compared to complex secular theories, yet it is true, gloriously true. It is a heavenly reality, the realm above reaching down to renew the realm below. Truly, this unity in the Gospel is not from man. It is from God. And it is no small or mean thing. This Gospel unity is powerful. Churches united around Christ do not easily crumble. They are the centers of the "increase" or spread of the Word (Acts 6:7), now just as in days long past. These effects cannot be controlled and marshaled by human cunning; they unfold as the Bible is preached, believed, and declared in all the world. Try as a sinful order might, it cannot stop the growth of the Church and the realization of true unity in Jesus.

Fifth Truth: The Nations Praise the King in Eternity

The book of Revelation shows that God does indeed fulfill all His promises to build His Church. Indeed, the Bible ends with one gathered and reconstituted holy people—and one united song of praise. In the heavenly places, the four living creatures and the twenty-four elders bow before Christ the Lamb. They lift their voices in worship of the crucified, resurrected, and reigning Messiah:

You are worthy to take the scroll and to open its seals, because
you were slaughtered, and you purchased people for God by
your blood from every tribe and language and people and
nation. You made them a kingdom and priests to our God,
and they will reign on the earth. (Revelation 5:9–10)

The world is full of people from every φυλή (tribe) and γλῶσσα
(tongue) and λαός (people) and ἔθνος (nation). The Father's ultimate
desire is for a redeemed people from across the earth, purchased for God
by Christ's blood, to join Him in the new Heaven and new Earth and
reign forever with Him. This redeemed people are not devoid of a past
or a background. They are from distinct cultures, they speak distinct
languages, they hail from a certain tribe, and they come from different
nations.[27] John's use of these terms shows us that there is such a thing as
ethnicity—belonging to a group that has a unique culture, language,
heritage, and certain practices. "Race" is not a biblical category, as if
there are distinct species of humanity based on differing skin pigmentation, but ethnicity is. Ethnicity, though not of ultimate importance,
reveals (as we have expressed already) how diversity owes to God and
glorifies God in glorious fashion. The Church is unity in diversity—one
family from many peoples.

We glimpse the distinctive beauty of ethnicity in a second text in
Revelation 21, as the people of God stream into the New Jerusalem and
the kings bring their treasure with them. As with the previous passage,
this text is dripping with glory, so we quote it at length:

And I saw no temple in the city, for its temple is the Lord God
the Almighty and the Lamb. And the city has no need of sun
or moon to shine on it, for the glory of God gives it light, and

---

27   Robert Mounce notes that the same four terms "are used (but always in a different order) in 5:9; 7:9; 11:9; 13:7; and 14:6." Robert Mounce, *The Book of Revelation*, revised edition, New International Commentary on the New Testament (Grand
Rapids, Michigan; Cambridge, United Kingdom: Eerdmans, 1997), 136.

its lamp is the Lamb. By its light will the nations walk, and the kings of the earth will bring their glory into it, and its gates will never be shut by day—and there will be no night there. They will bring into it the glory and the honor of the nations. But nothing unclean will ever enter it, nor anyone who does what is detestable or false, but only those who are written in the Lamb's book of life. (Revelation 21:22–27)

There is much to savor here. For our purposes, we note that the "kings of the earth" do not only bring themselves, but carry "the glory and the honor of the nations" with them (24, 26). What this specific glory and honor is we do not know. We do not need to know, exactly, because the text shows us regardless that there is such a thing in God's counsel as "national glory and honor." We read this rightly, I believe, as the distinctive contributions made by different redeemed peoples across the globe. Ethnicities have their own food, their own material products, their own artistic works, their own styles, and their own culture more generally. As embraced by Christians and with right recognition of biblical morality, these are not problematic realities. Ethnic or communal uniqueness is not erased as people trust in Christ. Instead, God's Church celebrates the diversity God's creative mind has yielded in the world of men.

In no sense do we rejoice in what is "unclean," now or in eternity to come. This passage is not taking a morally neutral approach to global culture; it is not teaching an "anything goes" approach to the same. Neither unclean artifacts (whatever they are) nor unclean persons can enter God's eternal rest (verse 27). Only what is righteous can. These different affirmations thus reveal that earthly culture coming from redeemed peoples is brought to honor God and is not rejected. In a broader sense, becoming a Christian need not mean losing all trace of one's manhood, womanhood, background, or heritage. It means, by contrast, that God is glorified in the saving of sinners from all over the world. He forms a people from them, and they do not need to pretend they are an amorphous, gender-neutral, culturally undefined blob of believers, but image-bearers showing the signs of God's beautiful making who have been gathered into one gloriously diverse family.

Passages like this teach us to avoid extremes. We should not obliterate our ethnic background; nor should we relativize it and make it untouchable to the Gospel. Instead, we should embrace a richly textured and appropriately balanced vision of human distinctiveness. It is not bad to hail from somewhere (we all do), appreciate our given background, and retain markers of that heritage as a born-again man or woman. But we cannot make the consequential mistake of placing earthly citizenship or membership of any country or people above our heavenly citizenship and membership. Our secular age urges us to do this, telling us our sex, our skin color, our language, our economic status, our educational pedigree, our looks, and many other factors matter most about us. While these characteristics are a part of our story, they are not and must never be ultimate in our Christian identity.

To reiterate what we have stated already: There is no such thing as "race" in the modern sense. There are not different forms of humanity constituted by different skin colors. At the same time, our ethnic background is not nothing—to God or to us. It is part of God's sovereign providential rule of our lives. Yet as we note this, we must not fail to see that our ultimate identity is not in belonging to a tribe or people in natural terms. We must remember that Jesus takes embittered and hostile ethnic groups and makes them one.[28] Our ultimate identity is only and always in Christ. William Hendriksen beautifully reminds us:

> The reason why there is so much strife in this world, between individuals, families, social or political groups, whether small or large, is that the contending parties, through the fault of either or both, have not found each other at Calvary. Only

---

[28] Strachan, *Reenchanting Humanity*, 242–43.

then, when sinners have been reconciled to God through the cross, will they be truly reconciled to each other.[29]

How true this is. When sinners trust Christ, they find peace with God. When sinners find peace with God, they find peace with all who love God. Neither hostility nor division remains in the biblical mind following regeneration and conversion. "Reconciliation" across all backgrounds is not a possibility; as we have seen, it is a reality. When you meet a Christian, you are meeting someone whom you are objectively—by God's own action—united to, much as we may try to frustrate such bedrock truth. We are not responsible for accomplishing such work; we are responsible for living out of the overflow of this glorious salvific accomplishment. Reconciliation is not on our shoulders; it is the work of God, and though it sounds too good to be true, it is *done*.

Sadly, in this world we can resist the truthfulness of this divine deed. We all can. We can let worldly boundary markers seem to diminish the oneness of the body of Christ. We can choose to live in strife, to quote Hendriksen. Yet this does not do anything to lessen the power of God's work. We may resist it, but what God has done, no man can undo. No one can overcome it, no one can edit it, and no one can hold back the plans of God from coming to perfect fruition in God's own timing. This is what Revelation 5 communicates to us. It reminds us where we are headed. Soon the nations will *not* rage. Soon our cities will *not* bleed. Soon our churches will *not* suffer attack and division. Soon the people of Christ will gather. They will do what they never have done previously on such a massive scale: they will come together as in Revelation 5 to praise Christ. He is worthy of their worship "precisely because he was slain."[30]

So we conclude, in joy and in hope: For the Church, the scattering has ended. God is gathering His people to Himself. Sin's power has been

---

[29] William Hendriksen, *New Testament Commentary: Exposition of Ephesians* (Grand Rapids, Michigan: Baker, 1967), 136.
[30] Mounce, *Book of Revelation*, 135.

broken by the cross of Christ, the most powerful event in history. The work of salvific recreation is more powerful even than the original creation, majestic as that was. God is making a way out of this depraved world. His people have suffered many things and committed many sins. They have walked, and are even now walking, through a fallen order that hates God, denies human image-bearing, ignores divine grace, focuses its attention on man-made justice and man-driven eschatology, pays no mind to the cross as the power of God to cleanse and unify His people, and ultimately shakes its fist at God all the way unto destruction.

But sin does not have the last word in this story. It may have had the last word in human interactions in this divided and depraved place. But it has no such privilege in the Kingdom of God. The Father has sent His Son. The Son has made atonement for sin. The Spirit has applied the blood to the Church and gathered the family of God. The work is finished. No burden or condemnation remains for Jesus's Bride. The peoples of Earth separated so long ago find unity in the Gospel. Babel is undone.

We do not have to yearn for our God to pay attention to us. We have a heavenly Father, and soon and very soon, the children of God will be home.

DISCUSSION QUESTIONS

1. What were some of the barriers between Jews and Gentiles in the first century AD?
2. How did Jesus unite Jews and Gentiles?
3. In Ephesians 2:11–22, what are some metaphors that Paul uses for the Church? What do these metaphors tell us about life together in the local church?
4. What kind of vision for human history does Revelation 5:9–10 display when contrasted with CRT's vision?

CHAPTER 7

Hard Questions on American History and Other Hot Topics

My pains are great; but, blessed be God, they are not eternal.

—Lemuel Haynes

In this final chapter, we will consider some common questions that come in response to the material presented in this book. In some cases, we have touched on these matters in earlier chapters. I raise them again here because it is right and good to ask questions about difficult matters. Our goal in the discussion over wokeness, after all, is never to shut conversation down. It is always to stimulate pursuit of the truth. Toward that end, we turn now to several reasonable queries and to my relatively brief responses to them.

Does the Bible Endorse American Race-Based Slavery?

No, the Bible does not endorse American slavery. The Bible prohibits "man-stealing" in the most straightforward terms (1 Timothy 1:10), and American race-based chattel slavery was founded in and dependent on man-stealing.[1] In various African nations, slave traders stole families,

---

[1] The uniqueness of American slavery was its genesis in race-based man-stealing. "Chattel" slavery, though, which is defined as the ownership of a human being as property by a master who solely determines the slave's rights (or lack thereof), is not unique to the American institution; this characteristic has been an integral part of

brought them to market, and sold them to merchants trafficking in human beings. The people in bondage were then taken to America, where they were bought in public auctions and sold as human goods. The Bible gives no encouragement to the iniquitous agents, buyers, and sellers of this evil institution. No slaveowner working in this system could open his Bible, read passages on slavery, and think that he had gotten his slaves in a righteous and fair way. He had not.

To understand in greater depth why we must handle Scripture thoughtfully on slavery, we must make clear that the Bible—including the New Testament—does not prohibit it. We might expect God's Word to condemn it without nuance, but it does not do so. In both the Old and New Testaments, slavery is presented with depth and subtlety.[2]

Considering first the Old Testament, slaves were generally household laborers. Though in a state of bondage, they were not subhuman, but were protected according to God's law, particularly from life-threatening acts (Exodus 21:20). From ancient times, it was wrong for God's people to steal fellow human beings and enslave them (Exodus 21:26). There were numerous opportunities for slaves to find freedom: purchase, sabbatical year law, the Year of Jubilee, or when their master died. Though slaves' experiences varied, they "were considered part of the owner's family" and "had the right to the sabbath rest and to participate in the

---

systems of slavery for much of human history. Chattel slavery existed in numerous nations in the Ancient Near East, in ancient Athens, and in ancient Rome. Paul Copan, *Is God a Moral Monster? Making Sense of the Old Testament God* (Grand Rapids, Michigan: Baker Books, 2011), 132–34. See also N. R. E. Fisher, *Slavery in Classical Greece*, reprint edition (London: Bristol Classical Press, 1998), 5–6; and Sandra R. Joshel, *Slavery in the Roman World* (New York: Cambridge University Press, 2013), 7–8, 80–81.

[2]   John Murray makes an interesting observation: "Though the Scripture exercises an eloquent reserve in refraining from the proscription of the institution [of slavery], and though it does not lay down principles which evince its intrinsic wrong, nevertheless the Scripture does encourage and require the promotion of those conditions which make slavery unnecessary." John Murray, *Principles of Conduct: Aspects of Biblical Ethics* (Grand Rapids, Michigan: Eerdmans, 1957), 100.

religious feasts.".³ Though it is a strange judgment in our time, wives and slave-concubines were in many cases indistinguishable.

Israelite slavery was, relatively, a notably humane institution. The New Testament went further, framing slave and master relationships in a Gospel light. Masters and slaves alike had responsibilities to one another. Masters had to treat slaves with full human dignity and do good to them (Ephesians 6:5–9); they could not threaten their slaves and were called by God to treat them "justly and fairly" (Colossians 4:1). Slaves were to obey their masters, working hard for them, honoring God as they honored their masters (Colossians 3:22–25). Serving one's vocational authority reflected the way the believer served one's metaphysical authority (Ephesians 6:9; Colossians 3:24).⁴

In these texts we see that the day-to-day experience of slavery countenanced by the New Testament was akin to the duty of Christian labor more broadly. Slaves were to be treated much like non-slave workers of the Greco-Roman world, few of whom knew a fraction of the "rights" that workers claim today. Masters could not treat their slaves as human cattle; they could not do with their slaves whatever they wanted. Slaves were not subhuman or inferior to their masters in any fundamental way. Instead, masters were to do good to those who labored under them and not create a climate of fear and easy retribution for disappointed expectations.⁵ The end picture of slavery as shaped by apostolic decree is one remarkably similar to broader biblical teaching on vocation. Those in

---

³   Walter A. Elwell, ed., *Evangelical Dictionary of Theology*, 2nd edition, Baker Reference Library (Grand Rapids, Michigan: Baker Academic, 2001), s.v. "Slavery," by W. N. Kerr.

⁴   For helpful exegesis of Ephesians 6:5–9, see Frank Thielman, *Ephesians*, Baker Exegetical Commentary on the New Testament (Grand Rapids, Michigan: Baker Academic, 2010), 404–10; for Colossians 3:22–4:1, see Douglas J. Moo, *The Letters to the Colossians and to Philemon*, Pillar New Testament Commentary (Grand Rapids, Michigan: Eerdmans, 2008), 308–17.

⁵   Copan sums up the Apostle Paul's position on slavery as follows: "(1) he repudiated slave trading; (2) he affirmed the full human dignity and equal spiritual status of slaves; and (3) he encouraged slaves to acquire their freedom whenever possible (1 Corinthians 7:20–22)." Paul Copan, *Is God a Moral Monster?* (Grand Rapids, Michigan: Baker Books, 2011), 152.

authority should be humane, knowing they were subject to God; those under authority should work hard and well, knowing they ultimately were serving not man but God.

All this is quite distinct from the institution of slavery as commonly practiced in America. Not all American slaveowners were the same. Some treated their slaves humanely and even sought to win them to Christ. But the American slave system as a whole differed in several important ways from the biblical portrait sketched above. First, American slavery was based in man-stealing, showing its evil roots. Second, American slavery was race-based or race-driven, grounded for many in the perceived inherent "inferiority" of Africans. Third, American slavery was often conducted outside the bounds of biblical morality, as masters treated their slaves in subhuman ways. Fourth, slaves in many cases could not buy or work their way out of slavery but were bound to their condition indefinitely (against the Old Testament code, even).[6]

Ancient slaves generally entered their state as a result of defeat in war. The slavery discussed in both the Old and New Testament proceeds from this reality. Whole populations entered slavery not because of perceived anthropological inferiority (as the cause), but because of civilizational eclipse. Nor were slaves always considered below the line of ordinary personhood. Ancient slaves could rise to positions of immense power, could make serious money, and in a good number of cases found themselves better off than freedmen. None of this means that ancient slavery was a picnic, for it surely was not. But it does color our understanding of slavery and show us the uniquely dark nature of American slavery as practiced by many.

For this reason, we conclude that American race-based chattel slavery differs considerably from the institution Scripture engages. Ancient slavery was in several ways different from American race-based slavery, and both the Old and New Testaments humanized the institution in important ways. In the final analysis, the New Testament in no

---

[6]   For many of these observations, see Copan, *Is God a Moral Monster?*, 124–34.

way mandates slavery, nor does it prohibit it absolutely.[7] Instead, it is best to think of the New Testament (building on the Old) as reshaping slavery in a distinctly God-centered way. The Old Covenant law, so often unfairly maligned, made considerable provision for the release and liberation of slaves, a theme that recurs throughout the Old Testament, coming to a crescendo during the exodus. The New Covenant law does not outlaw slavery, but in enhancing the moral dimensions of acceptable slave-owning brings the theme of the salvific exodus of God's people to its peak. In Christ, we are free, gloriously free. Yet the one freed from slavery to sin is the same one who becomes a *doulos Christou*—a slave of Christ.[8]

The New Testament, then, gives cold comfort to defenders of racist American slavery. But it leaves us in a place that perhaps surprises us regarding slavery as a whole. The Scripture does not end up condemning *any* form of slavery, but firstly reshapes our conception of slavery along Christian lines and secondly teaches every believer that our discipleship to Christ is not the discipleship of an equal to an equal, but that of a subject under bondage—the glad bondage of the Church to its gracious Lord and Master. Christ, the true master, is no cruel and tyrannical overlord, but is the King who rules His subjects with grace and truth, never failing to minister tender mercy to His blood-bought people.

Is It True That Christian Churches Were All Pro-Slavery in Past Days?

No, this is not true. As is often the case, there is more to the story than an easy one-sided narrative. There are at least two significant streams within nineteenth-century American Christianity: a pro-slavery

---

[7] Murray Harris notes: "Since the New Testament draws both positive and negative images from slavery, we conclude that it neither endorses slavery (given the negative imagery) nor rejects slavery (given the positive imagery)." Murray J. Harris, *Slave of Christ: A New Testament Metaphor for Total Devotion to Christ*, New Studies in Biblical Theology, vol. 8 (Downers Grove, Illinois: InterVarsity Press, 2001), 53.

[8] Ibid., 139–56.

wing and an anti-slavery wing. Some accounts tell the story of American church history as if only one side existed, but this is not the case. Both groups vied for influence and clashed repeatedly and unpredictably in the nineteenth century, as the evils of slavery came to light in the young nation and across the Atlantic in England.

The contingent that we hear much about today from woke voices is the pro-slavery faction.[9] We make no effort here to whitewash the real failings of pro-slavery evangelicals in days past. To be sure, some believed earnestly that Scripture supported their views, and some Christians who practiced race-based slavery did so believing that they should treat their slaves humanely and even evangelize them. It is necessary to recognize that slaveholders were not monolithic in their practice, and that there was a clear spectrum of action among professing evangelicals that ranged from more humane to decidedly less humane. On the "more humane" side, some treated their slaves in terms consonant with the description of New Testament slavery given above.

But all too many Christians defended race-based slavery and the racist views it stood upon. They failed to recognize that American race-based slavery was distinct from the institution engaged and reshaped by the Old and New Testaments, and they enabled the subhuman treatment of slaves. They failed to condemn the evil practice American slavery was founded in (man-stealing), and they failed to speak up for the full personhood and dignity of slaves once they came to America. In this way we see that a good number of churches and Christians defended and promoted an institution that they should have opposed and opposed to the full. American slavery did not occur without the support of a solid portion of American churches. In this we see that many Christians failed to challenge a wicked institution based in unbiblical ideology. The Church all too often followed the world, and

---

[9]   The pro-slavery side included prominent Presbyterian theologians Robert Lewis Dabney and James Henley Thornwell. There was considerable tension in the Presbyterian movement over slavery; the Old School and New School stood apart on this issue in the nineteenth century, with long-ranging consequences.

in doing so exchanged an enchanted vision of the human person as a God-made image-bearer for a secular vision that rendered slaves subhuman due to the color of their skin.

Praise God, this is not the full story, however. In both the eighteenth and especially the nineteenth centuries, protest arose against slavery and the slave trade among a wide range of professing Christians. Here we see the second major stream of American Christian response to this evil institution: the anti-slavery wing. We must recall what great odds this side faced. A sizeable but not monolithic percentage of the nation was pro-slavery. Being pro-slavery meant following the spirit of the age. It was generally assumed by many that slavery was justified due to the fundamental inequality of the "races."[10] To go against this consensus that reached across societal and cultural lines was a fearsome thing indeed. It is always a fearsome thing to stand against the world, against the devil's own lies, and against evil.

But this is what a good number of Christians did, both in America and Great Britain. The greatest of the champions in the West was William Wilberforce. Wilberforce represents the evangelical abolitionist wing at its peak. Though the fight against slavery and the slave trade was a losing issue politically in many respects, Wilberforce was driven by his biblical convictions to campaign for abolition and cessation of the dreadful institution, a campaign he fought for decades.[11] In America, a loose coalition of Christian groups rallied against slavery and the slave trade. All the way back in the early 1700s, Puritan New England witnessed the publication of *The Selling of Joseph*, an ardently anti-slavery tract by

---

[10] Dabney, for example, repeatedly deemed the "black" race to be "morally inferior" and those of white ethnicity to be the "superior grade" and the "nobler race." Robert Lewis Dabney, *A Defence of Virginia (and through Her, of the South) in Recent and Pending Contests against the Sectional Party* (New York: E. J. Hale & Son, 1867), 54, 260, 281.

[11] For a popular biography of William Wilberforce, see Eric Metaxas, *Amazing Grace: William Wilberforce and the Heroic Campaign to End Slavery* (New York: HarperOne, 2007). For a more academic treatment, see William Hague, *William Wilberforce: The Life of the Great Anti-Slave Trade Campaigner* (London: HarperPress, 2007).

Samuel Sewall.[12] Some decades later, Jonathan Edwards Jr. published abolitionist material, and numerous "New Divinity" clergymen agreed with his stance.[13] In the nineteenth century, others joined the cause: Quakers, Moravians, and Pietists all spoke against slavery and the slave trade. William Lloyd Garrison caused a stir with his quest for "immediate abolition," with figures like Lyman Beecher (an evangelical leader) supporting this drive.[14]

The story of the two sides in Christian circles deserves further telling and exploration. This book is not a history of American Christianity, nor of the complex dynamics of racism in the American past. With these brief comments offered, for our purposes it must suffice to say that the historic narrative about Christians and slavery is neither triumphalist nor desolate. Too many otherwise sound pastors and theologians stood for the wrong side of this matter. Others fare better in the counsel of history.

We are admonished by this sobering complexity to recognize that we are all tempted, as past Christians were, to follow the culture in our thinking. A significant portion of America was pro-slavery, or at least not set against it. Too many evangelicals drank this cultural water. Thankfully, though, others did not, and a past witness unto liberty and human dignity persists in the Church.

This analysis leaves us freshly aware that America has real sin in its past and that we must avoid any conception of this country that ignores this reality. There is no perfect country, and surely the material we have introduced here shows that. But we must take care as well on this count.

---

[12] Samuel Sewall, *The Selling of Joseph: A Memorial* (Amherst, Massachusetts: University of Massachusetts Press, 1969).

[13] Jonathan Edwards Jr., "The Injustice and Impolicy of the Slave Trade, and of the Slavery of the Africans," in *Early American Abolitionists: A Collection of Anti-Slavery Writings, 1760–1820*, ed. James G. Basker (New York: Gilder Lehrman Institute of American History, 2005), 135–71.

[14] Beecher was the father of the famed author of *Uncle Tom's Cabin*, Harriet Beecher Stowe. For a penetrating analysis of how Beecher gradually came to his abolitionist position, see J. Earl Thompson Jr., "Lyman Beecher's Long Road to Conservative Abolitionism," *Church History* 42, vol. 1 (1973): 89–109.

We should not *hate* America or the West after dealing with these hard historical truths. We should see instead that this country overcame slavery, albeit after a long and terrible war, with much violence and pain and evil following after it. Racism was no easy thing to oppose and face down, a point we see enforced in postbellum and twentieth-century history, with the rise of Jim Crow laws, lynching, segregation, and other evils. But in the common grace of God, this nation did after much travail and much hardship rid itself of numerous racist policies and practices.[15] It is not that racism went away, nor that every effect of racism was washed out in the 1960s as the Civil Rights Movement won numerous victories. But America did go through real and shaking change in this time, and this country made real gains as segregation, Jim Crow laws, and other racist policies were overturned and overcome.

The ideology that fueled such wickedness eventually lost traction in regions of America where it predominated. People came together across common boundaries to stand against evil and stand for justice. Again, in God's common grace, these costly efforts bore fruit. The America of today is not the America of 1800, or 1880, or 1960. Racism is not gone, not by a long shot, but it has been addressed in our society at the level of law, policy, and the public square in many respects. It is no longer tenable to be a traditional racist in America.[16] Policies or practices that produce racism draw censure and legal attention, as is only right. We give thanks to God for these developments, even as we remember that we must always remain vigilant to fight racism.

All the foregoing reminds us just how expensive and punitive it is to give evil a foothold. Because racism festered and took root in America, many had to pay a heavy price to fight it. This included a good number

---

[15] Thomas Sowell, *Black Rednecks and White Liberals* (New York: Encounter Books, 2005), 50.

[16] The very fact that ongoing expressions of "white guilt" have become all the rage in our present day demonstrates that promoting a white racist agenda in public policy is unacceptable. Shelby Steele, *White Guilt: How Blacks and Whites Together Destroyed the Promise of the Civil Rights Era* (New York: HarperCollins, 2006), 27.

of Christians, whether slave or free. They had to think scripturally about a matter that had already been settled according to the spirit of the age. Their witness challenges us today to know the difference between biblical thinking and cultural thinking and to side with those who stand for truth in our own time. Many who spoke against slavery and the slave trade—and many more who suffered unduly as slaves—were treated shamefully and unfairly, but the judgment of wisdom vindicates them on this count.

Beyond our own assessment of past eras, there will be a much greater judgment, and by God's grace a much greater vindication, on the last day. All that is now buried in the earth of the past will come to light; all the wickedness that no one saw will be seen and weighed; all the righteousness that drew persecution and suffering will be rewarded. Much as we strive for justice now, much as justice was secured at the cross of Christ, we know that it is the last day that brings justice to complete resolution. The Christian does not live so as to be found on the right side of history as defined by men. The Christian lives so as to be found on the right side of God when He calls all to account before the Great White Throne.

If We Shouldn't Hate America, How Should We Think about Racists?

I have mentioned this in numerous places but need to treat it briefly. I do not encourage people to hate America for many reasons. Yet I would be remiss not to connect ungodliness with racism. We hear little on such matters today, but this is an important area to consider. The media and the academy put Christians continually on the back foot. Over and over again, they attack the Church for its past failings. As I have done here in no uncertain terms, we should not dodge such hard conversations. We should handle them well, think soberly about our tradition's failings, acknowledge those failings with humility, and learn from them. Christians, after all, are not a people engaged in PR, fundamentally. We are not trying to spin any challenge to our movement. We know that past

Christians all stumbled in many ways, as we do (James 3:2). Our weakness is actually part of the strength of the Christian faith. *We* are not the point. We are not sinless, and we are not the Savior. Like every sinner, we are the ones who need the Savior—and need Him desperately.

There is another point we must make alongside the Gospel point. The history of elite Western intellectuals is replete with racism, ethnocentrism, eugenicism, and partiality of every kind. This is not unique to the West; every group of people in human history is chock-full of sin, and thus manifests partiality in all sorts of ways. Even as the Western tradition has much good in it and produced many fierce opponents of actual white supremacy and the mechanisms that supported it, it also includes many prominent leaders who denied the presence of the *imago Dei* in all people. It was not at all only evangelicals who fell prey to this. Some evangelicals did, and some did not.

In the non-Christian realm, the list of offenders, and influential culture-shapers at that, is not short. We think of Charles Darwin, whose theory of evolution included the cornerstone idea that white European society was humanity at its peak. What was the original title of Darwin's famous work? It was *On the Origin of Species by Means of Natural Selection, or the Preservation of Favoured Races in the Struggle for Life* (the book debuted in 1871). This original proposal is not an accident; it is a tell. It reveals that Darwin was not only concerned with his conception of macro-evolution. Not in the least: he had a social goal in mind.[17]

Darwin's defenders today often try to distance him from "social Darwinism," the view that the survival of the fittest not only can be applied to society but should be applied to it. No such move can be made, however. Surveying his material, two noted biographers of Darwin conclude as follows on this point: "But his notebooks make plain that competition, free trade, imperialism, racial extermination, and sexual

---

[17]   To read more, see Ken Ham and A. Charles Ware, *Darwin's Plantation: Evolution's Racist Roots* (Green Forest, Arkansas: Master, 2007); see also Ken Ham and A. Charles Ware, *One Race, One Blood: The Biblical Answer to Racism* (Green Forest, Arkansas: Master, 2019).

inequality were written into the equation from the start—'Darwinism' was always intended to explain human society."[18] This was progress in the common Darwinian outlook. Stephen Jay Gould, a Harvard professor and the preeminent secular scientist some decades ago, made this surprising admission along similar lines: "Biological arguments for racism may have been common before 1859 but they increased by orders of magnitude following the acceptance of evolutionary theory."[19]

This perspective both influenced and reinforced common secular biases in Darwin's day. It had a monumental effect on Western thought and policy in the next several decades. Seeing "white" Europeans as more civilized than other "races," entrepreneurs brought "exotic" people to polite society, hosting them in human zoos. William McGee, one-time president of the Association for the Advancement of Science, took thousands of indigenous people from their homes and toured the world with them. Supposedly, these people represented part of the "bridge" species between ape and human, the view at the burning center of evolutionary thought.

The links here are well-established but need stating again: such ideas had consequences, tragic and wide-ranging consequences. Hitler and the Nazis believed in the superiority of their Aryan "race" and sent millions of people to their deaths from such a stance. In America, Margaret Sanger, the founder of Planned Parenthood, viewed "black" children as "weeds." Abortion was not a "choice" one could contemplate while reading a pastel-colored pamphlet in a waiting room; abortion for Sanger was a moral imperative, a way to cleanse America of its basest elements. In a less physically destructive way, elite Western institutions that had long since lost their Christian moorings worked hard to keep the student body Anglo-Saxon "white," barring many

[18] Michael Flannery, "Distancing Darwin from Racism Is a Fool's Errand," Evolution News, November 23, 2020, https://evolutionnews.org/2020/11/distancing-darwin-from-racism-is-a-fools-errand. See Adrian Desmond and James Moore, Darwin: The Life of a Tormented Evolutionist (New York: W. W. Norton, 1994).

[19] Stephen Jay Gould, Ontogeny and Phylogeny (Cambridge, Massachusetts: Belknap, 1977), 127.

people groups from entry. This helped mold the American upper class, which to this day even in "progressive" and "leftist" circles is one of the least integrated areas of American life.

What is the point in all this? It is not, as has been made clear, to argue that only one group has fallen prey to the unbiblical and thoroughly evil sin of partiality along "racial" or ethnic lines. That is not the case. But it is to note that when Christians fell prey to "racism," they were only thinking in a worldly way, not a scriptural way. They were being *cultural*, not *theological*. They were letting the world and its ideologies influence them, not God. Western culture, but also every culture, may easily be influenced by partiality. This does not render every person in such a context as personally guilty of a given culture's sins; as we have noted earlier in the book, if this were so, then Christ would have been guilty for his own context's failings. However, it does tell us that "racism" is a Satanic ideology, not a cultural one.

Our survey is only a very brief one, but a broader overview of non-Christian partiality in America (and most anywhere) would tell this tragic story at length. "Racism" is not Christian; it is demonic. Hence why Christians must stay vigilant not only about past forms of partiality, but new forms of it, for like itself, partiality does not stay static, but morphs and changes over time as the devil forges new strategies for sending sinners to hell and dividing Christ's blood-bought people.

What about Racism Today? If It's Still a Present Threat, Isn't It Fair to Conclude That It Really Is Everywhere, as Wokeness Argues?

Racism has not vanished. It is not possible to end racism in human terms; only Christ will end the reign of sin in the age to come. A society that opposes racism is achievable; a society that ends all racism is a utopian fiction. Racism is one form of human partiality, a sinful condition of a fallen heart. Until Christ makes the earth right, people of every background will suffer from partiality, and some will experience real prejudice for the color of their skin and the heritage of their family.

We have to be realistic about the prevalence of sin in a fallen world. Christianity is not a faith that promises that the world will be made right on our terms. Christianity will influence societies, and can even transform them in some instances, but this is not the core message or purpose of Gospel faith. The biblical message of salvation saves sinners, gathers them into local churches, and releases them as salt and light in the world.[20] We give thanks wherever God allows the influence of the Church to have a real effect in a country. On the other hand, when the Church grows through evangelism and discipleship, but a given nation persecutes the Church and limits its public effect, we do not read such an outcome as a failure of the faith. Instead, we remember that Christianity is a religion of the heart, and that God has promised not that our cause will overwhelm the darkness in all places, but that the gates of Hell will not prevail against Christ's blood-bought people.

We need to remember this truth. If we do not, we will be tempted to a paradisical version of Christianity that "immanentizes the eschaton"— in other words, one that reads the end-times remaking of this realm as occurring once and for all time in our age. Much as we yearn for eternity, we must recall that we are not in our final home. Christ has not returned. All is not yet made right.[21] This means for our purposes that, much as we oppose this, people will still experience racism and ethnocentrism. But we must think carefully before we jump to the conclusion that such partiality reveals that our society is "systemically unjust." It could be. But it also could be the case that we are living in a fallen world and experiencing the normal effects of that condition.

---

[20] The words of Murray Harris are instructive on this topic: "Christianity in its essence is concerned with the transformation of character and conduct rather than with the reformation of societal structures. Its primary focus is on the individual ethics within the Christian community rather than on corporate ethics within society at large, on interpersonal relationships rather than on social reformation through institutional change." Harris, *Slave of Christ: A New Testament Metaphor for Total Devotion to Christ* (Downers Grove, Illinois: IVP Academic, 2001), 67–68.

[21] Owen Strachan, *Reenchanting Humanity: A Theology of Mankind* (Fearn, Scotland: Mentor, 2019), 312.

Let me illustrate. If I am mocked for being short, I might react to that unpleasant experience by lamenting that society is stacked against me. I might argue that "tall privilege" exists and that it creates a condition of "systemic injustice" for short people. This could be the case, but it also could be the case that society is not systemically unjust in terms of public policy, law, and societal structures, but that I am experiencing the kind of non-mandated sinful partiality that is found throughout our earthly existence. On the one hand, my claim might seem valid because of repeated mockery over the years for shortness. But on the other, I would likely struggle to find an existing policy, law, or public square initiative that targets short people.

So: Is America "systemically unjust" toward short people? This is a possibility, yes. But it is also quite likely that there is no overarching mechanism that oppresses short people, even though a fair number of short people would, if polled, report that they have experienced mockery and partiality because of their lack of height. In the end, unless clear proof of actual measures to inhibit and harm short people emerges, then we should avoid the claim of "systemic injustice." Similarly, where we find tangible proof of overarching organized prejudice against people of color, we may conclude that sin has systemic form. But where we do not find such proof, we should exercise great care before we assume that the American system in its present-day form is evil and harmful. The people of a society may well express sin even where the public "system" in no way intentionally fosters such wickedness.

The claim of "systemic injustice" and "systemic racism" is a very large claim indeed. It is also often made in a fuzzy and undefined way. For this reason, Voddie Baucham Jr. has noted that

> the Bible may help you with a number of things, but it simply cannot help you even begin to understand systemic racism. That is because "systemic racism" is a moving target.[22]

---

22 Voddie Baucham Jr., *Fault Lines: The Social Justice Movement and Evangelicalism's Looming Catastrophe* (Washington, D.C.: Salem Books, 2021), 129.

As a concept, it sounds sensible based on past American failings to allege that it reigns today. We may be able to point to discrepancies in our public order that seem to back the claim up. But as noted above, we must be careful before concluding that intentional, coordinated partiality is operating at the public level. As we pointed out in past chapters, the existence of differences between communities or ethnic groups does not in itself automate the conclusion of racism. Differences can reveal inequities, including skin-color-based prejudice. But differences can also owe to complex factors that do not neatly reduce to ongoing color-based partiality. We must make room for "complex causality" in our analysis of society, even as we remain vigilant about partiality of a sinful kind.[23]

In Theological Terms, Doesn't the Concept of "Total Depravity" Affirm "Systemic Injustice"?

The section above represents a society-driven response to the concept of "systemic injustice." We need to think more about another dimension of this concept, the theological angle. Many Christians like me affirm that sin has so affected the world that it's fallen, cursed, and that we all sin by nature. We do not glorify God in fundamental terms (though God's design still stands and is still good). Sin reaches into every part of our lives; there is no corner of this world that is vacuum-sealed such that sin cannot enter it.

So far, it sounds like we can affirm what woke voices claim by "systemic racism"—their argument is that if sin is everywhere per total depravity, then racism (one form of sin) is everywhere. When people make this claim, it has a kind of immediate force that sometimes closes conversations down. But it deserves further consideration. We Christians surely know that societies can embrace evil at the macro-level, as covered above. But while always acknowledging such a possibility, and while

---

[23] For ruminations on "multiple causation" and concrete examples of this reality, see Thomas Sowell, *Wealth, Poverty and Politics* (New York: Basic Books, 2016), 392–405.

never making the mistake of thinking a given community or country is sin-free, we must also handle this with care at this point.

Let me illustrate with a reference to ancient Corinth, as mentioned in a footnote in Chapter 3 (I'm expanding here on my remarks there). Ancient Corinth was an evil place by all reports. The city famously "Corinthianized" visitors, inducting them into debauchery, paganism, and idolatrous sexual worship at the temple. This culture clearly exerted an effect upon the Corinthian church, as Paul's two biblical letters to it reveal. In a city of sexual license, the Corinthians were giving in to temptation of various kinds (see 1 Corinthians 5–6). They were without question letting the city influence them.

In one sense, then, the "systemic" nature of Corinth's depravity affected the church. But here is where we need clear boundaries and sharp distinctions. The sexualized culture of Corinth did not *make* any church members sin. They alone were responsible for their sins of thought, desire, word, and action. Yes, they faced great temptation by virtue of living in Corinth, and also because of their own indwelling sin. But Corinth as a city could not force them to disobey God. This was something only individual Corinthian Christians could do. Though they found themselves in a compromised and pagan place, the Corinthian believers were not held guilty because of the worship cult featuring gender-bending temple prostitutes. It is surely true that the presence of such blasphemy would affect the environment in which the Corinthians lived, but that is a different matter altogether than holding the Corinthian church guilty for such evil.

We are not softening the sound doctrine of "total depravity" here. We are instead distinguishing it from a fuzzy and undefined form of systemic sin that wrongly implicates believers in a culture's failings. While always comprehending the ways that a fallen culture puts pressure on us to conform to it—often tremendous pressure—and while being honest about the sinful propensity of our hearts to give in to external and also internal temptation, we must also take great care that we do not indict Christians for the sins of their region. For example, our pro-abortion culture puts great pressure on us all to affirm a pro-death worldview over a pro-life one. But are we Christians guilty for living amidst such a culture? If we live in a city that is flooded with sexual sin, are we ourselves automatically guilty of some form of participation in "systemic" evil? Are our children?

The point here is not to deny that sin can easily influence us and co-opt us. It surely can. But we must choose our steps very precisely here in a theological sense. To put it as plainly as I can: You and I are not automatically guilty of the crimes of our surrounding environment. You and I are held accountable for our engagement of our environment. Our thoughts, desires, words, and actions all are seen by God and all either glorify Him or dishonor Him. But I am not guilty automatically of the sins of my city, state, country, or world. I am guilty for my failure to resist temptation by the power of God's Spirit, whether that temptation is *around me* (and I embrace it) or *within me* in the form of ungodly instinctual thoughts, desires, words, and actions.

The clincher to this argument is Jesus Christ. If it is sinful to live in a context that has serious "structural" sins, then Jesus was sinful. He lived, after all, under the boot of ancient Rome, a pagan empire. Yet Jesus was not sinful at all. He was not only *not sinful*; He was *impeccable*—as the Son of God become man, He could not sin. He lived and moved among all sorts of transgressors, and in fact sought out their company in order to witness to them and win them to faith, but He was in no way complicit in any of their failings. Rome had all sorts of evil components to its societal life, but Christ had no participation in them and accrued no guilt before God for them.

This little exploration reveals a few things, in sum:

1. We should always beware the sins of our context and know that we are all too susceptible to them.
2. We should live alertly, being mindful of both external and internal temptation.

3. We should continually pursue a transformed mind as believers, taking every thought captive to Christ (Romans 12:1–2; 2 Corinthians 10:3–6).

4. We should fight injustice wherever we see it, living as salt and light (Matthew 5:13–16).

5. We should be very careful with claims of "systemic" sin and indictment of individuals in those systems. It is surely possible that "systems" are influencing us, but living in a fallen context is in no way synonymous with participating in "structural" evil.

6. We should, if in ministry, train people to fight their sin at all levels, but we should also make sure that the sin they fight is genuine sin as defined by God's truth, not generic sin as defined by our culture.

Is There a "Black Way of Thinking" and a "White Way of Thinking"?

There may be some overlap between the experiences of people who have similar skin color and background. We can understand why that would be the case, especially in places where there is a strong "majority culture," as we have discussed previously.

But we should be ever wary of classing people according to stereotypes. When I was a boy, American culture expended a great deal of energy to discredit such thinking and behavior. Today, however, we have witnessed the revenge of the stereotype. We learn from many that the most important part of human identity is skin color or a related identifier. We are told that we can know a great deal about people based upon these limited characteristics. This extends even to assuming that having a certain pigmentation, or being from a certain community, predetermines our way of thinking, our forms of expression, our preferences, our experiences, and our very personhood itself.

We should think hard about this sentiment. We may not want to outlaw any and all generalizations (I just gave one, after all), but we as Christians need to take pains that we do not assume that we know people based only on their skin color.[24] God has made every person. God has formed each one of us according to His own infinite wisdom. God has given us a distinct heritage, background, appearance, personality, and life. There is an unhealthy individualism today that some fall prey to, believing that they are so unique as to be little gods, essentially. But if this Disneyfied conception of the self is troubling, so too is what we could call conformist collectivism—a grouping of people according to certain traits that diminishes their God-given selfhood. Image-bearers are not robots. Human beings are not stereotypes. We are not faceless members of the collective. We are individuals made by God to know God.

Alongside this fundamental theological truth, we all have our own story. Looking like someone else may signal a common life path. But it also may not. So too with sharing a background; two individuals from the same zip code, the same neighborhood, even the same household lead different—even radically different—lives. In scriptural terms, was it not Jacob that God loved and Esau that God hated (Romans 9:13)? Though these two brothers shared so much in natural terms, their paths diverged sharply even unto eternity itself. Going back still further, did not Cain hate Abel and the God who made Abel, and did not Abel love God and do no harm to his brother? Right from the very start, if we read Scripture with real care, we see that commonality of family, bloodline, heritage, training, and background guarantees nothing of shared theology and character. Nor does it mean that any two people live the same life or see the world God has made in the same way. From the earliest pages of the Bible, the attentive reader gains vital clues about the uniqueness of every person, the often-stubborn individuality that is such a hallmark of life in this God-made realm.

---

[24] Contra Robin DiAngelo, who admits to sociological generalizing: "I am proceeding as if I could know anything about someone just because the person is white." Robin DiAngelo, *White Fragility: Why It's So Hard for White People to Talk about Racism* (Boston, Massachusetts: Beacon Press, 2018), 11.

In the same way, we err if we think we know a person's mind or heart because of how they look or where they grew up. Perhaps we can guess their core convictions or past experiences, but perhaps not. There is no one way that people of any given region or area or (again) even family think or act or live.[25] Ironically, in an age that celebrates diversity continually, there is little cultural attention to just how rich intellectual diversity is in our country. Some who are "black," for example, vote Democrat in typical terms. Many do. But a lot do not. It is always shocking to hear someone critique a critique of wokeness, for example, because it does not represent what "our African American brothers and sisters believe." When I hear this, particularly from a "white" person, I have to stifle laughter. Though such a statement may proceed from a genuine attempt at good intentions, it represents a surprising stereotyping of a large group of people, many of whom will not agree on all sorts of matters, religious or otherwise.

So too with "white" people. Though we hear much about this group today as covered earlier in the book, there is no one "white" mind. To drill down not by fictional racial identity but by tangible ethnicity, there is no "Irish" mind, or "South African" mind, or "Siberian" mind, or "Japanese" mind. Can we in different cases observe commonalities in majority cultures? Yes, I think so. But that is a far cry from assuming there is a body of ideas that everyone in a given people group or region shares. It is equally troublesome to believe that, beyond locality, we may size someone up within two seconds through identifying their essential physical characteristics and think we have them mapped out. As anyone who actually talks with strangers knows, few things in life are more surprise-filled than taking the time to engage a fellow human being, learn their story, gauge their views, and experience their personality. Doing so

---

[25] This lack of a monolith is why Robert Woodson maintains that one of the defining marks of effective grassroots leaders or "neighborhood healers" in inner-city contexts is flexibility. He recounts, "They know that every person cannot be reached in exactly the same way." Robert L. Woodson Sr., *The Triumphs of Joseph: How Today's Community Healers Are Reviving Our Streets and Neighborhoods* (New York: Free Press, 1998), 92.

is rarely dull, and one never comes away thinking, "I knew everything there was to know about that person by sizing them up in two seconds." Instead, we commonly think afterward, "What a unique person and a fascinating encounter—I had no idea who I was talking to!"

Christians know why this is so. We know that God made every person, and without slipping into a kind of therapeutic wonderment project, that God has made each of us as a little display of Himself. That's the wonder of being made in God's image, as we saw earlier. Yet wokeness, as with all ideologies, does not start with the wonder of image-bearing. It starts with the dull stereotypes of Marxist collectivism. It breaks people down by how they look and where they're from. It robs the human person of dignity, uniqueness, and a sense of lingering enchantment even in a world ruined by the Fall. It does not teach that we are all bound by the common bond of image-bearing, but rather that we live in fundamental alienation from one another.[26] This alienation as covered elsewhere is truly impossible to overcome—unless one belongs to an underprivileged group, and then one does not live in alienation with members of the group. But here again wokeness compromises biblical truth and fails to capture reality. The miracle of salvation is that people who have nothing in common end up as spiritual family members, while very often people who have massive natural overlap end up living very different lives and holding very different views.

Are there common genetic traits among people of a certain skin color? Yes, there are. Does this point to ethnicity being a meaningful reality? It does. Can there be common experiences that people of certain backgrounds share? Yes. But do those common experiences shape our

---

[26] Kimberlé Crenshaw, one of the founders of the academic discipline of intersectionality, in her famous essay "Mapping the Margins" asserts race to be of greater social importance than any notion of a common shared humanity. Crenshaw remarks, "We all can recognize the distinction between the claims 'I am Black' and the claim 'I am a person who happens to be Black.'" Crenshaw wants the former description to define her, not the latter. Her fundamental identity is in being black, not in being human. Kimberlé Crenshaw, "Mapping the Margins: Intersectionality, Identity Politics, and Violence against Women of Color," *Stanford Law Review* 43, no. 6 (1991): 1297.

identity in the most important way? No. Does the Bible present us with a Church in which one's natural background constitutes one's identity, necessitating different churches for affinity groups? No, not at all. Though we do fall prey to such self-sorting behavior, the New Testament church is "one new man" in Christ Jesus (Ephesians 2:15). The blood of Christ was sufficient to overcome the covenantal distinctions between included Jews and excluded Gentiles; in a similar way, the blood of Christ is sufficient to unite people of every people group, however divergent our past paths may be. In Christ, we do not have many different faiths based on our pigmentation or heritage; we each have a God-charted past, yes, but we share the very mind of Christ, we all feed alike on the one Gospel of Christ, and we are baptized with the baptism of Christ.[27] Neither are there separate crosses or separate resurrections for distinct groups. As believers, we are washed by the same blood and will be raised by the same Lord.

Distinctiveness is no bad thing and is, in truth, a gift and blessing of God—but unity will be our song in all the ages to come.

What If I Believe That CRT Is Bankrupt, but Grant That "Oppression" Is Still Occurring in America? Where Does That Leave Me?

As I have made clear, oppression has not magically disappeared from Earth. It's a live and dangerous possibility lurking at all times in a world destabilized by the real historical Fall of a real historical Adam. But in order to grant that racial oppression is still occurring today, we need proof of this claim—definitive proof. Note that pointing to discrepancies between communities or "races" alone will not do. Statistics can reveal many things; for example, if poor middle-aged white men commit suicide at the highest rates of any group, I could reasonably come to numerous conclusions based on this data. A simplistic conclusion would be that this

---

[27] David F. Wells, *The Courage to Be Protestant: Reformation Faith in Today's World*, 2nd edition (Grand Rapids, Michigan: Eerdmans, 2017), 52.

group lives under oppression. A more thoughtful approach would include such a possibility but would range across different potential causes and explanations. It is perennially tempting to come to one-factor conclusions about different social realities, but it is often best to step back, coolly think about what is before us, and not predetermine our analysis.

We must remember at this point that the major argument CRT makes is that America oppresses people of color and underprivileged groups. We engaged the idea of "systemic racism" earlier; suffice it to say that disavowing CRT but affirming the presence of racist societal oppression means you end up affirming what you denied. Said differently, it is possible to deny the ideology of CRT in technical terms but still use the categories and ideology that CRT promotes. If we do this, we're not meaningfully anti-CRT. In the most basic and honest sense, we're pro-CRT. It frames the way we think, which is just as great a victory as employing the concepts of the system.

The very category of "oppressor" and "oppressed" as the differentiators of humanity is found in CRT but is especially promoted by intersectionality.[28] As covered previously in this book, Christians have a healthy understanding of the possibility of oppression in this cursed place. One group *could* act as oppressor to another, yes. Yet we do not fundamentally slot people into these positions, nor should we ever do so based only on skin color or personal background. When we hear an issue framed this way, we are listening to an intersectional system. So it is with those who would argue that some people are inherently unjust, while others are just, or with those who are either innately racist or anti-racist. Intersectional categories account for each of these pairings and will color any and all conversations to follow. Such discussions cannot really be fair or unbiased; instead, the whole dialogue is conducted under the assumption that one group—the group in power—has wronged the other and has

---

[28] The terms "oppress," "oppression," and "oppressive" are found over a dozen times in Kimberlé Crenshaw's seminal essay on intersectionality, "Mapping the Margins." See Crenshaw, "Mapping the Margins," 1246, 1253, 1256n48, 1266n72, 1267 (twice), 1271 (twice), 1280, 1294, 1294n177, 1295n178, 1298.

done so by explicit words and discrete actions, but also simply by virtue of possessing power.

One issue that is often framed in these terms today is complementarity—male and female relationships and roles. Some evangelical leaders now commonly speak of male headship in the home and the Church as a "justice" issue and nuance their statements about such leadership by noting that complementarity can "oppress" women.[29] While we must always be honest about the failings of the Church, we should not frame issues in this way. If we do, we let an intersectional slant color people's thinking on the subject. We destabilize the goodness of the doctrines of God's Word by connecting them to "power dynamics." It is true that men are called by God to have authority in the home and Church.[30] It is also true that even the godliest men must regularly repent of sin. But intersectionality's critique of power is not a helpful one; it is a destructive one. It encourages us to read any power or authority distinction as a matter of oppression on the part of leadership. That is an unsound approach to biblical authority.

From numerous angles, wokeness encourages us to distrust the order God has created in the world He has personally made. As an ideology, it reads our society as fundamentally oppressive along racial lines, but often stops short of substantiating this claim. Furthermore, it conflates individual experience with societal structures, training people to read real wrongs done against them as necessarily part of a broader public square campaign. In addition, wokeness is fundamentally an anti-authority system, but as we have noted, it is itself deeply authoritarian. Though it speaks against "oppression," it actually creates injustice, for it teaches us to distrust God-made order and God-given authority. Though CRT gets

---

[29] To give one recent example, evangelical New Testament scholar Esau McCaulley states that black feminist ("womanist") scholars have raised "valid concerns...about the imagery and depiction of women in biblical texts." Esau McCaulley, *Reading While Black: African American Biblical Interpretation as an Exercise in Hope* (Downers Grove, Illinois: IVP Academic, 2020), 181.

[30] Voddie Baucham Jr., *Family Shepherds: Calling and Equipping Men to Lead Their Homes* (Wheaton, Illinois: Crossway, 2011), 101.

most of the headlines, it is in truth intersectionality that really brings the pain. People who will never read a sentence from an intersectional author nevertheless buy into and express an intersectional framework when they view our society as oppressive and read leadership in terms of power imbalances.

Should we always watch for oppression? Indeed, we should. Evil does not sleep. In fact, we should watch out for authoritarian evil from every corner, knowing that it is all too easy for those who are supposedly "anti-authoritarianism" to end up oppressing others. Surely a good number of those inclined to wokeness do not start out with such intentions. But movements are strange and unpredictable things, and they are especially ripe for exploitation when not grounded in sound principles and Christian ideas.

Complex Societal Matters Aside, How Does Wokeness Affect Our Spirituality?

I have seen little attention to this question in the considerable body of material engaging CRT, intersectionality, and wokeness more broadly. Yet with everything considered and covered thus far in this little book, I actually think this area matters as much as many other subjects we've treated. My primary focus in this book is on the *intellectual* consequences of embracing wokeness. But we must briefly consider the *spiritual* consequences of the same. We don't want this analysis to get too heady; wokeness is an ideology, but like every ideology, it affects our daily Christian faith in a serious way.

Toward that end, let me list out a few spiritual effects of a woke takeover. In what follows, I am not considering how wokeness takes an unbeliever captive (which is a subject unto itself), but some ways in which it overtakes a believer, a born-again Christian, over time. In a good number of cases (though not all by any means), this is a gradual process; furthermore, it is not a one-size-fits-all experience. Whether instantaneous or long-term, however, this takeover occurs as people *let themselves be taken captive* and *fail to take every thought captive* (Colossians

2:8; 2 Corinthians 10:5). This does not happen by accident, and it is not a neutral occurrence. We are all responsible for vigilantly watching over our heart and mind (Proverbs 4:23).

First, wokeness divides us from others. It causes us to see them in unbiblical terms—as either oppressor or oppressed.

Second, wokeness causes us to despise others. We not only see certain people in the category of oppressor, but we hate them for it.

Third, wokeness leads us to condemn others in pride. We bring the charge of guilty to people who are not necessarily guilty of what we allege. We are quick to speak, quick to weigh in, quick to give a definitive answer, quick to silence others, quick to anger, quick to dismiss, quick to stereotype, and slow to listen. We proudly assume that we have nothing to hear from others we disagree with, and we lecture older and wiser Christians in the faith, wrongly assuming the role of teacher over them.[31]

Fourth, wokeness robs us of joyful peace. This terrible alchemy works in us and robs us of our joy in Christ. We are not at rest. We are at war with brothers and sisters—wrongly. We churn with uncontrolled passion.

Fifth, wokeness directs us away from the Gospel. We don't see people in light of the Gospel. We don't seek to share the Gospel, the biblical Gospel. We instead pursue the mission of social justice, which is no justice at all.

Sixth, wokeness makes us bitter. As we pursue this unbiblical program, we sever relationships, change churches out of a divisive (not righteous) spirit, spread slander, and generally live a judgmental and embittered life.

Seventh, wokeness makes moving on from wrongs very hard. We do not live in the freedom given us through repentance and forgiveness,

---

[31] As just one biblical example of why this is wrong, we think of Paul's words to Timothy: "Do not rebuke an older man but encourage him as you would a father" (1 Timothy 5:1). Paul's admonition cannot mean that Timothy fails to lead with conviction. He does not avoid speaking with older men. But when he must correct his elders, he does so with real humility and in a manner appropriate to their station.

first at the vertical (divine) level, and secondly at the human level. Instead, in practical terms we deny the power of repentance and forgiveness, thinking it less important than a reparational scheme. In perhaps subtle ways, we focus more on figuring out an intricate (and unbiblical) system of wrongdoing and repayment for aggrieved peoples than we do in practicing—and celebrating—the biblical call to forgive, overlook offenses, and move on from past wrongs (real ones).[32] On this count, we must remember the stunning counsel of Scripture. "Good sense makes one slow to anger," Proverbs 19:11 teaches, "and it is his glory to overlook an offense."[33]

Eighth, wokeness veils God's providence. We fail to focus on God's sovereignty in all things, especially the life of the Church. Instead of embracing the board as God has set it up, we feel unceasing anger over the past, and we go into attack mode in the present. We lose sight of God's providential working; our focus is this-worldly, not pointed upwards.

Ninth, wokeness makes man big and God small. To sharpen the point, humanity grows large, and God becomes small. Man's concerns end up dominating our lives; God's cause, and God's wisdom, and God's infinite kindness to sinners like us, and God's solutions to our problems become relatively small things.

Many of us are seeing the takeover described above play out in different forms. To use a biblical metaphor, the diseased tree of wokeness is bearing bad fruit. Here I mean that the spirituality mentioned above, the attitude and actions, is nothing other than the fruit of the tree, the

---

[32] As we did previously, we must distinguish making real *restitution* in material terms (when you've robbed someone, for example) from a therapeutic or judicial scheme of *reparations* (in which the effect of real injustice is not calculable in material terms).

[33] There is much more to think through on this specific point. Wokeness as a system is in truth the rejection of such biblical teachings as this. We think as well of Proverbs 17:9. "Whoever covers an offense seeks love, but he who repeats a matter separates close friends." And this is to say nothing of the call of Ephesians 4:32, which commands us to "Be kind to one another, tenderhearted, forgiving one another, as God in Christ forgave you." What of the fruit of the Spirit, furthermore? It is "love, joy, peace, patience, kindness, goodness, faithfulness, gentleness, and self-control" (Galatians 5:22–23).

ungodly system. In making this observation, I am only passing on the teaching of Christ, who warned His disciples along these lines some two thousand years ago:

> So, every healthy tree bears good fruit, but the diseased tree bears bad fruit. A healthy tree cannot bear bad fruit, nor can a diseased tree bear good fruit. Every tree that does not bear good fruit is cut down and thrown into the fire. Thus you will recognize them by their fruits. (Matthew 7:17–20)

We must engage systems on their own terms. We should handle their claims, listen to their ideas, test their views, and sift their conclusions. But we must also look closely at the results of ideologies. What does this body of thought yield? How does it affect its adherents? Do they end up closer to Scripture? Or do they end up bearing bad fruit, dividing churches in an unrighteous way, calling people to unbiblical "repentance," bewildering friends and family members and church members with their accusations? We must all test the fruit.

Say I Believe That CRT and Wokeness Aren't Sound. What Exactly Do You Suggest I Do Practically to Work for Unity in the Church and Broader Society?

This is one of the most common questions asked, and it's a good one. As an activist social religion, wokeness specializes in mobilization. It creates a false society-wide sin pattern, raises the alarm to solve it, marshals support in the public square, and then agitates for sweeping social and cultural change to combat it.[34] When people distinguish such falsehood from true biblical justice, which always involves combating sins like partiality, they sometimes feel like they have nothing left to do.

---

[34] Ibram Kendi's activist program calls for nothing less than achieving full "power and policy change." Ibram X. Kendi, *How to Be an Antiracist* (New York: One World, 2019), 209.

Wokeness, after all, supplies intense and unending marching orders. By contrast, biblical justice seems almost tame.

There are in truth several priorities for the Christian who rejects wokeness and embraces biblical justice. I'll list and describe them in brief.

First, be a happy and unitive member of a local church. Remember that the local church is the display of God's glory and the place where people will see that the Gospel saves people of every background, every sin pattern, and every skin color. The local church as we studied earlier is not an afterthought in God's plan. It is the centerpiece of His plan.[35] Working to build up the body in all sorts of ways through membership, service, prayer, attendance, and godly trust is crucial. If our local churches bring people who have little in common together, the power of the Gospel will pop in our embittered world. This isn't just one place of many where we desire unity; the local church is never perfect, but it is created by God to enflesh theological unity. Such a reality takes real work, real forbearance, and real fruits of the Spirit. Be a church member (and a Christian in public beyond your local church) who lives as if the Gospel creates real unity—because it does. The Gospel creates the only true unity there is—unity that lasts not just for a few fleeting decades, but for all eternity to come.

Second, be salt and light. Anywhere you see it, fight injustice. Anywhere you can, spread the hope of Christ. When you have a chance to befriend someone who is not like you (in most ways), take it. Where there are weak points in your community, where you see people struggling to get by, get involved. Recall here that mercy is not shallow and inexpensive, but deep and often costly. Extend forgiveness when someone wrongs you and repents. There are many more ways to stand out as a Christian in a fallen world; avail yourself of them. A Christian motivated by joy and propelled by the Holy Spirit is a powerful thing indeed.

---

[35] John Hammett rightly notes that the Church is "God's [i.e., the Father's] creation, Christ's body, and the special instrument of the Holy Spirit in the world today. Because the church is so important to God, it should be a primary concern to every Christian." John S. Hammett, *Biblical Foundations for Baptist Churches: A Contemporary Ecclesiology*, 2nd edition (Grand Rapids, Michigan: Kregel Academic, 2019), 11.

Third, stand against woke utopianism. Speak up against wokeness—not out of harsh anger, but out of love for those who may be falling prey to an ungodly ideology. When we are convicted by the falsehood of any system, we may easily fall into the trap of speaking too strongly and without love. All of us are indicted here. Yet even as we must watch our speech, we must also think, and act, and speak. We cannot fall silent. We cannot stand by as people around us are taken captive by wokeness or any ungodly ideology. [36] We must instead tell the truth, all the truth, and pray that God will grant repentance and faith to those who are embracing lies. Our outreach is not to soulless people; our loving outreach is to image-bearers. Furthermore, as we covered in Chapter 1, not all people are in the same place regarding wokeness. We don't want to bring a blowtorch into a conversation where a candle is needed.

Fourth, if needed, make the necessary hard decision to leave a compromised church. If your church is not proclaiming the woke gospel, rejoice and be glad. But if your church is moving in this direction, and if the church leaders are in the third category that I mapped out in Chapter 2, then you have a few things to sort out. Instead of inflammatory posts on social media, make an appointment to talk with your elders or church leaders. Express your thankfulness for these figures and then walk through your concerns regarding wokeness. Pray for your pastors after you do so and give them time to think and pray themselves. If your church leadership does not repent of woke preaching and teaching, then it is time for you to find a new church. This is no small thing; it will no doubt prove painful in certain ways. Yet it is time for such action in evangelical circles. Wokeness is advancing far too quickly to treat this matter lightly or to assume that these issues will simply "go away."

---

[36] Commenting on the downgrade controversy in his own day, Charles Spurgeon pointedly proclaimed: "The house is being robbed, its very walls are being digged down, but the good people who are in bed are too fond of the warmth, and too much afraid of getting broken heads, to go downstairs and meet the burglars.... One way or the other we must go. Decision is the virtue of the hour." Charles Spurgeon, *The Sword and the Trowel*, September 1887, as cited in Iain H. Murray, *The Forgotten Spurgeon*, 2nd edition (Edinburgh, Scotland; Carlisle, Pennsylvania: Banner of Truth Trust, 1973), 143.

No—they will not go away. As we have argued throughout the book, strongholds and false ideologies must be destroyed, not ignored or treated with a soft-shoe approach.

It will require finding a body of pastors and leaders willing to go to war against false ideology. Search for an assembly led by strong and godly men. Search for a church that preaches expository messages from all of Scripture, that promotes the true biblical Gospel, and that celebrates genuine oneness of all redeemed sinners in Christ. Do not drag your feet about joining such a church. Search for one, find one, and join one for the good of your soul. Some may label you as divisive for doing so, but you will need to remember that it is not you who is leaving Christ, but woke leaders who are departing from the truth.

It is not going to get easier to be a Christian in the days ahead. It will likely get more difficult. This is a sad reality, but it actually means that strong and sound congregations will stand out all the more. Faithful pastoring will shine all the more brightly. Sheep that believe the truth and reject every counterfeit will only emerge as healthier and more loving. Again, do not delay in finding a biblical church. You and your loved ones have souls that will go to either eternal life or eternal damnation. Choose wisely. Life is too short to sit under unsound doctrine.

Fifth, protect and help your children. We face different decisions as Christian fathers and mothers: What school should we send our kids to? Should they attend a Christian college or a secular one? What about youth group? Many others confront us as well. Even as we seek to handle gray areas well and charitably, Christians fathers and mothers must protect their children from wokeness. At an absolute minimum, this means shepherding in the home from a godly father, discipleship in the care of a strong biblical church (see previous point), and very careful attention to what children are learning in school, whatever model of education your family embraces. As a believing father or mother, you *must not* assume that your child is being well trained in various settings today, whether secular or spiritual. You must take ownership of their education, shepherd them best you can, and disciple them comprehensively in the things of God.

This is not only true for younger children. It applies as well to the place you send your children to college, if they go. Do not make the common mistake of thinking that a university is sound because it says it is Christian. You must investigate these things, and you must choose wisely for your children. In addition, they need to be linked to a strong local church wherever they go. I hear regularly from fathers and mothers who grieve over their child's embracing wokeness, many of them after studying at "Christian" schools. We cannot save our children; only God can. Our goal as fathers and mothers is not to get them saved, but to glorify God by making disciples as He moves and leads. Nonetheless, the absolute sovereignty of God in no way cancels out human responsibility. Do all you can to train your child well, protect your child, disciple your child, build a theological worldview for your child, and love your child.

Sixth, pray for good to come in the Church and beyond. Our special focus as Christians is the Church of Christ. That's what we give our greatest effort to preserve and strengthen. (Hence this humble book!) But we cannot consign the world to its fate, washing our hands of any responsibility to witness to unbelievers, speak for the wronged, and promote the truth in public. This is not a proper understanding of the Church or the Christian life. What did Jesus do—hide out in a Galilean kitchen all His ministry? What about the apostles—did they only concern themselves with hidden meetings in far-off places? No, the faith once for all delivered to the saints was a public faith. Jesus died in public. The apostles preached in public. Before he lost his head, righteous John the Baptist spoke against Herod's sexual sin in defense of his wronged wife. The Gospel is a public gospel, and the Christian faith must ever go public.[37]

All this biblical material shapes our prayer life. Our first burden is the Church, and we must pray hard and regularly for the doctrinal health and spiritual vitality of God's people. But we must also pray for unbelievers, for communities, for towns and cities, for nations, for the very world

---

[37] For insightful practical wisdom into how the Church should speak and publicly engage in an intolerantly "tolerant" culture, see D. A. Carson, *The Intolerance of Tolerance* (Grand Rapids, Michigan; Cambridge, United Kingdom: Eerdmans, 2012), 161–76.

itself. Our prayer life feels small, and in one sense it *is* small. It's just us in our living-room chair, in our car on our morning commute, in a forest as we walk and petition the Lord. All that is small: just one person praying. But the Scripture teaches us that even one person praying is able to summon all the armies of Heaven. One person praying has the very attention of God. One person praying is all that is needed.[38] Let us pray amidst the spread of wokeness and evil. Let us ask God to save, and strengthen, and cast down, and liberate, and rule.

Again, praying—like the other steps—may feel insignificant. What is one action, one church, one conversation of loving warning, one time of prayer? The things of God often feel so light and glancing. But they are not. The things of God look weak to the natural man, but the natural man does not think rightly. He does not know what is true, ultimately. And what he does know that is true he does not value or esteem as he should. He thinks the world is heavy, and God is light. But God is great, and he is nothing. God is true, and all the counsels of evildoers will fail. God is undefeated, invincible, and perfectly wise. We must invest our lives in the very work of God, small though it may be. For it is in small things, and only in small things, that the great work of our great God goes forth.

What about you, Reader?

Before this little book concludes, I want to pause for a moment. I want to ask you, Reader, if this material has convicted you—not because of my thinking, but ultimately because of God's truth as presented here?

Consider a few questions and points of application before you finish the book:

- *Have you ever despised someone for their skin color, background, financial status, or other markers?* If yes, you have committed sins as—in different senses—we all have.

---

[38] For a stirring account of how God miraculously answered the prayers of one singular saint time and time again, see George Mueller, *Answers to Prayer*, Moody Classics (Chicago, Illinois: Moody Publishers, 2007).

- *Where you see this sin of "partiality" (treating people unfairly based on their personal identity markers) in your past and present, you should repent of it.*
- *You should repent both in a particular sense, turning from these targeted sins, but also in a much bigger sense.* Our individual sins show us that we in fact have a much bigger problem: we're sinners by nature, and we deserve God's just judgment for our sin.
- *Claim the forgiveness that is available to you in Christ.* Don't claim it as if it's a prize at a fair. Claim it as a gracious pardon from a forgiving King. That is, in fact, what it is.

Turn to Christ now, while there is time. Don't let the sin of partiality in any form send you to Hell. There is hope, infinite hope and forgiveness, in Christ.

Conclusion

Wokeness may feel great and powerful now. But it is only having its day. Its limits, like the popularity curve of every ungodly ideology, are already appointed. Its eclipse is already secured. Though the world seems to bow to this body of thought, we must not. We must trust that God is working all things out according to the counsel of His will. The end result of this "working out" is not mere cessation of evil, glorious as that is. The end result is the vindication of God, God's truth, and God's people. Our vindication, like evil's end, is already appointed. It is already secured. No one can shake it or undermine it. We *will* be vindicated on the last day (Isaiah 62:2).

The truth of God will ring out then, and the angels will rise in worship of the victorious King of the earth, and a Church of every tribe and tongue and nation and people will sing praise to God with tears of joy in their eyes. That song of praise will never end. That unity in Christ will never die. And the great God we worship, the Maker and Redeemer of His people, will never cease to be our God.

Until that day, do not forget the abiding refrain of this book, and one of the key pairings of Scripture: *Do not be taken captive by evil ideology.* Instead, by the grace of God, *take every thought captive for Christ.*[39]

---

[39] Colossians 2:8; 2 Corinthians 10:5.

Afterword

hakespeare was right. The "tide in the affairs of men" is real, as we observed in the Introduction. Over three years after this book originally came out, I can clearly see the tidal pull of wokeness in the West. Over the last several years, many were taken out to sea by woke ideology. This was true in American culture, and this was true in the American Church. Colleges were shipwrecked; once-respected pastors embraced godless ideas and lost their pulpits; many sheep migrated to new churches, creating an explosion of church growth in some unlikely places. The sea is a powerful force indeed, and so wokeness has proved to be.

For that reason, it still seems rather incredible to me that this book exists at all. In a strange providence, it was in the city where George Floyd died that this book found its genesis. After being asked in February 2020 by a faithful pastor to give messages on Critical Race Theory (CRT), I traveled to the Minneapolis area in October 2020 and gave six messages on that subject. With no promotion or marketing, the series—titled "Christianity and Wokeness"—found an audience on YouTube. From that point, things moved quickly, and I endeavored to write a book with the same title. In the midst of doing so, I had a moment in seminary chapel when I looked out a window and thought, "My whole life is about to change because of this book." So it was, in ways I could scarcely have imagined.

In 2020 and 2021, I worked doggedly on this text (even as my research assistant, Jeff Moore, was a great help to me). As one can imagine, it was a lonely book to write. In 2020, aside from the lionhearted Voddie Baucham Jr., I knew of no other Christian writer penning a response to wokeness. Little did we know that his book would become a massive bestseller and that mine would get some traction as well. To this day, I am grateful for Tim Peterson, then of Salem Books, for his prescience in publishing both *Fault Lines* and *Christianity and Wokeness*. (I offer thanks as well to Karla, Jennifer, Katie, and the team at Salem that worked so hard on my project.)

Fast forward to our time. Though wokeness is still tolerated in some corners of the Western Church, the viscerally evil nature of this system has been laid bare. Christians who had no idea what CRT was now know that it is vicious Marxism with a thin veneer of academic jargon sprinkled on top. They know that it is a terrible thing to assume that "white" people are "white supremacists." They know that Scripture teaches that reconciliation, whether "racial" or otherwise, is no human project, but the accomplishment of Christ's atonement. They know that they must not stand mute as unsound philosophies enter the Church but must speak. In all these ways, God has acted to protect His sheep and drive wolves from His Church.

This does not mean, however, that evangelicalism in late 2024 is in a place of quiet tranquility. Ironically, the widespread embrace of wokeness led to a visceral backlash that has metastasized into a serious problem on the other side. Wokeness taught "white" people to hate themselves; a counter-movement teaches "white" people to venerate Anglo-Saxon culture and preserve the homogeneity and even ethnic purity of their familial bloodline and their country. These polar ideologies each represent a grave corruption of Gospel oneness in Christ (Ephesians 2:11–18). They must be resisted.

In all these ways, conditions have changed since I wrote *Christianity and Wokeness*. For my part, I ended up changing jobs, moving to a new state, and walking with my beloved wife through a fresh set of blessings and trials. Salem Books was sold, and now I am privileged to work with Skyhorse Publishing, a vital champion of free speech and free thought (a major thank you to Kathryn Riggs of Skyhorse for her partnership on this project).

Much has changed, yes—but much remains the same. While wokeness has had many effects, it has not in any way altered the Church's calling. Our charge, even in these tumultuous times, is to be faithful in Babylon. Contra what we hear from some, we are not to seize upon extreme measures in these evil moments. We are, as the Lord God once said to the Israelite exiles, to build homes, strengthen families, and plant gardens. We are to seek the good of the city in which God has placed us (Jeremiah 29:4–7). In a new covenant sense, this means that we make disciples by faithful proclamation of the Word and Gospel (Matthew 28:19–20). No ideology, however virulent, can stop the advance of this mission.

Yes, there is a "tide" in our current affairs. The strongest current in this world is not godless evil, though. It is love. Bitterness, after all, is satanic. But love, especially love that creates unity through the blood of Christ, is divine.

Dr. Owen Strachan
June 2024
Conway, Arkansas

Glossary of Terms

Antiracism: In woke thought, dedicated opposition to hidden, race-based injustices through social demonstration and political activism; a white person cannot ever completely escape *internal* racial bias but can perform *outward* actions that seek to dismantle white power.

Color-Blindness: In woke thought, the false claim often voiced by white people that they do not evaluate others based on ethnicity or skin color.

Critical Race Theory (CRT): The system of thought founded by legal scholars such as Richard Delgado and Derrick Bell (circa 1989) which asserts that hidden racism is pervasive throughout society, all whites are racist, blacks (and other minorities) are not racist because they lack the power to be so, and one's racial group determines one's core identity; CRT's "solution" to the problem of racism is (A) to deconstruct white power and (B) to redistribute power to minorities.

Critical Theory: The social philosophy pioneered by the work of Max Horkheimer and the Frankfurt School in Germany (circa 1930) which seeks to define and dismantle power imbalances that reside in the institutions and structures of society.

Ethnic Gnosticism: Per Voddie Baucham, secret insider knowledge that a person possesses by being a member of a minority race; there are certain realities in society that a person can only know if he or she has a particular skin color.

Intersectionality: The crisscrossing of categories of oppression in society, including race, class, gender, sexuality, age, ability, citizenship, and body type; in intersectional thought, the most oppressed person is a black, poor, LGBT, young, disabled, undocumented, fat woman.

Microaggression: The voicing of a subtle and unintended stereotype (for example, "I don't see color") that implies power over ethnic minorities and elicits a negative reaction.

Racism: Historically, this term refers to any unfavorable or hostile attitude harbored by an individual based on a person's skin color; in woke thought, this term denotes race-based prejudice against someone *only* when it is coupled with power (that is, prejudice *plus* power), such that an individual cannot display racism if he or she is an ethnic minority.

Social Justice: Historically, this phrase refers to broad attempts to fight against unfair inequalities that exist in civic life and to hold unjust perpetrators accountable; in woke thought, this phrase alludes to the twofold practice of deconstructing white power and redistributing power to minorities.

Standpoint Epistemology: The view that an individual's minority status gives him or her the unique ability to see truth in society, a perspective which is not able to be seen by a person in the majority group (see also "Ethnic Gnosticism").

Systemic Racism: Historically, this phrase refers to any explicit and sweeping societal policies that intentionally limit or segregate human beings based on race (for example, Jim Crow laws, neighborhood redlining, etc.); in woke thought, this phrase denotes the idea that race-based injustices are secretly embedded in the laws, policies, values, histories, institutions, language, and even thought categories created by the dominant white race.

White Fragility: In woke thought, the defensive reaction that white people display when confronted with the reality of their racist attitudes; such a reaction can manifest in outbursts of anger, tears, anxiety, or even flight from the conversation.

White Guilt: In woke thought, the shame that a white person feels for being part of the oppressor race.

White Privilege: In woke thought, the natural, inborn advantages and benefits that all white people possess simply by virtue of being members of the dominant race.

White Supremacy: Historically, this phrase refers to overt declarations of racial superiority by advocates of race-based segregation, including movements such as the KKK and alt-right pro-Aryan groups; in woke thought, this phrase denotes the unspoken assumption possessed by all white people that they are the ideal race and all other ethnicities are inferior.

Whiteness: In woke thought, the mindset and lived reality of people with Indo-European ancestry and light-colored skin who view themselves, whether consciously or subconsciously, as the superior race and the embodiment of what every human culture should become.

Wokeness: The state of being consciously aware of and "awake" to the hidden, race-based injustices that pervade all of American society; this term has also been expanded to refer to the state of being "awake" to injustices that are gender-based, class-based, etc.

Recommended Reading

To Understand Wokeness from Proponents:

DiAngelo, Robin. *White Fragility: Why It's So Hard for White People to Talk about Racism*. Boston, Massachusetts: Beacon Press, 2018.

Kendi, Ibram X. *How to Be an Antiracist*. New York: One World, 2019.

Tisby, Jemar. *The Color of Compromise: The Truth about the American Church's Complicity in Racism*. Grand Rapids, Michigan: Zondervan, 2019.

To Understand Wokeness from Non-Christians:

Pluckrose, Helen, and James Lindsay. *Cynical Theories: How Activist Scholarship Made Everything about Race, Gender, and Identity—and Why This Harms Everybody*. Durham, North Carolina: Pitchstone Publishing, 2020.

Rothman, Noah. *Unjust: Social Justice and the Unmaking of America*. Washington, D.C.: Gateway Editions, 2019.

Scruton, Roger. *Fools, Frauds, and Firebrands: Thinkers of the New Left*. London: Bloomsbury Continuum, 2017.

Sowell, Thomas. *Discrimination and Disparities*. New York: Hachette, 2019.

To Answer Wokeness (for Christians):

Ascol, Tom, and Jared Longshore, eds. *By What Standard? God's World...God's Rules*. Cape Coral, Florida: Founders, 2020.

Baucham Jr., Voddie. *Fault Lines: The Social Justice Movement and Evangelicalism's Looming Catastrophe*. Washington, D.C.: Salem Books, 2021.

Caldwell, Richard. *A Biblical Answer for Racial Unity*. Houston, Texas: Kress, 2018.

Johnson, Jeffrey. *What Does the Bible Teach about Social Justice?* Free Grace Press, 2021.

The *Just Thinking* podcast, hosted by Darrell Harrison and Virgil Walker (and the broader B. A. R. network; note that here I'm encouraging listening, not reading).

Bibliography

Alexander, Michelle. *The New Jim Crow: Mass Incarceration in the Age of Colorblindness.* 10th anniversary edition. New York and London: New Press, 2020.

Anyabwile, Thabiti. "We Await Repentance for Assassinating Dr. King." The Gospel Coalition, April 4, 2018, https://www.thegospelcoalition.org/blogs/thabiti-anyabwile/await-repentance-assassinating-dr-king.

"Are the Police Racist?" PragerU, August 22, 2016, https://www.prageru.com/video/are-the-police-racist/?fbclid=IwAR0a7lBv5v57-Cp6TRm tdmpV71Mvd6FgyzbhDjRYJ-CzZopKjkbQobfsoMQ.

Aristides. *The Apology of Aristides: Translated from the Syriac.* In *Ante-Nicene Fathers,* 9:263–79. Edited by Alexander Roberts and James Donaldson. Peabody, Massachusetts: Hendrickson, 2012.

Ascol, Tom, and Jared Longshore, eds. *By What Standard? God's World...God's Rules.* Cape Coral, Florida: Founders, 2020.

Atkinson, David. *The Wings of Refuge: The Message of Ruth.* The Bible Speaks Today. Downers Grove, Illinois: InterVarsity Press, 1983.

Bahnsen, Greg L. *Van Til's Apologetic: Readings and Analysis*. Phillipsburg, New Jersey: Presbyterian & Reformed, 1998.

Baptist, Edward E. *The Half Has Never Been Told: Slavery and the Making of American Capitalism*. New York: Basic Books, 2017.

Barnett, Paul. *1 Corinthians: Holiness and Hope of a Rescued People*. Focus on the Bible. Fearn, Scotland: Christian Focus, 2011.

Baucham Jr., Voddie T. "Ethnic Gnosticism." In *By What Standard? God's World... God's Rules*. Edited by Jared Longshore, 17–30. Cape Coral, Florida: Founders Press, 2020.

———. *Family Shepherds: Calling and Equipping Men to Lead Their Homes*. Wheaton, Illinois: Crossway, 2011.

———. *Fault Lines: The Social Justice Movement and Evangelicalism's Looming Catastrophe*. Washington, D.C.: Salem Books, 2021.

Beale, G. K. *The Temple and the Church's Mission: A Biblical Theology of the Dwelling Place of God*. New Studies in Biblical Theology. Downers Grove, Illinois; Leicester, United Kingdom: IVP Academic, 2004.

Beckert, Sven. *Empire of Cotton: A Global History*. New York: Alfred A. Knopf, 2015.

Bell, Derrick A. *Faces at the Bottom of the Well: The Permanence of Racism*. New York: BasicBooks, 1992.

Block, Daniel I. *Judges, Ruth: An Exegetical and Theological Exposition of Holy Scripture*, vol. 6. New American Commentary. Nashville, Tennessee: B&H, 1999.

Bolar, Kelsey. "Justice for Breonna Taylor Isn't Indicting Police Officers for Acting in Self-Defense." The Federalist, September 25, 2020, https://thefederalist.com/2020/09/25/justice-for-breonna-taylor-isnt-indicting-police-officers-for-acting-in-self-defense.

Borysenko, Karlyn. "Shocking Images Show Coca-Cola Is Training Employees to 'Try to Be Less White.'" YouTube, February 19, 2021, https://www.youtube.com/watch?v=FRWfSoSmNqw.

Bowell, T. "Feminist Standpoint Theory." *Internet Encyclopedia of Philosophy*. No date, https://iep.utm.edu/fem-stan.

Bremner, Jade. "Coca-Cola Faces Backlash over Seminar Asking Staff to 'Be Less White,'" *Independent*, February 24, 2021, https://www.independent.co.uk/life-style/coca-cola-racism-robin-diangelo-coke-b1806122.html.

Brooks, Arthur. *The Conservative Heart: How to Build a Fairer, Happier, and More Prosperous America.* Northampton, Massachusetts: Broadside Books, 2015.

Bruce, F. F. *The Epistles to the Colossians, to Philemon and to the Ephesians.* New International Commentary on the New Testament. Grand Rapids, Michigan: Eerdmans, 1984.

Caldwell, Richard et al. *A Biblical Answer for Racial Unity.* Houston, Texas: Kress, 2018.

Calvin, John. *Commentaries on the Epistles of Paul to the Galatians and Ephesians.* Translated by William Pringle. Vol. 21 of Calvin's Commentaries. Grand Rapids, Michigan: Baker Books, 1999.

Card, Michael. "Underneath the Door." From the album *Scribbling in the Sand: The Best of Michael Card—Live.* Word Entertainment, 2002, compact disc.

Carden, Art. "Slavery Did Not Enrich Americans." American Institute for Economic Research, June 25, 2020, https://www.aier.org/article/slavery-did-not-enrich-americans/.

Carson, D. A. *The Intolerance of Tolerance.* Grand Rapids, Michigan: Eerdmans, 2012.

Chapman, Thandeka K. "Origins of and Connections to Social Justice in Critical Race Theory in Education." In *Handbook of Critical Race Theory in Education.* Edited by Marvin Lynn and Adrienne D. Dixson, 101–12. New York: Routledge, 2013.

Charles, H. B. *On Pastoring: A Short Guide to Living, Leading, and Ministering as a Pastor.* Chicago, Illinois: Moody Publishers, 2016.

Chou, Abner. *The Hermeneutics of the Biblical Writers: Learning to Interpret Scripture from the Prophets and Apostles.* Grand Rapids, Michigan: Kregel, 2018.

Chrysostom, John. *Homily on Ephesians* 5.2.16, as quoted in M. J. Edwards, ed. *Galatians, Ephesians, Philippians*. Vol. 8 of *Ancient Christian Commentary on Scripture: New Testament*. Downers Grove, Illinois: InterVarsity, 1999.

Cleveland, Margot. "Why Kenosha Police Officers' Use of Force on Jacob Blake Was Justified." The Federalist, August 31, 2020, https://thefederalist.com/2020/08/31/why-kenosha-police-officers-use-of-force-on-jacob-blake-was-justified.

Coates, Ta-Nehisi. *Between the World and Me*. New York: One World, 2015.

———. "The Case for Reparations." *The Atlantic*, June 2014, https://www.theatlantic.com/ magazine/archive/2014/06/the-case-for-reparations/361631/.

———. *We Were Eight Years in Power: An American Tragedy*. New York: One World, 2017.

Collins, Patricia Hill. *Intersectionality as Critical Social Theory*. Durham, North Carolina: Duke University Press, 2019.

Collins, Patricia Hill, and Sirma Bilge. *Intersectionality*. Key Concepts. Cambridge, United Kingdom; Medford, Massachusetts: Polity Press, 2016.

Cone, James H. *God of the Oppressed*. Maryknoll, New York: Orbis, 1997.

———. *A Theology of Black Liberation*. 40th anniversary edition. Maryknoll, New York: Orbis, 2010 [1970].

Copan, Paul. *Is God a Moral Monster? Making Sense of the Old Testament God*. Grand Rapids, Michigan: BakerBooks, 2011.

Crenshaw, Kimberlé. "Demarginalizing the Intersection of Race and Sex: A Black Feminist Critique of Antidiscrimination Doctrine, Feminist Theory and Antiracist Politics." *University of Chicago Legal Forum*, vol. 1989, article 8. Available at https://chicagounbound.uchicago.edu/cgi/ viewcontent.cgi?article=1052 &context=uclf.

———. "Mapping the Margins: Intersectionality, Identity Politics, and Violence against Women of Color." *Stanford Law Review* 43, no. 6 (1991): 1241–99.

Crenshaw, Kimberlé et al., eds. *Critical Race Theory: The Key Writings That Formed the Movement.* New York: New Press, 1996.

Dabney, Robert Lewis. *A Defence of Virginia (and Through Her, of the South) in Recent and Pending Contests against the Sectional Party.* New York: E. J. Hale & Son, 1867.

Delgado, Richard, and Jean Stefancic. *Critical Race Theory: An Introduction.* 2nd edition. New York and London: New York University Press, 2012.

Desmond, Adrian, and James Moore. *Darwin: The Life of a Tormented Evolutionist.* New York: W. W. Norton, 1994.

DiAngelo, Robin. *White Fragility: Why It's So Hard for White People to Talk about Racism.* Boston, Massachusetts: Beacon, 2018.

Dolezal, Rachel, with Storms Reback. *In Full Color: Finding My Place in a Black and White World.* Dallas, Texas: BenBella Books, 2017.

Dumas, Michael J. "Doing Class in Critical Race Analysis in Education." In *Handbook of Critical Race Theory in Education.* Edited by Marvin Lynn and Adrienne D. Dixson, 113–25. New York: Routledge, 2013.

"East Harlem Resident and Professor Jessica Krug Admits She Is Not Black (Update)." *Harlem World Magazine,* September 8, 2020, https://www.harlemworldmagazine.com/east-harlem-resident-and-professor-jessica-krug-admits-she-admits-she-is-not-black.

Edwards Jr., Jonathan. "The Injustice and Impolicy of the Slave Trade, and of the Slavery of the Africans." In *Early American Abolitionists: A Collection of Anti-Slavery Writings, 1760–1820.* Edited by James G. Basker, 135–74. New York: Gilder Lehrman Institute of American History, 2005.

Elwell, Walter A. *Evangelical Dictionary of Theology.* 2nd edition, Baker Reference Library. Grand Rapids, Michigan: Baker Academic, 2001.

Emerson, Michael O., and Christian Smith. *Divided by Faith: Evangelical Religion and the Problem of Race in America.* Oxford: Oxford University Press, 2000.

Epistle to Diognetus. In *Early Christian Writings: The Apostolic Fathers.* Revised edition. Translated by Maxwell Staniforth. Penguin Classics. New York: Penguin, 1987.

Fisher, N. R. E. *Slavery in Classical Greece.* London: Bristol Classical Press, 1998.

Flannery, Michael. "Distancing Darwin from Racism Is a Fool's Errand." *Evolution News,* November 23, 2020, https://evolutionnews.org/2020/11/distancing-darwin-from-racism-is-a-fools-errand.

Fung, Ronald Y. K. *The Epistle to the Galatians.* New International Commentary on the New Testament. Grand Rapids, Michigan: Eerdmans, 1988.

Gates Jr., Henry Louis. "Let Them Talk: Why Civil Liberties Pose No Threat to Civil Rights." *The New Republic,* September 20, 1993, https://newrepublic.com/article/149558/let-talk.

Gentry, Peter J., and Stephen J. Wellum. *Kingdom through Covenant: A Biblical-Theological Understanding of the Covenants.* 2nd edition. Wheaton, Illinois: Crossway, 2018.

Gould, Stephen Jay. *Ontogeny and Phylogeny.* Cambridge, Massachusetts: Belknap, 1977.

Grudem, Wayne A. *Christian Ethics: An Introduction to Biblical Moral Reasoning.* Wheaton, Illinois: Crossway, 2018.

———. *The First Epistle of Peter: An Introduction and Commentary.* 1st edition. Tyndale Old Testament Commentaries. Leicester, United Kingdom; Grand Rapid, Michigan: InterVarsity Press; Eerdmans, 1988.

Hague, William. *William Wilberforce: The Life of the Great Anti-Slave Trade Campaigner.* London: HarperPress, 2007.

Ham, Ken. "Are There Really Different Races?" Answers in Genesis, November 29, 2007, https://answersingenesis.org/racism/are-there-really-different-races.

Ham, Ken, and A. Charles Ware. *Darwin's Plantation: Evolution's Racist Roots*. Green Forest, Arkansas: Master, 2007.

————. *One Race, One Blood: The Biblical Answer to Racism*. Green Forest, Arkansas: Master, 2019.

Hamilton, Victor P. *The Book of Genesis: Chapters 1–17*. The New International Commentary on the Old Testament. Grand Rapids, Michigan: Eerdmans, 1990.

Hammett, John S. *Biblical Foundations for Baptist Churches: A Contemporary Ecclesiology*. 2nd edition. Grand Rapids, Michigan: Kregel Academic, 2019.

Harris, Murray J. *Slave of Christ: A New Testament Metaphor for Total Devotion to Christ*. New Studies in Biblical Theology (Volume 8). Downers Grove, Illinois: InterVarsity Press, 2001.

Hays, J. Daniel. *From Every People and Nation: A Biblical Theology of Race*. New Studies in Biblical Theology (Volume 14). Downers Grove, Illinois: Apollos, 2003.

Hendriksen, William. *New Testament Commentary: Exposition of Ephesians*. Grand Rapids, Michigan: Baker, 1967.

Henry, Carl F. H. *God, Revelation, and Authority* (Volumes 1–6). Wheaton, Illinois: Crossway, 1976–1983.

Henry, Matthew. *A Commentary upon the Holy Bible*, vol. 6. London, United Kingdom: Religious Tract Society, 1888.

"Here's What Ta-Nehisi Coates Told Congress about Reparations." *New York Times*, June 19, 2019, https://www.nytimes.com/2019/06/19/us/ta-nehisi-coates-reparations.html.

Hill, Daniel. *White Awake: An Honest Look at What It Means to Be White*. Downers Grove, Illinois: IVP Books, 2017.

Hodge, Charles. *Ephesians*. Crossway Classic Commentaries. Wheaton, Illinois: Crossway, 1994.

Hoehner, Harold W. "Ephesians." In *Bible Knowledge Commentary: New Testament Edition*. Edited by John F. Walvoord and Roy B. Zuck, 613–45. Wheaton, Illinois: Victor Books, 1985.

Hoekema, Anthony. *Created in God's Image*. Grand Rapids, Michigan: Eerdmans, 1994

Hughes, R. Kent. *Genesis: Beginning and Blessing*. Preaching the Word. Wheaton, Illinois: Crossway, 2004.

InterVarsity Christian Fellowship USA. "Michelle Higgins—Urbana 15." YouTube, January 26, 2016, https://www.youtube.com/watch?v=XVGDSkxxXco.

Jensen, Robert. *The Heart of Whiteness: Confronting Race, Racism, and White Privilege*. San Francisco, California: City Lights, 2005.

Jesionka, Natalie. "Social Justice for Toddlers: These New Books and Programs Start the Conversation Early." *Washington Post*, March 18, 2021, https://www.washingtonpost.com/ lifestyle/2021/03/18/social-justice-antiracist-books-toddlers-kids.

Johnson, Dennis. *Him We Proclaim: Proclaiming Christ from All the Scriptures*. Phillipsburg, New Jersey: P&R, 2007.

Johnson, Jeffrey. *What Does the Bible Teach about Social Justice?* Conway, Arkansas: Free Grace Press, 2021.

Jones, Timothy Paul. *Four Views of the End Times*. Peabody, Massachusetts: Rose Publishing, 2006.

Joshel, Sandra R. *Slavery in the Roman World*. New York: Cambridge University Press, 2013.

Judson Memorial Church. "How to Be an Antiracist: Ibram X. Kendi in Conversation with Molly Crabapple." YouTube, filmed on August 15, 2019, https://www.youtube.com/watch?v=BhbbmjqcRvY.

Kaufmann, J. E., H. W. Kaufmann, Aleksander Potocnik, and Patrice Lang. *The Maginot Line: History and Guide*. Barnsley, United Kingdom: Pen & Sword Military, 2011.

Kendi, Ibram X. *How to Be an Antiracist*. New York: One World, 2019.

Kidner, Derek. *Genesis: An Introduction and Commentary*. Tyndale Old Testament Commentaries. Carol Stream, Illinois: Tyndale, 1967.

Kilner, John F. *Dignity and Destiny: Humanity in the Image of God*. Grand Rapids, Michigan: Eerdmans, 2015.

Krumholz, Willis L. "Bloomberg's Plan for Black Americans Doubles Down on the Left's Failures." The Federalist, January 22, 2020, https://thefederalist.com/2020/01/22/bloombergs-plan-for-black-americans-doubles-down-on-the-lefts-failures.

Kuyper, Abraham. Lectures on Calvinism. Grand Rapids, Michigan: Eerdmans, 1931.

Lehman, Charles Fain. "The Wages of Woke: How Robin DiAngelo Got Rich Peddling 'White Fragility.'" Washington Free Beacon, July 25, 2020, https://freebeacon.com/culture/ the-wages-of-woke-2/.

Lemon, Jason. "Why Ibram Kendi Is Facing a Backlash over a Tweet about Amy Coney Barrett's Adopted Haitian Children." Newsweek, September 27, 2020, https://www.newsweek.com/why-ibram-kendi-facing-backlash-over-tweet-about-amy-coney-barretts-adopted-haitian-children-1534507.

Lewis, C. S. The Weight of Glory. San Francisco, California: Harper-One, 2001 [1941].

Lincoln, C. Eric, and Lawrence H. Mamiya. The Black Church in the African-American Experience. Durham, North Carolina: Duke University Press, 1990.

Longfield, Bradley J. The Presbyterian Controversy: Fundamentalists, Modernists, and Moderates. Religion in America. New York: Oxford University Press, 1993.

Loury, Glenn. "Unspeakable Truths about Racial Inequality in America." Quillette, February 10, 2021, https://quillette.com/2021/02/10/unspeakable-truths-about-racial-inequality-in-america.

Lumpkin, Lauren, and Susan Svrluga. "White GWU Professor Admits She Falsely Claimed Black Identity." Washington Post, September 3, 2020, https://www.washingtonpost.com/ education/2020/09/03/white-gwu-professor-admits-she-falsely-claimed-black-identity.

Mac Donald, Heather. "There Is No Epidemic of Fatal Police Shootings against Unarmed Black Americans." USA Today, July 3, 2020, https://www.usatoday.com/story/opinion/ 2020/07/03/police-black-killings-homicide-rates-race-injustice-column/3235072001.

Machen, J. Gresham. *Christianity and Liberalism*. Grand Rapids, Michigan: Eerdmans, 1923.

Magness, Phillip W. "The New History of Capitalism Has a 'Whiteness' Problem." American Institute for Economic Research, December 10, 2019, https://www.aier.org/article/slavery-did-not-enrich-americans.

Mahoney, Daniel J. *The Idol of Our Age: How the Religion of Humanity Subverts Christianity*. New York: Encounter Books, 2018.

Marx, Karl, and Friedrich Engels. *The Communist Manifesto*. New York: Penguin Classics, 2002 [1848].

Mason, Eric. *Woke Church: An Urgent Call for Christians in America to Confront Racism and Injustice*. Chicago, Illinois: Moody, 2018.

Mathews, Kenneth A. *Genesis 1–11:26*. New American Commentary 1A. Nashville, Tennessee: Broadman & Holman, 1996.

McCaulley, Esau. *Reading While Black: African American Biblical Interpretation as an Exercise in Hope*. Downers Grove, Illinois: IVP Academic, 2020.

McWhorter, John. "The Neoracists: A New Religion Is Preached across America. It Is Nonsense Posing as Wisdom." Persuasion, February 8, 2021, https://www.persuasion.community/ p/john-mcwhorter-the-neoracists.

Mesa, Ivan. "7 Books on the White-Black Racial Divide You Should Read." The Gospel Coalition: Current Events, September 22, 2016, https://www.thegospelcoalition.org/ article/7-books-on-the-white-black-racial-divide-you-should-read.

Metaxas, Eric. *Amazing Grace: William Wilberforce and the Heroic Campaign to End Slavery*. New York: HarperOne, 2007.

Mitchell, Craig. "Rev. Michael Eric Dyson: An Analysis." In *Keep Your Head Up: America's New Black Christian Leaders, Social Consciousness, and the Cosby Conversation*, ed. Anthony B. Bradley, 197–214. Wheaton, Illinois: Crossway, 2012.

Moo, Douglas J. *The Letters to the Colossians and to Philemon.* Pillar New Testament Commentary. Grand Rapids, Michigan: Eerdmans, 2008.

Mounce, Robert. *The Book of Revelation.* Revised edition. New International Commentary on the New Testament. Grand Rapids, Michigan; Cambridge, United Kingdom: Eerdmans, 1997

Mueller, George. *Answers to Prayer.* Moody Classics. Chicago, Illinois: Moody Publishers, 2007.

Murray, Douglas. *The Madness of Crowds: Gender, Race, and Identity.* London: Bloomsbury, 2019.

Murray, Iain H. *The Forgotten Spurgeon.* 2nd edition. Edinburgh; Carlisle, Pennsylvania: Banner of Truth Trust, 1973.

Murray, John. *Principles of Conduct: Aspects of Biblical Ethics.* Grand Rapids, Michigan: Eerdmans, 1957.

———. *Redemption Accomplished and Applied.* Grand Rapids, Michigan: Eerdmans, 1955.

Niemietz, Kristian. *Socialism: The Failed Idea That Never Dies.* London: London Publishing, 2019.

Nitzberg, Alex. "Black Lives Matter's Agenda Is about More Than Race." *The Hill,* September 6, 2016, https://thehill.com/blogs/pundits-blog/civil-rights/294451-black-lives-matter-agenda-is-about-more-than-race.

North, Gary. *Crossed Fingers: How the Liberals Captured the Presbyterian Church.* Tyler, Texas: Institute for Christian Economics, 1996.

Nussman, David. "'All White People Are Racist Demons.'" Church Militant, September 10, 2020, https://www.churchmilitant.com/news/article/all-white-people-are-racist.

Packer, J. I., and Mark Dever. *In My Place Condemned He Stood: Celebrating the Glory of the Atonement.* Wheaton, Illinois: Crossway, 2008.

"The Parties on the Eve of the 2016 Election: Two Coalitions Moving Further Apart." Pew Research Center, September 13, 2016, https://

www.pewresearch.org/politics/ 2016/09/13/2-party-affiliation-among-voters-1992-2016.

"Religious Landscape Study." Pew Research Center, https://www.pew-forum.org/religious-landscape-study/racial-and-ethnic-composition/white.

Paul, Rand. *The Case against Socialism.* Northampton, Massachusetts: Broadside Books, 2019.

Piper, John. *Bloodlines: Race, Cross, and the Christian.* Wheaton, Illinois: Crossway, 2011.

Pluckrose, Helen, and James Lindsay. *Cynical Theories: How Activist Scholarship Made Everything about Race, Gender, and Identity—and Why This Harms Everybody.* Durham, North Carolina: Pitchstone, 2020.

Poe, Edgar Allan. *The Tell-Tale Heart and Other Writings by Edgar Allan Poe.* New York: Bantam Books, 1982.

Pratt Jr., Richard L. *Every Thought Captive: A Study Manual for the Defense of Christian Truth.* Phillipsburg, New Jersey: P&R, 1980.

"Racial and Ethnic Disparities." Suicide Prevention Resource Center, https://sprc.org/scope/racial-ethnic-disparities.

"The Racial Wage Gap Persists in 2020." Payscale, https://www.payscale.com/data/racial-wage-gap.

Raguse, Lou. "New Court Docs Say George Floyd Had 'Fatal Level' of Fentanyl in His System," KARE11, August 26, 2020, https://www.kare11.com/article/news/local/george-floyd/new-court-docs-say-george-floyd-had-fatal-level-of-fentanyl-in-his-system/89-ed69d09d-a9ec-481c-90fe-7acd4ead3d04.

Rah, Soong-Chan. *Prophetic Lament: A Call for Justice in Troubled Times.* Downers Grove, Illinois: IVP Books, 2015.

Ramsey, Donovan X. "Being Antiracist Is Work, Even for Ibram X. Kendi." *Wall Street Journal Magazine,* July 6, 2020, https://www.wsj.com/articles/being-antiracist-is-work-even-for-ibram-x-kendi-11594039803.

Ridderbos, Herman N. *The Coming of the Kingdom*. Philadelphia, Pennsylvania: Presbyterian and Reformed, 1962.

Riley, Jason. *Please Stop Helping Us: How Liberals Make It Harder for Blacks to Succeed*. New York: Encounter, 2015.

Rippee, Ryan. *That God May Be All in All: A Paterology Demonstrating That the Father Is the Initiator of All Divine Activity*. Eugene, Oregon: Pickwick, 2018.

Roden, Sitara. "Dr. Ibram Kendi, Amy Coney Barrett and Evangelical Adoption: Transracial Adoption Doesn't Make You Non-racist; but It Doesn't Make You Racist Either." *The Exchange with Ed Stetzer*, September 30, 2020, https://www.christianitytoday.com/edstetzer/2020/september/kendi-barrett-adoption.html.

Ross, Allen P. *Psalms*. In *Bible Knowledge Commentary*. Edited by John F. Walvoord and Roy B. Zuck, 779–899. Wheaton, Illinois: Victor Books, 1985.

Rothman, Noah. *Unjust: Social Justice and the Unmaking of America*. Washington, D.C.: Gateway Editions, 2019.

Schaeffer, Francis. *The Francis Schaeffer Trilogy*. Wheaton, Illinois: Crossway, 1990.

Schreiner, Thomas R. *Galatians*. Zondervan Exegetical Commentary on the New Testament (Volume 9). Grand Rapids, Michigan: Zondervan, 2010.

———. *Romans*. 2nd edition. Baker Exegetical Commentary on the New Testament. Grand Rapids, Michigan: Baker Academic, 2018.

Scruton, Roger. *Fools, Frauds, and Firebrands: Thinkers of the New Left*. London: Bloomsbury Continuum, 2017.

Sewall, Samuel. *The Selling of Joseph: A Memorial*. Amherst, Massachusetts: University of Massachusetts Press, 1969.

Shakespeare, William. *Julius Caesar*. Mineola, New York: Dover Publications, 2009.

Shenvi, Neil, and Pat Sawyer. *Engaging Critical Theory and the Social Justice Movement*. Lafayette, Indiana: Ratio Christi, 2019.

Sowell, Thomas. *Black Rednecks and White Liberals*. New York: Encounter Books, 2005.

———, *Discrimination and Disparities*. New York: Hachette, 2019.

———, *Wealth, Poverty and Politics*. New York: Basic Books, 2016.

Staniforth, Maxwell. *Early Christian Writings: The Apostolic Fathers*. Revised edition. Penguin Classics. New York: Penguin, 1987.

Steele, Shelby. *Shame: How America's Past Sins Have Polarized Our Country*. New York: Basic Books, 2016.

———, *White Guilt: How Blacks and Whites Together Destroyed the Promise of the Civil Rights Era*. New York: HarperCollins, 2006.

Stott, John R. W. *God's New Society: The Message of Ephesians*. Bible Speaks Today. Downers Grove, Illinois: InterVarsity Press, 1979.

Strachan, Owen. *Reenchanting Humanity: A Theology of Mankind*. Fearn, Scotland: Mentor, 2019.

Strachan, Owen, and Gavin Peacock. *The Grand Design: Male and Female He Made Them*. Fearn, Scotland: Christian Focus, 2016.

———, *What Does the Bible Teach about Homosexuality?* Fearn, Scotland: Christian Focus, 2020.

———, *What Does the Bible Teach about Lust?* Fearn, Scotland: Christian Focus, 2020.

———, *What Does the Bible Teach about Transgenderism?* Fearn, Scotland: Christian Focus, 2020.

Straub, Jeffrey. *The Making of a Battle Royal: The Rise of Liberalism in Northern Baptist Life, 1870–1920*. Eugene, Oregon: Pickwick, 2018.

Sussman, Robert Wald. *The Myth of Race: The Troubling Persistence of an Unscientific Idea*. Cambridge, Massachusetts: Harvard University Press, 2016.

Swift, Art. "Blacks Divided on Whether Police Treat Minorities Fairly." Gallup Social and Policy Issues, August 6, 2015, https://news.gallup. com/poll/184511/blacks-divided-whether-police-treat-minorities-fairly.aspx.

Tatum, Beverly Daniel. *Why Are All the Black Kids Sitting Together in the Cafeteria? And Other Conversations about Race.* New York: Basic Books, 2017.

Thielman, Frank. *Ephesians.* Baker Exegetical Commentary on the New Testament. Grand Rapids, Michigan: Baker Academic, 2010.

Thompson Jr., J. Earl. "Lyman Beecher's Long Road to Conservative Abolitionism." *Church History* 42, no. 1 (1973): 89–109.

Tisby, Jemar. *The Color of Compromise: The Truth about the American Church's Complicity in Racism.* Grand Rapids, Michigan: Zondervan, 2019.

Van Til, Cornelius. *The Defense of the Faith.* 3rd edition. Philadelphia, Pennsylvania: Presbyterian and Reformed, 1955.

———. *An Introduction to Systematic Theology.* 2nd edition. Phillipsburg, New Jersey: Presbyterian & Reformed, 2004.

———. *The Reformed Pastor and Modern Thought.* Phillipsburg, New Jersey: Presbyterian & Reformed, 1971.

Vos, Geerhardus. *Biblical Theology: Old and New Testaments.* Carlisle, Pennsylvania: Banner of Truth Trust, 2000.

Washington, Raleigh, and Glen Kehrein. *Breaking Down Walls: A Model for Reconciliation in an Age of Racial Strife.* Chicago, Illinois: Moody Press, 1993.

Wells, David F. *The Courage to Be Protestant: Reformation Faith in Today's World.* 2nd edition. Grand Rapids, Michigan: Eerdmans, 2017.

Williams, Walter E. *Race & Economics: How Much Can Be Blamed on Discrimination?* Stanford, California: Hoover Institution Press, 2011.

Woodson Sr., Robert L. *The Triumphs of Joseph: How Today's Community Healers Are Reviving Our Streets and Neighborhoods.* New York: Free Press, 1998.

Wright, Matthew. "Black Lives Matter Removes Page Encouraging the 'Disruption' of the 'Western Nuclear Family' during a Massive Cleanup of Their National Website." *Daily Mail,* September 22, 2020, https://www.dailymail.co.uk/news/article-8759959/BLM-removes-page-mentions-disrupting-Western-nuclear-family-website.html.

Acknowledgments

I am grateful to my heavenly Father, who by the Spirit's power has given a wretched sinner like me saving faith in my Lord and Master, Jesus Christ. I am nothing, and Christ is everything; I have no reputation, no image, no brand but Christ. He is "my all" (Colossians 3:4).

Considerable thanks go to my wife, who is a helper to me in more ways than I can quantify, and altogether lovely besides; Jeff Moore, who gave excellent assistance on this project (in too many ways to count, truly) as my research assistant; Jason Wredberg, who asked me to give the talks at Redeemer Bible Church of Minnetonka, Minnesota, that became the initial foundation for this book; Trent Hunter, who gave early and needed encouragement about taking my "Christianity & Wokeness" videos and turning them into a book; Tim Peterson, for his partnership in publishing this book, and his personal bravery; Grant Castleberry, who gave wise counsel and brotherly support throughout; Rick Holland, my pastor at Mission Road Bible Church, a congregation that loves sound doctrine, and is thriving for it; Mike Dixon, who provides valuable assistance to me through his work for the Center for Public Theology; Jeff Johnson, for his sound thinking and example of scholarly courage; Phil Johnson, for his help in securing a foreword from John MacArthur; Philip DeCourcy, for his friendship and example of Irish Baptist doctrinal passion; Gavin Peacock, for his encouragement and discerning advice; and the endorsers of this book, brothers all.

My previous institution, Midwestern Baptist Theological Seminary, supported my writing projects and made space for faculty members like me to write. I thank President Jason Allen, Provost Jason Duesing, and the MBTS trustees for the culture of scholarship they established to the glory of God. I had six good years at MBTS, and I am thankful for them.

This book is dedicated to two men who are lions for the truth. They did not know I was dedicating this book to them when I reached out to them about this project. Their involvement is in no way coming as the result of any kindness to me they have shown. Nor have I known these men closely, speaking of the past; yet I have followed them for years and learned from them in numerous ways.

No, my dedication of the book to John MacArthur and Voddie Baucham Jr. is because of one reason alone: courage. Specifically, theological courage born of love for Christ's blood-bought people. These men have taken ferocious heat as a result of their stand against wokeness. In an age that generally despises strong biblical manhood, they have been called terrible things; they have been attacked and undermined and campaigned against; at times, they have stood alone, or nearly alone; they have paid the price, a heavy price indeed, to defend the Gospel of God, the justice of God, and the oneness of the Church.

They are men of clay like I am; we are all unprofitable servants (Luke 17:10). But the stand for God's Word these brothers—and a company of faithful men including Tom Ascol, Josh Buice, Tom Buck, Jared Longshore, Michael O'Fallon, and others associated with the 2018 Dallas Statement, among other works—have taken has been historic. It has been essential. It has enabled the Church to find her balance, recover from Satan's terrible assault, and regain her courage. This stand has been costly in our day, but it will be vindicated on the only day that counts: the last day.

Like ancient Israelites in the halls of their kings, we rise and give thanks for these faithful men. MacArthur and Baucham remind me of what David said in tribute regarding Saul and Jonathan in 2 Samuel 1:23. Truly, by God's amazing grace, MacArthur and Baucham are swifter than eagles, and stronger than lions.

Index